New Feminist Library

*Dedicated to the memory of Sarah Eisenstein, 1946–1978,
activist, scholar, friend*

IMMIGRANT WOMEN
IN THE
LAND OF DOLLARS

LIFE AND CULTURE
ON THE LOWER EAST SIDE
1890–1925

◇

ELIZABETH EWEN

MONTHLY REVIEW PRESS • NEW YORK

Grateful acknowledgment is made to the following for permission to use photographs: page 19, Museum of the City of New York; pages 59, 129, photos by Jacob A. Riis, from the Jacob A. Riis Collection, Museum of the City of New York; pages 75, 93, 207, photos by Byron, from the Byron Collection, Museum of the City of New York; pages 29, 49, 111, 147, 185, 241, photos from the U.S. History, Local History, and Genealogy Division, New York Public Library, Astor, Lenox, and Tilden Foundations; page 165, photo courtesy of the Library of Congress; pages 225 and 263, from the author's family collection.

Library of Congress Catalog-in-Publication Data
Ewen, Elizabeth.
    Immigrant women in the land of dollars.

    (New feminist library)
    1. Italian American women—New York (N.Y.)—History.
2. Women, Jewish—New York (N.Y.)—History.   3. New York (N.Y.)—
Social life and customs.   4. New York (N.Y.)—
Biography.   I. Title.   II. Series.
F128.9.I8E83   1985   305.4'885107471   85-15408
ISBN 0-85345-681-X
ISBN 0-85345-682-8 (pbk.)

Monthly Review Press
122 West 27th Street
New York, N.Y. 10001

Manufactured in Canada
10 9 8 7 6

For Rosa Campanile, Hortense Wunderlich,
Anna Scott, Sylvia Ewen

and especially for

Frances Campanile Wunderlich

I'm one of the million of immigrant children, children of loneliness
wandering between worlds that are at once too old and too new to
live in. . . . I can't live with the old world and I'm yet too green for
the new. I don't belong to those who gave me birth or to those with
whom I was educated.

—Anzia Yezierska

To be a poor race is hard, but to be a poor race in the land of dollars is
the very bottom of hardship.

—W.E.B. DuBois

CONTENTS

ACKNOWLEDGMENTS

The author of a book like this, which was written over a long period of time, cannot help but incur profound debts. To a very large extent Herbert Gutman pointed the way in the early stages of the book's development. His generosity and friendship, his vast knowledge and unique perspective, breathed life into my work and that of countless other "younger" historians. Sadly, in the final months before the publication of this book, Herbert Gutman died. I will always remember his passion for history and his dedication to the idea that working people help to shape its contours.

The City University of New York Oral History Project, under the direction of Herbert Gutman and Virginia Yans, was an essential resource. Oral histories conducted by Karen Kearns, Santa Cigliano, Louise Mayo, and other members of the project made an invaluable contribution to the book. Laura Schwartz lent me useful materials from the archives of the WPA oral history collection. Vicki Friedman and Joan Kaufman conducted additional excellent interviews.

Isabel McKeever was a supportive friend in the preparation of the manuscript. Maria Spicciatie offered me technical assistance and advice. For their efforts, I offer deep-felt thanks.

Several people read the manuscript in its various stages and parts and offered me valuable editorial suggestions and criticism: Laura Schwartz, Onita Estes-Hicks, and Catherine Stimpson, and the members of the New Feminist Library Editorial Board, in particular Meredith Tax, Ellen Ross, Liz Phillips, Ruth Milkman, Dotty Zellner, and Debbie Bell.

Over the years I have been enlightened and encouraged by discussions with Fina Bathrick, Paul Brienes, Wini Brienes, John Ehrenreich, Phyllis Ewen, Sol Ewen, Naomi Glauberman, Linda Gordon, Allen Hunter, Paul Lauter, Gail Pellett, Sam Rosenberg,

Naomi Rosenthal, Margaret Schrage, Elaine Scott, Harry Scott, and William Taylor.

I have benefited from a more than twenty-five-year discussion of American history with Roger Wunderlich, my first teacher and colleague.

My mother, Frances Campanile Wunderlich, first pointed out to me the adaptability of Old World traditions when, after a heated argument, she agreed to chaperon me—then thirteen years old—to my first rock-and-roll show at the Brooklyn Paramount. My aunt, Letitia Feltrinelli Serpe, shared the intimate details of her immigrant experience. My brothers Roger and Michael offered me continual support, as has my brother-in-law Andy Ewen.

My children, Pauly-Dee and Sam T. Ewen, tried valiantly to keep me in touch with the late twentieth century. They also kept me company into the long hours of the night, and when I became too obsessed with turn-of-the-century details they dragged me away from my typewriter and forced me to listen to contemporary rock or watch MTV. Ironically, like the second-generation children in this book, they became my guides to the future.

Susan Lowes, my editor at Monthly Review Press, showed me the true value of the editing process. Patient and firm, she taught me a great deal and is a master at her craft.

Through the years Rosalyn Baxandall has been an inspiration and a faithful friend. At every turn she has been a source of ideas and material, determination and strength. She gave me constant support and made me laugh at my fears. My sister in spirit, I thank her for her confidence.

Stuart Ewen, my foremost intellectual collaborator, has provided me with sustenance, criticism, and guidance over the long haul. Without him this book would not have been possible. To me, he embodies the essence of the old Jewish proverb, "In between a *luftmensch* and a *macher* is a *mensch*."

Preface

I never saw my grandmother dressed in anything but black. During the time I knew her she stood a tall 4'10". I barely understood a word she said. She spoke Italian. I pretended to understand. She would talk and I would nod my head in agreement.

When I visited her she was either in the kitchen, about to go out shopping, or in church. Sometimes she would ask me to come with her on her errands. Together, we would walk down the washed-out streets of Beacon, New York, a small factory town populated by Italians who had moved there in better days. She greeted her neighbors and haggled with the shopkeepers. I would hold her hand, fantasizing about life as a girl in an Italian village.

My grandmother lived in a house desperately in need of a coat of paint. The inside was dimly lit; family crests and rosary beads dangled from the mantle, all-night candles burned on the sideboard. A lace tablecloth graced the dining-room table. Only the kitchen was bright.

My favorite room was upstairs. Although my grandmother shared the house with my grandfather, she had her own bedroom. He, of course, had the master bedroom, a large imposing room with an enormous bed in the middle. She had the smallest room, the size of a large closet. I loved her room; it became my hideaway. It was sparsely furnished—a single bed, a vanity—but there was a closet full of her possessions. Its size didn't matter. What did matter was what was inside the vanity and the closet, what she kept there.

During every visit there was a huge feast: antipasto, soup, pasta, meat, vegetables, and dessert. I never made it past the pasta. I'd sneak up to her room and daydream until someone found me in time for dessert. My grandmother let me sleep in her room at night—a sacrifice on her part. She knew how I felt about her room; it was the place where we shared secret rituals.

When I was little, it was difficult to imagine my grandmother as anything but old. Small, hunched, wearing black, she fulfilled the standard stereotype of an old immigrant woman. There were, however, aspects of her physical being that went against the stereotype: her silver hair was thick and beautiful, her eyes doelike hazel, her face unwrinkled, her skin smooth and soft.

In her room, the door closed, she would open the closet. Whenever she did that, her youth seemed to transcend her age. The closet contained remnants of her past: old work dresses and shirtwaists, work shoes, shoes to dance in, shawls, and, most memorable, beautiful hats—hats she had made herself. By trade, she had been a milliner.

She would sit me on the bed and then retire into the closet, motioning for me to cover my eyes. She always started with a hat, especially the one with the big purple plume. Ready, she stood over me, beaming. From behind her back she'd take out another hat, a brown one that looked like an old-fashioned double-boiler pot turned upside down and tied under the chin. She'd put it on me, and we'd both stand in front of the mirror laughing ecstatically. "Like two fine American ladies," she'd say.

Pleasure made her face come alive. Under these hats, looking into the mirror, we looked like twins: same height, same face. After the hats came the shawls, brightly colored, covered with sequins and embroidery. In her hat and shawl, her age erased, rubbed off her body. In baby Italian, I would try to say, "How can you be so old when you look so young?" Delighted, she'd respond in baby English, "What difference does it make?"

Sometimes we'd try on the shirtwaists and skirts. Then she'd pull out an old head form and we'd pretend to be working. At such moments she would become serious, making make-believe hats at a furious pace. She'd say to me, "Hurry, hurry, boss is coming." I would laugh and her mood would change. She'd dart back into the closet and bring out an old bustle and we'd take turns putting it on and waddling around the room. At the end of the ritual, she would open a drawer in the vanity, take out a bag, jingle it, and extract two pieces of silver which she would lay in my hands. To her this was real money, unlike the paper she gave to the shopkeepers—money like her jewelry, bright, shiny, and silver. "You keep," she would say. Somehow I always felt guilty when I spent it.

Years after my grandmother died I was "adopted" by Anna Scott, my husband's grandmother. Initially she was suspicious of the match, fearful of what would happen to her grandson if he married a non-Jewish girl. He tried to appease her fears by appealing to her immigrant heritage. When he told her that my mother was Italian, she responded, "Italian. Then it's alright. My next door neighbor in the Bronx was a nice Italian man."

We became fast friends. Anna reminded me of my own grandmother, although in many ways she was different. She too was small in stature—sometimes I imagined that she slept in a shoebox. But she was worldly and talkative, feisty and brittle, and a vivid storyteller. Her stories reflected a strength of character, a pride in herself and her secular culture. She could close her eyes and use her voice to take you back to the Russia she came from, the sweatshops she worked in, the little store she ran with her husband, the neighborhood she loved, and the movies that impressed her. And she was generous. She was always giving me things—pots, hairpins, candy, even clothes. She opened up her drawers like my grandmother opened her closet, to pass on the pieces of her past, a skirt, a blouse, a sweater: gifts of love.

In a sense this book began as an attempt to re-enter my two grandmothers' closets, to ferret out the fragments of a past when women made the journey from the fields of southern Italy and the market towns of Eastern Europe to the world's most modern metropolis, New York City. It traces the historical experiences of women who were born roughly between 1870 and 1890, spent their childhoods in Europe, and then migrated, worked, married, and raised children in one of the most densely populated parts of the globe, Manhattan's Lower East Side.

This story has been told many times and in many different guises. It has been converted into a national myth—the myth of the melting pot. This is the twentieth-century version of the Horatio Alger story, but here groups, not individuals, rise from rags to riches, reaffirming the basic values of American life: hard work leads to economic rewards and social success. The myth has been presented as a model for other groups. Blacks and other more recent arrivals to the metropolis are asked to accept their place at the bottom of the ladder until they too can pull themselves up by their bootstraps.

But while the main tendency of historians of the American immigrant past has been to chart the journey from miserable beginnings to great success, something important is missing from this perspective: history, after all, is filled with jagged edges. If part of America's tale is deliverance, another—perhaps more telling—part is the continued presence of people living, working, and trying to survive at the bottom of society. This was the case with the people I am writing about in this book, as it was a part of the sacred treasury my grandmothers kept in their closets, and it continues to be the case today. Other groups have taken the place of the turn-of-the-century immigrants whose story is told here, but many of the features of their existence remain the same.

This book differs from other treatments in several important ways. Most American myths—the frontier, the Protestant success story, or the melting pot—focus on the heroic male who struggles against adversity, nature, poverty, or the mores of a strange country to triumphantly conquer the obstacles in his way. In the melting pot version of the myth, this male subject sheds his past, loses touch with his family, and adopts American values as part of his new identity: the immigrant male becomes "Americanized" when he accepts the ideology of progress. He is no longer bound by past loyalties but instead defines himself as an "individual," free to choose his future. The reward of Americanization is upward mobility. And if he cannot Americanize, he will remain within the army of cheap labor, demoralized and dominated by his past.

Recently, some social historians have rejected this myth and begun to chart a different trajectory. They argue that rather than either adapt or become demoralized, these immigrants maintained many of their own traditions and institutions and used them as tools in their struggle for a decent life. They see immigrant family patterns, kinship networks, and local organizations as important aids in the fight for upward mobility. Old-world relationships flowered in the new world. Ethnic solidarity has been an important component of success.[1]

But this approach goes too far in the other direction: the immigrant emerges unscathed by his encounter with American life, unimpeded in his move upward by either the American economy or urban culture. He triumphs because of the plasticity of his past and his ethnicity. And with significant exceptions, he is a *he*—the new history continues to take a male subject for granted.[2]

This book places women and children at the center of the historical stage. While ethnic history is, as historian Herbert Gutman has noted, labor—and therefore class—history, class does not end at the factory gate: working-class history is shaped by a totality of experiences, including work and home, mothering and child-rearing, family relations, community activities, shopping, leisure, and recreation—in short, all the details and rhythms of everyday life. The study of class encompasses the material life and culture of women and men, parents and children, engaging in creating a life under adverse conditions they themselves did not create.

While, as we shall see in chapter 2, Jewish and Italian women came from radically different circumstances, once they arrived in the new urban world they shared a similar history: they came to the same neighborhoods of the Lower East Side, they worked in the same factories, their daily lives were shaped by the same social forces. Together they constituted a new working-class presence in New York City. By examining the contours of their historical experience we can, therefore, begin to come to grips with the relationship between ethnic and class history, and to understand the dynamics of working-class immigrant life at the turn of the century.

In addition, by focusing on the history of working-class Italian and Jewish women, we can discover new aspects of the process that is usually called "Americanization." In many ways, Americanization is a deceptive term: it implies exchanging one nationality for another. But it is more than that: it is also the initiation of people into an emerging industrial and consumer society. In fact, the process to which this term is applied had an impact that went beyond the immigrants themselves and touched the lives of most of the people who might be called Americans, transforming the way of life of a large proportion of the population. And this was part of the still larger process of industrialization: people, whether "native" or immigrant, whose lives were rooted in agriculture or small-scale industrial production found themselves, by the beginning of the twentieth century, embroiled in a new and unfamiliar social universe. The growth of large-scale mass production and the emergence of a national market for goods together laid down the outlines of a modern consumer culture, one with which we in the last years of the twentieth century have become all too familiar.

But for those unwitting pioneers this was hardly the case. They were to undergo a tumultuous period of change, and it was the women in particular who bore the brunt of this. These women were initiated into the culture of daily life twice in their lives: they grew up in patriarchal European societies that narrowly defined the boundaries of female possibility, where family and community organized and maintained a customary culture, a world where women still produced goods in the home. As they grew to maturity, historical circumstances propelled them into a new urban society that redefined the nature of daily life and cultural expectation. This new world undermined the basis of traditional womanhood, forcing these women to look in two directions at once: to the past for the strength to sustain their lives in the present, and to the future to find a new means of survival. If the Old World has used their labor to convert raw materials into finished goods, here they confronted the industrial marketplace where money and wages were the key to survival.

This confrontation was not only economic but was cultural as well. The new world churned out ideas as fast as products: immigrant mothers were constantly under attack for being "old fashioned"; social modernizers and social workers complained of the old-world imprint on the ways in which mothers dressed, did housework, organized their days, gave birth, nursed infants, raised children, went shopping, or participated in community life. Their children, although touched by the experiences of the Old World, were far more the children of the metropolis, and this created problems too: their lives were torn between family obligations and new ways of being that went beyond the confines of old-world understanding.

The Lower East Side was an amalgam of old and new: it contained vital old-world institutions and the most modern cultural offerings. For mothers and daughters, the situation was contradictory and confusing: if most daughters respected the family economy and turned their wages over to their mothers, others demanded the right to be "American" and keep some of their wages for themselves. If the economic bonds between family members at times led mothers and daughters out into the streets to demand higher wages or lower prices, at other times the bonds unraveled, pitting generation against generation, as daughters struggled for the right to date or marry a man of their choosing. As Mary Simkhovitch, the founder of Greenwich House, observed, the Lower East Side was not a melting pot but a boiling kettle.[3]

Immigrant Women in the Land of Dollars examines immigrant households through the eyes of newly arrived mothers and their daughters as they confronted the urban metropolis. I have drawn on many different sources: autobiographies, fiction, letters; oral histories (taken mainly from the CUNY Oral History Project on Immigrant Life, gathered under the direction of Herbert Gutman and Virginia Yans-McLoughlin from 1973 to 1975); and the observations of contemporary social workers, particularly women, both in the pages of *Survey* magazine and in the early twentieth-century social work literature in general.

These sources contain the voices of women recorded and preserved. Oral history is the closest way to capture the expression of a lived experience, the subjective voice in the historical process. At times, the women's memories are so clear that the details of wages, prices, living conditions, neighborhoods, and social relationships emerge after fifty years as a litany of transformation. It is almost as if the jarring confrontation between radically different cultures made such a deep impression that it can be recalled in breathtaking detail.

Yet despite the wealth of material, I have had to reconstruct the social world of immigrant working-class women from bits and pieces, fragments of experiences culled from many places: a phrase in an interview, an observation in an official document, a written quote, an autobiography, a memory, a piece of a letter. When used together, these sources complement and reinforce each other, providing a montage through which we can see the development of one part of American culture from a new point of view. Together these fragments make coherent the lives of women who seldom wrote about themselves and left few traces of their experiences. It is to them that this book is dedicated.

1
◇
A Tale of Two Cities

IN 1895 A YOUNG JEWISH GIRL MIGRATED TO THE UNITED STATES with her mother. Her name was Maria Ganz and she was five years old. She had come from Galicia to join her father in New York City. One day her mother sent her out into her Lower East Side street to play. There she saw a stranger who was "wearing a cap and long coat and was standing behind an empty carriage and a pair of horses: I stopped to stare at him for he did not look as if he belonged to our neighborhood: there was too prosperous and important an air about him." The stranger invited Maria to come for a ride with him uptown. She had never been out of the Lower East Side; she accepted the ride because of the adventure it promised.

As they drove uptown, Maria Ganz marveled at the city she lived in but had never seen. She noticed that there were "no tenements now with fire escapes hung with bedding and where groups of women and children huddled in the doorways, but stately buildings that almost reached the sky and bore no sign of family life." Riding up Fifth Avenue, she saw "gorgeous carriages . . . and inside surely princes and princesses, such women and men and children all dressed most wonderfully, even the children decked with furs. On one side were beautiful trees, a forest of trees decked in autumn colors; on the other, palaces of brownstone and marble, solemn, mysterious, forbidding." It began to get dark: "All the windows of the palaces are throwing a magic glare over the streets and palaces." She felt uncomfortable: "Nothing seems real. Am I awake or dreaming? Even the crowds of people are shadows, not living things of flesh and blood. It is too weird and fantastic to last long."

As her confusion increased, they left the "magician's paradise" behind: "Again we are on the streets I know, the streets of the tenements and the walks are thronged with people of my own kind. Pushcart torches flare along the curbs; oil, gas and candle lights gleam feebly in tenement windows; mothers crouch gossiping together on tenement steps; to hurdy-gurdy music little girls are dancing. I have come back to my own world." The contrasts Maria had seen on her adventure—"All the splendors I had seen"—provided food for thought, forcing the realization of how "miserable our home was." The contrast was a cruel one: "I was beginning to know the meaning of poverty."[1]

On her odyssey, Maria Ganz discovered some of the dynamics of her new American home. The contrasts she saw—between uptown wealth and the poverty of the tenement districts—led her to see things in new ways. In the same city, there were worlds within worlds. On the one hand there was Fifth Avenue, surrounded by giant buildings that bore no sign of family life, and part of a world based on wealth, power, and elegance. On the other there was the Lower East Side—poor, enclosed, but intensely familial, gregarious, and alive.

Into this city of contrasts poured thousands of immigrants challenged by the promise of America, determined to realize their dreams. Beckoned by the lure of money and freedom, they entered a social universe distinctly different from the world from which they had come. Between 1890 and 1924, about 23 million people migrated from eastern Europe and southern Italy. Over 17 million began their journey across America through the port of New York. For a great many of these, the Lower East Side was to become their home, the place where they were initiated into American life: by 1920 there were over 480,000 Jews and 391,000 Italians living in New York City.[2]

By the turn of the century, the heyday of the wave of immigration, the United States was in the throes of rapid industrial change. Life was now centered in the metropolis—the city rather than the small town or frontier became the center of energy and progress. In New York, new wealth and commerce, located on Wall Street and Fifth Avenue, dominated the economic and cultural life of the city, and to most upper- and middle-class New Yorkers the Lower East Side seemed a dangerous and menacing place. According to social worker Lillian Wald, the very "words 'East Side' suggested an alarming picture of something strange and alien, a vast crowded area, a foreign city." These fears "reflected the popular indifference—almost contempt—for the living conditions of a huge population."[3] Nevertheless, it was this same middle class that benefited in countless ways from the products made by immigrant labor.

The city was the new frontier. Below Fourteenth Street, the sights and sounds of change were everywhere: the tumult of the sweatshop, the many-tongued babble of the marketplace, the cries of anguish and excitement, the poverty, the congestion. Above Fourteenth Street, in the quiet brownstone districts, signs of change were less visible but nonetheless present, as the wonders of modern industry and technology arrived in the home.

Between 1880 and 1930, an explosion of factory-made goods and services transformed the nature and quality of life in the United States. New industries developed a vast array of consumer products that altered the context of everyday life. Steam heat, hot water, indoor plumbing and sewage systems, electricity and refrigeration simplified household labor. Ready-made clothing, factory-constructed furniture, canned goods, store-bought bread, and such mundane necessities as soap, candles, and cardboard boxes could now be purchased rather than made at home.

By 1905 newly built apartment buildings provided middle-class families with such blessings of progress as central heating, electricity for light and telephone, electrically powered elevators, refrigerators, and gas pumped in to heat the stove. By the mid-1920s, most middle-class homes had such appliances as the vacuum cleaner and the washing machine.[4]

For those of means, the city also offered public spaces devoted to commerce and entertainment. Middle-class women, used to shopping in specialized stores or to being visited at home by local merchants, could now find the same goods and services in department stores. Sunday or evening meals could be eaten in elegant new restaurants designed to woo a middle-class population into their environs. Lavish in appointments and services, sumptuous in design, these new commercial enterprises were referred to as "palaces"—an ironic commentary, perhaps, on the new functions of business in a democratic society.[5]

Middle-class families, and particularly women, found the industrialization of everyday life both wonderful and bewildering. As the household moved from being a center of production and consumption to being a center of consumption alone, work demanded of middle-class women changed dramatically. Social workers, sociologists, and home economists saw the changes that mass production was creating. Ellen Richardson, one of the creators of the new field of home economics, wrote about some of them:

Years ago, when our country was a nation of country folks, women did little of the spending, but helped much in the production of wealth. Before the invention of machinery production of most of the needs of life centered around the home. Men raised sheep and cattle; women did the spinning and weaving. Men tilled the soil and harvested . . . women did their own work which did not end with the preparation of meals but covered the actual manufacture of many useful wares such as candles for lighting the house and soap. Then there were spinning wheels, now there are factories. Then the home loom was part of the furnishing of every house, now the mills do the work. The country has moved to the town. Women can now buy all the necessities they once had to manufacture. They are not producing, they have thrown over the yoke of economic production. They only spend.[6]

The new standard of living to which the upper and middle classes was becoming accustomed was, in fact, a double standard. If middle-class families were now able to consume what they had once produced, immigrant working-class families produced—although no longer at home—what they could not consume. The new consumer goods' industries demanded their labor, but their daily lives were still defined by a nineteenth-century standard for living. The tenement line divided not simply rich from poor, but those who had access to new products and new technology from those who did not. In the tenement neighborhoods there were few inside bathrooms, coal and wood were the main sources of fuel, kerosene provided lighting, blocks of ice a minimum of refrigeration. Two- or three-room apartments contained an overabundance of people—sometimes eight or nine occupied these cramped spaces.

The daily grind was punctuated by the need for money. Money was the secular God of the new metropolis, the calling card that enabled progress to be purchased. Back home, the immigrants had had access to nature to supplement their meager earnings, but in the large cities they needed money: access to nature was replaced by access to the marketplace.

The market in Europe had of course dealt in money, but it had also dealt in barter or kind. In the United States, and particularly in the city, everything was measured in money terms. Labor time was measured in money, work time became money time. Goods and services were computed in the language of money, from rent to food to health to recreation. Italians called America the land of *dolci dollari*—sweet money—a slang expression that succinctly described the new life.[7]

At the same time, however, city life created new opportunities for all classes. Nineteenth-century Victorian culture had given the same moral weight to home and family as did Eastern European Jewish or Italian peasant culture; for each, the home was the center of social life. But as people poured into the cities, the patterns of social life began to change. For the upper and middle classes, background and social status gave way to an emphasis on money and displays of wealth. The city offered opportunities "to see and be seen"; the home was eclipsed by more alluring and glamorous diversions— restaurants, cabarets, department stores, or promenades down New York's fashionable streets.[8]

For immigrants, too, street life and the commercialization of leisure held out new options. Billboards, movie posters, chromos of all varieties created beguiling images of social life. The new nickelodeons and dance halls provided new meeting places. "To see and be seen" was important, as important as for the middle class, though costly.

First existing on the margins, and then moving to center stage, an urban mass culture was in the making. Using the energy and desires of youth and ethnic people, this culture allowed a place for the elite to meet the street. The movies, for example, which began in the 1890s in working-class immigrant neighborhoods, had by the 1920s attracted an audience from every class; the nickelodeon became the movie palace. Street music, whether played by blacks, Jews, Italians, or Irish, fueled the cabarets, Tin Pan Alley, and the record industry. Coney Island and Luna Park offered weekend amusement for all.

Two conflicting forces were set in motion: an urban consumer economy created distinct classes, geographically set apart, while an urban mass culture carved out public spaces that made possible a limited degree of cultural integration. The new immigrants were caught up in this process of urban transformation; their story illuminates not merely a change from old to new, but a change in the fabric of American society and culture.

New York City was the printing center of the country, but its leading industry was ready-made clothing, which produced three-quarters of all women's clothing in the country and most of the men's clothing as well.[9] The new immigration coincided with the development of New York City as the capital of the ready-made clothing industry, and the immigrants provided a source of labor. It was in the garment trade that most immigrant women worked. The industry was organized on a contract system: a contractor would buy material from a textile manufacturer, and hire workers to cut and finish the garments. Thousands of experienced tailors arrived in the United States from Eastern Europe and went to work in their tenement apartments, helped by all the members of the family. The contractor either rented machines or had his workers buy them on the installment plan and set them up in their homes, paid little overhead and low wages—and either made a profit or went broke. As the industry expanded, new laws and increased specialization pushed workers out of the home and into shops and lofts. Here a form of mass production was adopted as tasks were subdivided and an almost assembly-line type of production evolved, although finishing work continued to be done at home.

By 1910 women made up over 70 percent of the garment industry workforce. The sexual hierarchy that had developed gave men the more privileged positions and women were the unskilled and semi-skilled workers. By 1913 over 56 percent of these workers were Jewish and over 34 percent were Italian—and about 50 percent were under twenty years old.[10] As a surprisingly candid manufactuer explained, "I want no experienced girls, they know the pay to get . . . but these greenhorns . . . cannot speak English and they don't know where to go, and they just come from the old country, and I let them work hard, like the devil, for less wages."[11]

The vagaries of fashion created a demand for specialty items, and this work too was in the hands of immigrant women. Hand embroidery, for example, was a skill that Italian women brought with them. Calling on this cheap source of labor, the fashion industry created styles that required this skill.[12] Willowed (ostrich) plumes and artificial flowers were other caprices of fashion that created work in the home for immigrant women.

Compelled by necessity and desire, young immigrant women were seduced by the offerings of mass production. Donning ready-made clothing was the most visible sign of Americanization. Greenhorns quickly learned to be ashamed of old-world clothing. Americans ridiculed them in the streets or in school, and some garment manufacturers refused to hire women dressed in "un-American" clothing. All around them, movie posters, billboards, and chromos adorned women in sumptuous fashionable garments.

But the ability to participate was limited. Wages were not sufficient to enable these young workers to consume the better items they produced; they purchased the cheapest of the line, not in the new palaces but from peddlers and shops in the neighborhood. Although the clothing was cheap, it was very much in style. What the East Side lacked in quality it made up in quantity: "Does Broadway wear a feather? Grand Street wears two. Are trailing skirts seen on Fifth Avenue? Grand Street trails its yards with a dignity all its own." On the Lower East Side, Grand Street was a sartorial marketplace and a fashion boulevard all in one. On the weekends it looked like "Broadway and Fifth Avenue only very much more so. Its wide sidewalks show more fashion to the square foot on Sunday than any other part of the city."[13]

None of this was surprising. The women who worked in the industry had easy access to the new styles. As a *New York Tribune* reporter put it in 1898:

> But, in the matter of dress, it is natural that the East Side should be strictly up to date, for does it not furnish clothes for the rest of the town? If my lady wears a velvet gown, put together for her in an East Side sweatshop may not the girl whose fingers fashioned it rejoice her soul by astonishing Grand Street with a copy of it next Sunday? My lady's in velvet, and the East Side girl's is the cheapest, but it's the style that counts. In this land of equality, shall not one wear what the other wears? Shall not Fifth Avenue and Grand Street walk hand in hand?[14]

The Lower East Side, the center of the garment industry, was also the first home of the newly arrived immigrants. Between 1900 and 1905, the greatest density of population in the entire country was on New York's Lower East Side—sections of the Tenth Ward had as many as 750 people per acre.[15] While there were other immigrant neighborhoods in Manhattan—most notably the Italian section of East Harlem—the Lower East Side was the area of greatest concentration.

The physical separation of classes into neighborhoods created two cities—two distinct and separate worlds—in one, a fact that Maria Ganz had recorded on her ride uptown. Largely to escape the incoming flood of new immigrants, the middle and upper classes gradually left the downtown area and began to build brownstones and apartment buildings farther north. For a while the shopping areas remained downtown. Tiffany's and Lord and Taylor—to name only two—were located on Fifth Avenue and Broadway. But this brought the wealthy into direct contact with the garment workers themselves,[16] and by 1915 the department stores had followed the lead of their customers, moving above Fourteenth Street. "Ladies Mile," as the new shopping district was called, moved to the stretch between Fourteenth and Twenty-third Streets.

As the middle class abandoned the Lower East Side, their houses were left to the poor. Each room, including the basement, was rented, and then houses were built in the backyards. The new tenement buildings, called "dumbbells," had few windows, no inside bathrooms or bathtubs, and poor ventilation, and were generally dirty and unhealthy. Nonetheless, rents were higher than anywhere else in the country.

During this period the subways, the Brooklyn Bridge, and Grand Central Station were built in order to create working-class immigrant neighborhoods outside of the central city, but the Lower East Side remained the center of the immigrant population. Even though both industry and immigrants fanned out into the other boroughs, new arrivals quickly took their place. The immigrant communities on the Lower East Side created a complex cultural universe within the areas allotted to them. And while the upper classes perceived this neighborhood as distinctly foreign, the new immigrants saw it as distinctly American.

Viola Paradise of the Immigrant Protective League captured this complexity when she wrote: "The very things which strike the native born [American] as foreign seem to her [the new immigrant] as distinctly American: the pretentiousness of signs and advertisements, the gaudy crowded shop windows, the frequency of fruit stands and meat markets, her own countrymen in American clothes, women carrying great bundles of unfinished clothing on their heads—she sums it all up as 'America.' "[17] But to understand this interaction, let us look first at the world from which the immigrants came.

2
◇

In the Old World

MOST NATIVE-BORN AMERICANS AT THE TURN OF THE CENtury lumped all incoming foreigners together as "immigrants." Yet the particular cultures of the immigrants shaped their experiences in intimate ways. While in the European context the lives of Jewish and Italian women had little in common—save that both were immersed in a preindustrial world of home production—they found themselves living together on the Lower East Side, sharing neighborhoods, work, and their "immigrant" status.

To unravel the world of these immigrant women—their own particular cultural positions, attitudes, and beliefs—as they stepped onto American soil, we must briefly examine their lives before they began their journey. Most Italian immigrants came from the peasantry of the *mezzogiorno* (the southern tier of Italy), while the Jews came from the more urban and artisanal environment of Eastern Europe. There were therefore obvious differences between the experiences of the Italian peasants, who had lived for generations rooted to the land, and the Jewish artisans, for whom anti-Semitism and the Diaspora had made uncertainty and a feeling of displacement part of everyday life. In addition, Italian peasants lived primarily in hillside villages unchanged by time, while the Jews lived in areas that offered a greater diversity of experience, which the women were sometimes able to take advantage of. These differences shaped the women's lives at home, as well as their ideas of what would be possible in the New World, in crucial ways.

Yet both Italian and Jewish women were affected by being part of patriarchical, preindustrial societies, and so the question of what it meant to be a *woman* in such a context is important. While all these women came from cultures that saw them as inferior, subordinate, and even ignorant, within these confines they were nevertheless able to shape the spheres of life that were relegated to them: in their own worlds, the women controlled the use of time and resources.

In addition, both Italian peasants and Jewish artisans occupied a somewhat similar place within the broader national context: Italian peasants from the *mezzogiorno* were at the bottom of the hierarchy of Italian society, a despised sector of the population. Jews, too, were forced to live as outcasts, a segregated and barely tolerated minority in the midst of Christian Eastern Europe.

In the overview that follows, the lives and labors of the women provide us with an understanding of the rhythms and textures of daily life in these women's lands of origin, and this in turn illuminates who these women were when they reached America.[1]

In southern Italy in the late nineteenth century, the land and its products were the source of life. The five provinces that experienced the greatest out-migration were marked by diverse and chaotic systems of landholding, ranging from outright ownership to tenancy to sharecropping to wage labor.[2] Most plots were small and only the wealthier could afford the tools, seed, animals, irrigation, and taxes that made farming profitable. The system of inheritance, which divided property equally among sons, furthered the process of fragmentation.

Ownership, tenancy, and sharecropping gave peasants access to chestnut trees (which provided flour), grape vines (for wine), olive oil (for cooking), and fruit. A tenant was expected to raise his food and provide the material for his clothing. Half of each crop went to the owner and half to the tenant, while any surplus was sold to obtain the necessities that could not be produced. The wages of day laborers, although partially paid in cash, also came in the form of food, salt, wine, grain, oil, and cloth. Many peasant families were at once owners, sharecroppers, and day laborers—living in the *mezzogiorno* was a precarious enterprise. Peasants were constantly in debt for seed, livestock, and other necessities. Although they paid their debts mainly in kind (produce), cash was necessary for rent and taxes, to buy a donkey, to build a well, and to do the many other things that were necessary to live at more than the subsistence level.

The women sometimes assisted their husbands in the fields or even worked as day laborers (Sicilian women were a significant exception), although they were paid less than men.[3] In general, however, in those areas where agriculture was extensive and the population congregated in villages, the employment of women was low.

Peasant households were generally close together, affording the possibility of cooperation and a sense of community among the women. The houses had no running water, and both fetching water and doing the wash in the nearest river or lake were social occasions.[4] In the summer the house became a place to sleep, and work moved out of doors. Cooking, sewing, weaving, and spinning were open-air activities, done within the sight of other women. In winter, however, the houses—generally only one room—had to accommodate both people and animals. Despite the lack of space, peasant households were immaculately clean, although the walls were darkened by the wood or coal fires; only on special occasions was the house whitewashed.

The work of the household was extensive and required a rigorous apprenticeship for the daughters. Instead of receiving a formal education, they were trained in sewing, spinning, cooking—the skills of life. By the age of ten they were expected to be proficient in the performance of household duties, including the care of younger children. One daughter described her education:

> When I was five or six years old, my father gave me a small scythe with which to help harvest the grain. Around the fingers of my left hand my mother placed five *cannedda* [a protective covering] so that I would not cut my fingers while learning. All the girls in my village worked as I did. We also did much housework, following our mothers around continuously. There was never an idle moment for girls or women. We all wanted the reputation of being good workers.[5]

As the daughter became a working member of the family, she gained in social status as well. She donned a shawl—a symbol of initiation into the adult world of women—and she was allowed to go to the public fountain and help on laundry day—prized activities because they provided a chance to get out of the house.

A more formal education was discouraged, especially for girls. Schools were poor, and even those who attended the three-year elementary schools barely learned to read and write. Peasants saw few benefits in being literate, and many drawbacks, including days lost in the field or house. Privately run schools, usually taught by nuns, generally emphasized fine lace work or embroidery at the expense of literacy.

Many families feared the effects of literacy on their daughters, feeling that this new power would enable them to communicate more freely with their boyfriends. One Italian-American who asked his mother why she was illiterate reported the following answer: "In her case it was the fear of my grandparents that she would write love letters to young men in the town and thus would trespass against the decorum of a well-brought-up Italian girl."[6]

Some daughters tried to pursue an education but their fathers forbade them. Carmella Caruso, for example, lived in a small town near Palermo. Her mother died when she was quite young and she was brought up by her grandmother—her father had migrated to America. Her grandmother sent her to school, and her teachers wanted her to continue and become a teacher. Her father intervened; he came home to tell her that she did not deserve an education because "women have to stay in a corner of the house."[7]

The meager economy was sustained by household production, for few of life's necessities came ready-made. The household was a small workshop where the women, assisted by various trained artisans, transformed raw materials into finished goods. The making of clothing, for example, was a household industry: a trained woman (a *meastra*) would do the cutting and fitting and the women of the household would do the finishing. This was also true for weaving. These services were often paid for in produce, and poor families minimized the cost by arranging for a daughter to learn the trade, even if only for the service of her family.

Childbirth was also in the hands of women. The midwife was considered an artisan, and in her shop she hung her sign, the symbol of an egg. She was hired to deliver children, and stayed in the house to help with the work of taking care of the newborn. As she went from house to house, she brought community news and information, creating a social link among the women.[8]

Another visitor was the hairdresser. Since water was scarce, hair was not washed frequently; instead, for a few cents a month the hairdresser came to the house to arrange, brush, and oil the women's hair. She too served as a town crier, carrying news and gossip around the village.[9]

The family was the basic unit of social life and organization, and membership was defined broadly. As Leonard Covello explained it, in peasant culture the family was

> a social group which included all blood and in-law relatives to the fourth degree. . . . The family was an inclusive social world, of and by itself. In a *contadino* [peasant] community, the population consisted of familial groups. There were frequent instances where one familial set-up embraced the entire population of a village, that is, the inhabitants were related by blood and marriage.[10]

The family system bound parents and children into a system of mutual obligation. Parents labored for their children: fathers taught sons how to work the land, mothers taught daughters the skills of the household. To ensure that this would continue, parents endowed both sexes, through inheritance and dowries, with the means to create families of their own. Children were expected to support their parents in their old age. Sons inherited property and worked the land with their fathers; daughters were given dowries when they left home to live with their husbands' families.

In this system, too many daughters could be an economic liability, and while the mother was universally respected, daughters and young wives were viewed with derision or suspicion. Male domination was embedded in family life. The father was the head of the family and the main breadwinner. He was the lawgiver, and no enterprise was undertaken without his permission. He represented the family, its honor and prestige, to the community and village. Fathers trained their sons to dominate their sisters—this practice would turn sons into proper husbands. As Leonard Covello reported:

> When I was about twelve . . . my father told me plainly that it was my duty to watch over my sisters. "Son," he would say, "your sisters are women, like any other women. Don't give them too much liberty. Don't let them get out of hand. They are incapable of exercising any freedom. A little gallantry is okay, but not in a lush manner. Always show them you are a man."

Mothers, however, tried to blunt the harshness of this attitude toward women:

> When my father would be away my mother would continue on the same topic. "Father is quite right," she would say. "You'll be married one day, and you'll want to be master in your own home. But son, you must learn to be considerate to your sisters. They are women.

Some day, they'll be mothers. It is good to be firm . . . but it is bad to be brutal toward a woman, especially your sisters."[11]

Although married daughters were expected to be obedient to their husbands, to be thrifty housewives, and to raise large families, they still felt an obligation to their parents. "Obey your husband, but do not forget that you owe a debt to your family" was a traditional marriage blessing, and it was not uncommon for daughters to help their parents, with either money or labor.

When the wife of the eldest son moved into the household, she was expected to take on the bulk of the work but remain subservient to his mother. The passage, over time, from daughter to wife to mother was accompanied by a growing sense of power. The mother was the center of the household. Although outwardly submissive to her husband, she had a real authority in the home. An Italian-American from Sicily explained: "If we obeyed our father, it was only because we were afraid of him. We had no fear of our mother, but we obeyed and respected her because she was first a mother." This was clear when the mother died:

> I cannot tell you why but when a mother died the family usually fell apart. The small children were taken over to the mother's relatives, and the older ones felt that they could not live at home anymore. . . . When the father died and the mother remained alive the family always remained like chickens around a hen.[12]

In addition to home production, the mother had two key responsibilities; she controlled the family purse and she was expected to find suitable marriage partners for her children. The husband "turned over his earnings to his wife for complete management. Except for reserving the right to intercede in the case of mismanagement or other crises, the father did not further concern himself with the family budget."[13] The children did not regard wages as their own, but as part of the family fund that would ensure their future.

Yet managing the family purse was an ambiguous power in a society where money was rarely used as a medium of exchange. Southern Italians made barter and bargaining into a fine art: so much wool would be exchanged for so much oil and so on. When wives were sought, a good "reputation for haggling was one of the most desirable traits."[14]

Marriage in *contadino* culture was not merely a question of social status, but a necessity, a means of guaranteeing the future. This gave parents the authority to control the sexuality and courtship patterns of their children. For young women, virginity was a requirement; its absence shamed the entire family. Most marriages were arranged—sex and love followed rather than preceded marriage—and the choice of a marriage partner was made by the mother, aided by the grandmother, aunts, and other female family members. The father retained a veto, however, and made the match official when he announced the selection.

Most families used the services of a female matchmaker who helped in the intricate negotiations, which involved dowries, gifts, property, and status. If sons were involved, the father took an active role as well.[15]

Family ceremonies allowed peasant families to express their social connections to each other. Relatives and close neighbors helped in weddings, donating gifts and sharing food. During the first few months after the wedding, relatives and neighbors helped the new family establish itself. Funerals were also rituals of solidarity. The practice in Italian funerals was for "all present [to] leave some money to lessen the expense and the burden of the remaining members of the family. Pauper graves were nonexistent. Even the poorest could count upon contributions by the neighbors." When family members died, women had special responsibilities: "[It] was the duty of the neighbors, primarily the women, to stay with the widow day and night. The neighbors would do the cooking and the housework."[16]

These acts and rituals signified that economic relations were subordinate to kinship networks or social relations. Economic exchange was a "connection between concrete personalities and every economic act . . . is merely one moment of this solidarity. Its full meaning does not lie in itself, but the whole personal relationship that it involves."[17] The social labor of women was vital to the exchange process. Gifts were made (or saved for) by women as a part of their familial responsibility. While this meant sacrifice and extra labor, obligation to family, relatives, and neighbors created ongoing social bonds that gave life meaning.

Women went to church more regularly then men, but Sunday mass was a community celebration. According to Leonard Covello:

During the week everybody was busy with work. Sunday mass was a welcome chance for relaxation, for vainglorious display of women's and girls' finery, even for romance. . . . Throughout the mass one heard a constant drone produced by whispers, pious Amens, giggles, sneezes, and coughs. . . . Women and men were separated. During the entire service glances between the two sections were exchanged. The young men usually stood in the back and ogled at their sweethearts, whom they could see and communicate with in the church better than at other times or places. It was a merry crowd.[18]

If Sunday was also a holiday for a local patron saint, the mass was followed by a "magnificent procession and a general spirit of festivity." The *feste* turned the world upside down; bands played, the town was lavishly decorated: "The event ended with dancing that usually lasted into the evening. . . . A feast often continued for several days during which no work was done."[19]

Peasant women in Italy, then, played a vital and productive role in their families and culture. Patriarchal custom may have confined their activities to the domestic sphere, but that was the sphere that produced and sustained the foundations of life and culture, and in that sphere they played a fundamental role.

If the rhythms of peasant life defined the landscape of possibility for Italian women, Eastern European Jewish women were caught up in the dynamics of a culture where the Jews living in market towns (called shtetls) constituted a large army of artisans and peddlers to the Christian peasantry. During the nineteenth century half of the world's Jewish population lived in the Russian empire, in the part that spread from the Baltic to the Black Sea, called the Pale of Settlement—an area made up of the twenty-five northern and western provinces. After the pogroms of 1880–1881, Czar Alexander II issued the notorious May Laws, officially reserving the land and its products for Christians, prohibiting Jews from owning or renting land, and expelling people from towns they had inhabited for generations.

Industrialization seriously undercut the economic viability of shtetl life, already severely affected by rampant anti-Semitism. The Jews moved to cities in the Pale where industry turned former artisans into factory workers.

Economic and religious oppression went hand in hand. The restrictions of shtetl life forced many to engage in peddling and artisan labor. Throughout the Pale, virtually all artisans were Jewish—cobblers, tailors, blacksmiths, harnessmakers, butchers, bakers, watchmakers, jewelers, and furriers.[20] Artisans both manufactured and marketed their goods, supplying town, village, and countryside.

A traditional aristocratic disdain for artisan labor left these occupations open to Jews, but the continual pressure of poverty, pogroms, and czarist policies made this livelihood extremely unstable. Eastern European shtetl life revolved around the difficulties of making a living in a society in which anti-Semitism was an everyday practice implemented by Christian officials.

The geography of shtetl life reflected the demands of a trading population. These densely populated towns were located close to cities like Kiev and Lublin, and extended to small towns that were interspersed among the peasant farms. In the shtetl itself, houses and streets were constructed around the center of shtetl life, the marketplace. According to one person quoted in *The Shtetl Book*, a collection of contemporaneous accounts of shtetl life: "Without a market all the Jews would starve to death and all the peasants would be naked and barefoot. The market is the pulse, the meeting ground, the center of action."[21]

The market dictated the rhythms of the work week. Fairs took place once or twice a week; on the off days, merchants traveled to the cities to obtain merchandise, artisans prepared their wares, and shops opened to serve the local community. On market day itself there was a "feverish commotion . . . when a townful of Jews had to obtain its livelihood, not only for two days, but sometimes an entire week." On these days, the marketplace came alive, "all the voices flowed together into a chorus expressing one word and one word only, *Par-no-se* (livelihood)."[22]

Peasants sold produce and livestock, as well as the things Jews needed for the Sabbath: parsley, little cucumbers with dill for pickling, and carrots. In exchange—sometimes in barter, often in cash—Jews sold everything to satisfy the needs of the peasantry.

Irving Howe, in *World of Our Fathers*, noted that "at the peak of its development the shtetl was a highly formalized society. It had to be. Living in the shadow of lawlessness, it felt a need to mold its life into lawfulness. It survived by the disciplines of ritual." Nationless and oppressed, the Jews living in the shtetls in a sense turned their backs on the world they inhabited; the community became "the manifestation of God's covenant with Israel, the family was the living core of the community."[23] Religion governed most aspects of daily life until the late nineteenth century when the *Haskala* (Jewish Enlightenment) movement and socialism began to challenge its supremacy.

Traditionally, Jewish culture reserved learning and religion for men; women were given the home, the garden, and the marketplace. In this gender-defined world, the highest goal a man could attain was to become a scholar. While few did so, it was the scholars who set the standards. The ideal man withdrew from the mundane world; it was women who organized the everyday life:

> The men made the important decisions; when the Messiah will come, what the Torah means, and what are the attributes of God. The wife decided how much money to spend on clothes, whether or not to pawn the family candlesticks, to apprentice the son, when the daughter would marry, and whether it was better to buy fish or chicken for the Sabbath meal.[24]

Some men divided their days between the sacred and the secular. Another account in *The Shtetl Book* describes a man who worked as a baker and a shoemaker:

> As soon as the baking was done, he would hurry off for morning prayer, leaving his wife with the job of selling crackers and rolls in the market. "I'm an artisan, not a salesman," he would argue whenever she put up a fight about having to stand on her feet with the baked goods all day. "And second of all, it's only a few mornings a week and a Jew has to pray with a *minyan* every day."[25]

As with Italian peasant women, here too the women managed the daily fiscal affairs of the family: it was assumed that a true scholar did not know one coin from another. Even where the husbands were not scholars, the woman usually managed the household cash; in addition, all women participated in some gainful occupation, even if they were not the main economic support of the family.

Although the women were home-centered, they were not homebound—while the husband would work at home tailoring or shoemaking, the wife would work as a petty merchant in the marketplace, leaving her children at home—most artisan families needed such a division of labor to make ends meet.[26] The more successful women had shops, but countless others either sold their wares in the marketplace or peddled them door to door. In the market the women had a better command of the local languages spoken by the peasants—Russian, Hungarian, and Polish—than did the more learned men. Some occupations were part of the religious tradition—matchmakers, *mikveh* bath attendants, yeast and matzoh makers—while others were more secular: midwives, folk medics, chicken feeders and sellers, pearl stringers, clothing workers, pickle vendors, rag dealers, to name a few.[27]

It was not uncommon to find female peddlers and small merchants on the road. If their businesses took them out of town, they would stay with relatives. Many developed reputations for being strong, if perhaps tougher than a woman should be. Take Zabalye the Coachwoman, for example:

> She was a woman, but with her unusual habits and vulgar behavior, she might as well have been a man. She could have taught ten men how to curse, drink, and brawl. Yet she lived from honest toil. She owned a horse and wagon, and she transported assorted loads, particularly merchandise. She herself was strong as a horse, and it was said that when part of her wagon broke down and lost a wheel, Zabalye lifted the entire wagon on her back and fixed what needed fixing.[28]

Some men gave up on the secular altogether. A memorist in *From a Ruined Garden* writes of Dvoyrr Miriam, who "fulfilled the male role, while her husband, Yosl, was the woman":

> Most days, her husband would kiss his wife at daybreak, pick up his religious articles and go to morning service. When he came home, he did the housework and let the goat out to graze in the meadow while he sang Psalms by heart. She went about the hamlets and peasant houses, buying whatever was available, a chicken, a calf, butter, cheese; later she would sell it to the summer people at the dachas or to her regular customers in town . . . she took care of every aspect of her business at once; buying, selling, bartering, and doing a little matchmaking on the side.[29]

In addition, the daily work of the household was extensive, a mixture of production for family and market. Women made their own and their children's clothes, as well as producing what they sold. Sarah Rothman, for example, who learned watchmaking from her grandfather and had her own trade (although she charged less for her labor than did male watchmakers), also helped her mother at home:

> We had a garden, we had a cow, which not everybody had, you know. We had milk. Through the calf, we used to have leather for shoes. The butter we used to sell; we couldn't afford to eat butter. My mother

used to weigh it—if it's a pound, it's all right, if it's not a pound, we're going to eat it. To churn it was a big bother. The cheeses we used to put in a little sack. . . . We used to have grease for the wheels of the peasants' wagons, and flour. We give him the flour and he used to bring mushrooms, food for the chickens. We used to hire the peasants to fix up the garden; my father used to pay in honey.[30]

Anuta Sharrow grew up in a village eighty miles from Kiev, where she lived on what she called " a miniature farm because we had a garden, an orchard, and a cow." She was lucky to have an orchard; most did not, and for many even access to the surrounding forests was difficult: "Whenever we had to go pick wood in the woods, or pick berries, they wouldn't let us. Because you see we were Jews. The *skutsim* [Christian hooligans] used to throw stones or take a nice long piece of wood and chase us."[31]

If the father's shop was in the home, and if he hired apprentices or workers, housework was even more of a burden. On top of cooking, laundry, tending cows and gardens, and producing a surplus for sale, the women had to wash clothes for nine or ten people and cook them three meals a day.

There was also the work of "domestic religion," that link between scholasticism and daily ritual. As described in Barbara Myerhoff's *Number Our Days*, "it was the woman who gave the moments of life into the family, in the holidays, in the tragic moments. She could do this because she was allowed to express herself more than the men. . . . A man's religious expression was the crowd, in shul. Uneducated she was, but the woman did the rituals."[32]

These rituals included keeping a kosher home, preparing for the Sabbath and holidays, lighting the Sabbath candles and taking a *mikveh* (purification bath). The rules governing these were handed down from generation to generation. Rachel, one of seven girls, learned the domestic religion from her grandmother: prayer and housework went hand in hand. When the boys went off early each morning to pray, Rachel's grandmother gathered the girls around her and led them in their own prayers. After prayer and breakfast, the grandmother then divided up the housework: "That speech . . . was made very carefully, as carefully as the prayers, so that one girl doesn't get more to do than the other, all arranged according to age. . . . Grandmother made such a nice division, in such a beautiful way, not commanded, just like it was a part of God, even if it wasn't in Hebrew."[33]

Some daughters resented this training. Fannie Shapiro, for instance, helped her mother while her brothers went to school: "I had to help her with the laundry. You can't picture how laundry was washed in that place. . . . I had to help her with a lot of things and she used to watch that I don't do anything wrong with *fleischig* and *milchik* [keeping kosher]." On one occasion, her mother went to the doctor in another town: "I had to take over the housework. And I didn't care, *milchik, fleischig*. I cooked, I made [things in the wrong pots] and when I got through I felt kind of funny. So I told my father. My father says to me, 'Wash all those pots and put them right back where you took them and never tell her anything.' "[34]

Preparing for the Sabbath was a vital task: the Sabbath was the one day of the week when work ceased and the family came together. It was also a test of a woman's skills: "No matter how, poor Mama always managed to find somehow a fish or chicken, even if she had to hock her pearls." The Sabbath turned the world on its head: "Everything was transformed into a different realm":

> When I was a little girl, I would stand besides my mother when she would light the candles. . . . We were alone in the house, everything warm and clean and quiet with all the good smells of the cooking coming in. . . . We were still warm from the *mikveh*. Whatever we had, we wore our best.[35]

Charity was tied to the Sabbath, and giving food to those who were poorer was the woman's responsibility. Anuta Sharrow remembered that every Friday her mother used to pack a big bag of food and send her to give it to the poor. In a memoir in *The Shtetl Book*, Gitl, the wife of the *shochet* (Jewish ritual slaughterer) would send her daughters to collect extra bread for the poor and help them divide the pieces into portions to hand out.

Gitl exemplified the spirit of traditional female Jewish charity. Her house was considered grand because "Gitl, alone among the slaughterers' wives, gave away the meager chicken remnants her husband brought home. . . . What no one knew was that after giving most of the giblets away to the poor, there was barely enough to feed her own family." Before Passover "she would send her daughters to relieve the workers at the matzoh bakery. The bakers had to work non-stop around the clock under the strict supervision of the rabbi. The hired bakers waited all year for the money they earned in these frantic weeks. But if it wasn't for the help of Gitl's daughters, they would hardly be able to stop, even rest."[36]

Gitl's story revealed another important person in the lives of orthodox women, the reader. During services, when the men were separated from the women, Gitl was always surrounded by other women who needed help finding the place in the prayer book. On Saturday, Gitl would read from the Tsene-rene, the first five books of the Bible in Yiddish, prepared especially for women: "She would read aloud to her eldest daughters. . . . This always attracted women from neighboring houses who sat around to listen." Sarah Rothman's mother did the same: "Saturday and Sunday my mother used to read the history of the Jewish people to a whole bunch of women." She also supplemented her income by teaching: "She used to get a class of children . . . and she used to read the Jewish history, and they used to pay her five rubles a week, very little. And if people couldn't pay, she used to let them stay in the class anyway. . . . She taught me to read and write."[37] Girls were expected to learn from their mothers; a female apprenticeship contained a double message—self-sufficiency and sacrifice.

Jewish patriarchy deemed boy children more valuable than girl children. Boys were encouraged to study and great sacrifices were made for their sake. As Ida Richter bluntly put it:

> In Russia, a woman was nothing. But a Jewish woman, when she had a boy, she was the cream of the crop. A boy was a very important thing in Jewish life for a lot of things. When my father used to pray in the morning with his prayer shawl, I used to hear him say in Hebrew, "Thank God, I'm not a woman." A girl wasn't much.[38]

Girls could still acquire some education, however: hired teachers, girls' schools, secular schools, and—if the family was wealthy and highly motivated—a high school education in a city were all available to those who persevered. Yet some mothers were not anxious to have their girl children educated. Fannie Shapiro, for instance, began her education with a rabbi who lived with her family and taught her Hebrew and Russian. After a while her mother thought she had had enough: "I didn't need any more . . . but the boys never had enough." Resenting this, Fannie apprenticed herself as a domestic to a family in a bigger city—against her parents' will—and found a socialist teacher. When Fannie's mother heard this, she said:

"We're going to take her home. I don't want her to be in the city. She'll become a socialist and drop religion."[39]

Some well-off parents sent their daughters to the cities to be educated. Anuta Sharrow, for example, was sent to Kiev even though she had to get a special visa: Jews were not allowed to live there without papers. Private tutors, some of whom were socialists, prepared her for high school. "We used to sit up till twelve o'clock and read all kinds of pamphlets." The high school was half Jewish, half Gentile, "but the Jewish girl or boy had to know twice as much to get a high mark." Still, in the city students breathed the air of enlightenment. They were "free, our life, our environment, already belonged to the next generation." But the past still had a hold: although Anuta Sharrow argued that the only women who went to a school in a big city like Kiev had a chance, in the end she returned to her hometown to become a tutor.[40]

Enlightened women students were sometimes seen as the "black sheep" of the family. Fradly, for instance, was a student in Zvihil. She liked to dress up and speak Russian, and when she visited her father, there were always arguments. To her nephew, the young woman from the strange city was like a visitor from a far-off planet: "I gasped when she took a cigarette from Uncle Joseph's box and let the smoke drift from her mouth." Her father did not punish her for her "un-Jewish ways" but told her she was wasting her time in school instead of staying home and accepting a match with an eligible man:

> Fradly shrieked in a way no decent Jewish woman would dare. . . . "Marry some Itse Meyer and rot in this dump? I'd rather jump in the river." Her father asked her what she was looking for. "To study and become a dentist," she shot back. The word "dentist" filled me with such an awe that I hardly dared to breathe.[41]

Arranged marriages were common in the shtetl, especially among the scholarly elite. According to convention, only the poorest Jews—or the wealthy Christian gentry—married for love; love was supposed to come after the babies and the home.[42] Most marriages were arranged by the parents, with the assistance of the *shadken* (matchmaker), who took into account piety, wealth, honor, and social status. Traveling matchmakers were invaluable to families who lived in small towns with a shortage of men.

Even so, for the women love sometimes figured in the decision to marry, and on occasion even tragically. For example, an account in *From a Ruined Garden* told the story of Sorele, the daughter in a well-to-do family who fell secretly in love with Shloyme, the son of a poor teacher. Shloyme was drafted soon after the couple had sworn undying love. One morning her parents, who knew nothing of the affair, "announced to her that she had become a bride. True, she did not know the groom yet, but there was nothing to worry about; she would, God willing, know her spouse . . . right after the ceremony like all respectable Jewish girls." After much weeping and pining, Sorele married the man her parents had chosen. "Schloyme committed the ultimate sin—he killed himself."[43]

If there was a courtship, it was under the watchful eyes of the parents. Beatrice Pollack, for example, was courted by a wealthy boy her father approved of, but "there was no place to go. . . . You'd come and sit around and the parents were watching you. My father always trusted me . . . all he had to do was look at me and it meant I had to come in." Even so, "everybody did everything they wanted to do, only the parents didn't know it. Sometimes at night before really dark, we'd take a walk. I'd see boys and girls hiding under the trees. I don't say I had sexual intercourse with my boyfriend, but he hugged and kissed me. . . . We didn't kiss on the mouth—just little innocent kisses on the cheek."[44]

Arranged marriages cemented occupational and religious alliances between families, and the dowry was an important component of the marriage agreement. In addition, since the draft and emigration made eligible men scarce, families needed money to secure marriageable men for their daughters. The most eligible brides came from scholar families or had ample dowries; poor women had to rely on what their mothers could save out of their earnings. In the first year of marriage, the couple lived with the parents of the bride, and the dowry provided room, board, and spending money; if the groom was a scholar the dowry was used to guarantee his education.

Many women resented the marriage system, and the dowry in particular. Too many daughters could be a liability, and matchmaking easily turned into commerce, a humiliating experience for some: "Thank God my father was more enlightened. One day one of these *shadkens* came into the house sniffing a good fee because there were two pretty girls. With my mother, she started in haggling about prices. My father started to yell: 'Do you think you're selling horses here?' . . . He threw her right out."[45]

Although weddings were joyous and elaborate festivities, they sometimes increased tension between families or generations. Those who did not approve of the match would vent their disapproval publicly. The bride might also show her anger and disgust at the match that had been made for her. *The Shetl Book* includes an account of how Itke, the family rebel and one of the leading lights of the *Haskale,* was married off to a man who was the heir in a hasidic dynasty. As the date arrived and people and goods accumulated, "Itke did not appear at all. . . . For hours on end she sat in her chair and allowed everything to be done for her." Her mother was upset: "At night she wept . . . and consoled herself with the knowledge . . . that God had created divorce to rescue the daughters of Israel." Despite the mother's prayers, the moment came and the bride "passed by the female relatives with wide-opened eyes that stared and saw nothing."[44]

After marriage Jewish women put on wigs, which formally signified their new status and covered their hair, which had been cut to make them unattractive to other men, and attended *mikveh* baths for the seven days following each menstruation. Regular visits to the *mikveh* were considered a duty without which "a woman cannot be a good Jew," washing away the impurities that were believed to be inherent in menstruation. This obligation was taken very seriously: Fannie Shapiro recalled that "one time my grandmother forgot and they had intercourse anyway. So my grandfather took it to heart and he started fasting; he fasted so long he died."[47]

The highly developed sense of community within the Eastern European shtetl was in part an attempt to offset the difficulties and dangers faced by an oppressed minority. The collective survival of the shtetl demanded that business be conducted within a framework of mutual aid. Women often cared for each other's children so that a living could be made. Small shopkeepers and peddlers also helped each other out; they lent their commodities to each other without the expectation of immediate repayment, gave credit, and made loans freely: it was assumed that repayment would be made, guaranteed by the informal community sanctions associated with default. The point was to keep money circulating within the community and for its benefit.

This attitude was especially revealing in relation to children:

Children are given money to spend, not to save. They are taught to spend rationally, however, not for silly things, but for some purpose. They are taught to distribute "social justice," allowed to put the coins in the tine boxes [for charity] to hand the Friday night dole to the beggars. They learn that constructive giving is a sure way to win approval.[48]

Similarly, food was also to be shared within the community: it was a blessing to make food for the sick, to provide a meal for a penniless yeshiva student, or to offer homemade jam to visitors.

The idea of accumulating money or food for its own sake was foreign to shtetl life, and there was in any case rarely a surplus. The mother saved for tangible ends: to give a boy a better education, to prepare a dowry for a daughter, or to buy clothing for the children for the holidays. Money was good when directed toward a definite end. Gifts took the form of money and the most frequent punishment imposed by a rabbi was a fine that was to be distributed as charity. Generosity varied, and brought high status within the community. Misers, on the other hand, were abhorred:

> The miser who puts money above all else and wants to hoard it rather than spend it is called by the shtetl's most scathing epithet. He is called a *pig*, with all the disgust and hatred that was lavished upon that animal. Miserliness, in the view of the shtetl, is worse than un-Jewish, it is anti-Jewish.[49]

Money-making as an end in itself alienated the self from the community: it denied the community and its collective needs.

Jewish women played a vital role in the life of the Eastern European shtetl community, even though their lives contained many paradoxes. While everyday life—the home, the garden, and the marketplace—were realms given over to women because of their inferior status, these realms also maintained the customs of Jewish life. Women's lives were bound by a system of patriarchal obligation, but their world in large part created the social cement that enabled the culture to continue.

3

◇

STEERAGE TO GOTHAM

B Y THE LATE NINETEENTH CENTURY, INDUSTRIALIZATION AND
urbanization had upset the already precarious economic
relationship between peasant agriculture and domestic hand-
icrafts in southern Italy. The unification of Italy under northern
control in mid-century had severely affected the ability of the southern Italian peasants to maintain themselves on the land. Increasingly
dominated by their landlords by an elaborate system of taxation,
mortgage payments, and competition over small landholdings,
peasant families found it more and more difficult to maintain themselves. Artisanal activities that had supplemented agricultural production began to disappear. An agricultural depression, caused
partially by increased cereal and citrus production in the United
States, led to a fall in prices, and many peasants went bankrupt. As
the international market economy made serious inroads into traditional life, southern Italians began to migrate in large numbers to
the United States and elsewhere.

The Italian peasant, faced with an increasing need for money and
an increasing inability to acquire it at home, had three alternatives:
"He could either resign himself to his *miseria* [misery], or he could
rebel, or he could migrate."[1] Most emigrated, hoping by doing so to
maintain the family on the land. The peasants thus saw emigration as
an obligation to their own kin—as a way of getting money necessary
for the family back home. Emigration was in one sense an act of
estrangement, but the motivation was familiar: to maintain the
family in its traditional mode of life.

The mass migration of the southern Italian peasantry—over 5
million to the United States between 1890 and 1910—also functioned
to alleviate the growing demographic pressure in the cities and
potential revolt in the countryside. Sometimes the act of migration
was a kind of revolt. Adolfo Rossi, a well-known journalist and
inspector of immigrants, recounted this story:

Some time ago, in a Sicilian village, a lot of peasants became dissatisfied with the medieval agricultural methods of the local "feudal lord." These peasants felt that they were neither chattels going with the land, nor serfs. So one fine morning they gathered in front of the lord's house, bunched their shovels in a heap and on top placed the following notice: "Sir, do your farming yourself—we are going to America."[2]

Emigration brought a good deal of money into the southern Italian economy—money that, while it did not change the essential conditions of agriculture, did enable some peasants to buy land, to pay their mortgages and taxes, and to buy donkeys.

The overall structure, however, prevented any basic change. Often returning peasants "found no other opportunity than once again to buy a small piece of property in the same deteriorated rural economy, which they thought, when they left, they had escaped for all time."[3] In 1905 *Il Proletario,* the Italian-American socialist newspaper, noted that "Italians come to America with the sole intention of accumulating money. . . . Their dream . . . is the bundle of money they are painfully increasing, which will give them, after twenty years of deprivation, the possibility of having a mediocre standard of living in their native country."[4] The returning migrant may have come back more prosperous but he returned to the same untenable economic position.

The migrant stream itself revealed a distinct pattern. In the years of peak migration, 1890-1910, approximately 80 percent of the emigrants were male: Adolfo Rossi reported that "excessive emigration is working harm to the nation at large in that it takes from us the flowering of our laboring class . . . 84 percent of Italians coming to the United States are between 18 and 45 years of age. They are . . . producers. This 'human capital' of fresh young men is the contribution of Europe to the new land."[5] Repatriation rates were high: by 1907 seventy-three of every one hundred immigrants were returning each year.[6]

Single women also left but their numbers were fewer. It was far more difficult for a single woman to emigrate by herself: custom militated against women traveling alone. Those who did thought of themselves as part of the family economy, and left to help their families, to make a better dowry for themselves, or to find a husband. Agnes Santucci, for example, left for the United States at the age of seventeen. Her sister was already there, about to get married: "And so my father says, who wants to go next, to make a living, to help. My father couldn't support us, so he wrote to my uncle that he wanted to send another daughter to his house." In New York two years later Agnes married a man she had known in her hometown.[7]

Occasionally widows or deserted wives emigrated to forget their sorrows and start a new life. Rosina Giuliani, for instance, lived in a small suburb of Bari, where she worked as a hat maker and seamstress. She was quite beautiful, and met the son of a wealthy northern family when he passed through town with the army. They married and quickly had a child. He brought his new wife back to his mother's house, but the mother found her unacceptable and threw her out. Rosina went back with her husband to Bari but he soon left, leaving her with two small children. Rather than living out her life in disgrace, and being equipped with a marketable trade, she migrated to the United States at the age of thirty.[8]

But such cases were rare: most women who migrated went to join their husbands, part of a growing process of establishing families in the United States. The husband, as part of his familial obligation, migrated and saved the money to bring over his wife and small children. After an average of three or four years, the family was reunited in the United States; older parents, however, rarely made the journey. During the separation period, the women generally stayed in their mothers' homes.[9]

Eastern European Jews, on the other hand, although responding to many of the same pressures, represented a different pattern of migration. Industrialization, the May Laws, the overcrowding of cities, and the rampant anti-Semitism created a severe crisis in the already oppressive conditions of Jewish life. Jews moved from the towns to the cities, from artisan to factory labor, and in the process developed a more cosmopolitan and radical perspective. Russia was on the verge of revolution, and repression grew. Many women joined the socialist *Bund*, becoming active in trade union and socialist politics. But it was not easy to subvert the long arm of the czarist police, and many were beaten and jailed. After the failure of the 1905 revolution, pogroms increased and migration became a necessity.[10] Between 1881 and 1914 approximately one-third of all Jews left Eastern Europe.

Jewish migration was primarily a family affair, with an almost even ratio between the sexes—58 percent male and 42 percent female. This was a distinctive pattern among the "new" immigrants to the United States, as was the fact that repatriation rates were low and that the migration was permanent from the beginning. Moving the entire family was an expensive proposition, however, one that required time and planning. Generally fathers, as well as older sons and daughters, came over first in order to accumulate enough money to send for the rest of the family; economics, fear, and religious preference meant that the grandparents often stayed behind.

Many of the younger women hoped to find men to marry. Bessie Polski was a typical example: she left because there were no Jewish men for the girls to marry.[11] In a story entitled "The Miracle," Anzia Yezierska, a Lower East Side Jewish novelist, told a story that had particular relevance for these women. The heroine was a poor undowered Polish girl whose chances for marriage were slim. Suddenly a letter from America kindled her dreams: "In America, millionaires fall in love with the poorest girls. Matchmakers are out of style and a girl can get herself married to a man without the worries of a dowry. . . . In America, there is a law called ladies first. . . . The men hold their babies and carry bundles for the women and even help with the dishes." The letter made the rounds of the village. The ticket agents for the steamship companies, seeing how "the letter was working like yeast in the air for America, posted up big signs by all the market fairs: Go to America, The New World, fifty rubles a ticket."[12]

Others married in order to get to America. The young husband would go ahead to earn money for the wife's ticket. But newlywed husbands who sent back divorces instead of tickets were a major problem. Fannie Shapiro recalled: "You got married, [he] took the money, and left you right away to America. Sometimes, he sent for you; sometimes he found somebody else that he liked better, and forgot you. Sent you a divorce."[13]

Some opposed migration, in particular orthodox, middle-class Jewish fathers who had been raised to maintain the religious traditions and practices of Eastern European Jewish life.[14] Many of these fathers considered America "*trayf,*" or not kosher. Mothers, on the other hand, often encouraged migration, feeling it was in the interests of their children—even though this decision was extremely painful. Motherhood, in Eastern European shtetl life, was always more connected to the ways of the world.

But it was, ultimately, pointless to oppose migration. As one memorist put it, "America was in everybody's mouth. Businessmen talked of it over accounts; market women made up their quarrels that they might discuss it from stall to stall; people who had relatives in the famous land went around reading their letters for the enlightenment of less fortunate folks . . . children played at emigrating."[15] But fact and fiction blended into myth; in all the talk, "scarcely anyone knew one true fact about this magic land."[16] America was even in mothers' lullabies:

> Your daddy's in America
>   Little son of mine
> But you are just a child now
>   So hush and go to sleep.
> America is for everyone
>   They say, it's the greatest piece of luck
> For Jews, it's a garden of Eden
>   A rare and precious place.
> People there eat challah
>   In the middle of the week.[17]

And people acted on their inclinations, despite the resistance represented by the old orthodoxy: "The migration of Eastern European Jews constituted a spontaneous and collective impulse, perhaps even decision, by a people that had come to recognize the need for new modes and possibilities of life."[18]

The promise of America was multiple: the crisis intensified the desire to remake Jewish life in a country that appeared to be a land of milk and honey. While middle-class Jews had a greater stake in staying, the majority of artisans and skilled and semiskilled workers made the decision to migrate.

Anzia Yezierska articulated the magical effect America had in a story entitled "How I Found America" (in her book *Hungry Hearts*). A letter that arrived one day from the husband of one of the townspeople was full of good news: his sun had begun to shine in America because he had become a "businessman": "I have for myself a stand in the most crowded part of America, where people are as thick as flies and every day is like a market day by a fair." At the end of the day he had made a $2 profit: "That means four rubles and before your very eyes . . . I, Gedalyeh Mindel (a water carrier in the old country) earned four rubles a day, twenty-four rubles a week." He continued with an analysis of his good fortune, reporting that he ate "white bread and meat . . . every day just like the millionaires" and that in America "there were no mud huts where cows and chickens and people live together"; most importantly, "there is no Czar in America."

The letter inflamed the passions of the family, which suddenly erupted into an all-engulfing fantasy. "Sell my red quilted petticoat that grandmother left me for my dowry. Sell the feather beds, sell the samovar. Sure we can sell everything, the goat and all the winter things. It must always be summer in America." That evening the family fetched the pawnbroker and, after much bargaining by the mother, sold all their treasures, which brought them just enough money to buy steamship tickets.[19]

In this story, we seen an important exchange: the past is sold off in order to purchase the new. To make the dream come true, the family hocked its old way of life, turning their valued objects into the currency of the New World—cash.

The image of America as the country where money could be made, more money than most people could imagine, was carefully cultivated by a public relations effort mounted by U.S. companies. In both Italy and Eastern Europe this image worked its way into small towns and villages, newly industrialized cities and peasant villages, cultivating a dream that affected everyone. It was specifically aimed at recruiting young men and women of working age and depicted life in America as an unending stream of money. One poster, distributed across Europe by the woolen companies of Lawrence, Massachusetts, depicted a mill on one side of the street, a bank on the other, and workers marching from one side to the other with bags of money under their arms.[20] The poster was designed to reach people who could not read but who could easily understand the image: America was the country of rich workers; money was the means to wealth.

Steamship companies, too, acting as a vanguard of industry, used advertising to recruit immigrants. They sent posters showing prices and sailing dates into even the smallest villages and included editorials and articles from the U.S. newspapers that extolled the prosperity of the United States. Local agents, working on commission, were recruited from "the most varied people who took it upon themselves to convince the future emigrants and to sell them tickets:

auditors, priests, pharmacists, and copyists."[21] Selling steerage tickets in fact became a major occupation for large numbers of people in southern and Eastern Europe. Tickets could be paid for in installments, but if the price was $15 in 1890, by 1900 it was between $34 and $37.

In order to present America as a place where the crisis of emigration could be resolved, the posters had to have a strong social aspect: "America was the promised land to the poor, as opposed to the old world where land was denied the peasant."[22] Money and America became synonymous and provided the basis for the realization of long-standing dreams.

This propaganda would not however have met a responsive chord if there had not been personal reports that the United States was the way out. Personal witness, in the form of letters "from persons who have emigrated to friends at home have been the immediate cause of by far the greater part of the remarkable movement from Southern and Eastern Europe in the last twenty-five years," concluded a report of the Immigration Commission of 1909. The report went on to argue that "recently arrived immigrants are substantially the agencies which keep the American labor market supplied with unskilled laborers from Europe. . . . It is these personal appeals, which, more than all other agencies, promote and regulate the tide of European emigration to America."[23] The immigrant's letters also regulated the flow of migration: information about wages, depressions, and job possibilities acted as a stimulus or a break. Tickets were often bought in the United States—again on the installment plan—and sent back home.

Returning migrants provided another incentive. In Italy, for instance, returning immigrants were called "americanos," a word meaning "someone who got rich, no one knows how—as if money alone is enough to change people." They became dispensers of "information and inspiration. The money they can show makes a vivid impression."[24]

If the idea of America was a mixture of myths and yearnings, these were necessary to help the potential immigrants make the move to the unknown America. For women the myth contained a transformation to a nonpatriarchal, classless world where millionaires married poor girls, and men took care of children and helped with housework. America represented what was repressed in the old and promised in fantasy. Both Italians and Jews responded to myths of their own making—fostered by American advertising— visions that expressed inner longings denied in a dying and oppressive world.

4
◇

First Encounters

O N A SIZZLING HOT DAY IN THE SUMMER OF 1895 MARIA Ganz and her mother walked off the boat onto a New York City pier. They had left their comfortable farmhouse in Galicia to join Lazarus Ganz, who had recently rented a rear tenement apartment in the Lower East Side. For weeks he had been busy preparing their new home; he was flushed with anticipation. Maria's mother walked into her new apartment, looked around slowly, turned to her husband and cried: "So, we have crossed half the world for this?" Maria recreated the scene in her memoirs:

> I can see her now as she stood facing my father, her eyes full of reproach. I am sure it had never occurred to poor, dreamy, impractical Lazarus Ganz that his wife might be disappointed with the new home he had provided for her. The look of pain as he saw the impression the place made on her filled me with pity for him, young as I was. A five-year-old child is not apt to carry many distinct memories from that age of life, but it is a scene I have never forgotten.[1]

On an autumn day in 1896 Leonard Covello, his brothers, and their mother landed in New York, worlds away from their native Avigliano, Italy. They had spent twenty days aboard ship. When the sea became rough, Leonard's mother held her sons close to her heart; the ocean storms mirrored the fear and torment locked inside her body. As Leonard reported later:

> And when finally we saw the towering buildings and rode the screeching elevated train and saw the long, unending streets of the metropolis that could easily swallow a thousand Aviglianese towns, she accepted it with the mute resignation as *la volonta di Dio* [the will of God], while her heart longed for the familiar scenes and faces of loved ones and the security of a life she had forever left behind.[2]

A story by novelist Anzia Yezierska captured a mother's lament: "*Oi Veh!* my mother cried in dismay, where is the sunshine in

America? She went to her tenement window and looked at the blank wall of the next house. Like a grave so dark. To greenhorns it seemed as if the sunlight had faded from their lives and buildings like mountains took its place."[3] In another mother's story, a question: "Where are the green fields and open spaces in America? A loneliness for the fragrant silence of the woods that lay beyond my mud hut welled up in my heart, a longing for the soft, responsive earth of our village streets. All about me was the harshness of brick and stone, the stinking smell of crowded poverty."[4]

Leonard Covello voiced a similar despair:

The sunlight and fresh air of our mountain home . . . were replaced by four walls and people over and under and on all sides of us. Silence and sunshine, things of the past, now replaced by a new urban montage. The cobbled streets. The endless monotonous rows of tenement buildings that shut out the sky. The traffic of wagons and carts and carriages, and the clopping of horses' hooves which struck sparks at night. . . . The clanging of bells and the screeching of sirens as a fire broke out somewhere in the neighborhood. Dank hallways. Long flights of wooden stairs and the toilet in the hall.[5]

Nothing prepared people for the immediacy of this experience. America, as myth or image, may have been the Big Rock Candy Mountain, a utopian dream, a piece of heaven, but this heaven turned out to be a concrete prison, a vast wall of steel that blocked out the familiar world of nature, replacing the sunshine with the gray stare of stone and brick and changing silence into an omnipresent screeching tune. Even in Eastern European cities, the woods were a walk away—a place to gather food or sneak away, a space to hide from the pogroms or hold secret revolutionary meetings. New York abolished the forests forever, leaving them retrievable only in memory or in the pictorial reproductions that hung on the walls of tenement apartments as reminders of a world lost but not forgotten.

Not only were the woods lost, but city life seemed to transform the natural rhythms of life, turning night into day. This is how two Italian immigrants put it: "Our first impressions of the brightly lit streets of New York at night time suggested that such excessive illumination was for the prevention of the commission of theft. In Italy, there was no need for street lighting because when it was dark, every good person was supposed to be asleep."[6] For women, the loss of nature also meant a loss of space. An Italian homeworker summed this up when she responded to a question posed by an American social worker in 1911. Did she like America?

> Not much, not much. In my country, people cook out-of-doors, do the wash out-of-doors, tailor out-of-doors, make macaroni out-of-doors. And my people laugh, laugh all the time. In America, it is *sopra, sopra* [up, up, with a gesture of going upstairs]. Many people, one house; work, work all the time. Good money, but no good air.[7]

Anna Kuthan, an immigrant from Czechoslovakia, described her first year in New York in much the same way: "I didn't smile for a long time. Why? Because this was a different country. Everybody was for himself, and there was always money, money, money; rush, rush, rush."[8]

How many first-generation mothers experienced their new environment, with its density of people, filthy crowded streets, and small apartments, as the negation of their previous poor but more natural life? How many times did they compare past and present as they paced the floors of their new homes, thinking, as Yezierska put it: "In America were rooms without sunshine, rooms to sleep in, to eat in, to cook in, but without sunshine." How many asked, "Could I be satisfied with just a place to sleep and a door to shut people out to take the place of sunshine?"[9]

For many, the loss of sunshine was a metaphor that described feelings of alienation and unfamiliarity, an image of mourning for a world left behind, a plaintive moan of entry into the unknown. The abrupt separation from the immediate past was probably hardest on the older generation, whose lives had been shaped in other worlds and different cultures. This separation also spoke to a primary difference between themselves and their children. After all, as Leonard Covello noted, "a child adapts to everything. It was the older people who suffered, those uprooted human beings who faced the shores of an unknown land with quaking hearts."[10]

In the cultures from which these women came, mothers existed within the confines of the home, but that home was the "center of the world, at the heart of the real."[11] For women with small children, pulling up the foundations of a known life was a severe shock, a shock that penetrated to the core of experience and the ways in which experience becomes codified as culture. The loss of the natural, as perceived by the first generation, also meant the loss of familiar social rituals that had given life meaning and value.

As the concrete walls of the tenement apartment closed in, announcing the new environment, the home itself changed irrevocably. It no longer looked out to nature but to thousands of other crowded rooms that opened to the urban street, to dirty hallways, to endless clotheslines, to fear and isolation. Some women never recovered. Jane Addams recorded the following incident, one of her first encounters with an immigrant woman:

> We were also early impressed with the curious isolation of many of the immigrants: an Italian woman once expressed her pleasure in the red roses that she saw at one of our receptions, in surprise that they had been "brought so fresh all the way from Italy." She would not believe for an instant that they had grown in America. She said that she had lived in Chicago for six years and had never seen any roses, whereas in Italy she had seen them in great profusion. During all that time, of course, the woman had lived within ten blocks of a florist's window; she had not been more than a five-cent ride away from a public park; but she had never dreamed of faring farther forth for herself and no one had taken her. Her conception of America had been the untidy street in which she lived and had made her long struggle to adapt herself to American ways.[12]

The street, however, held a promise. In the spaces of American life carved out for immigrants the only "roses" were other people, family, relatives, friends. Italian and Jewish settlement patterns on the Lower East Side reflected the absolute necessity for family and ethnic cohesion. Italians settled between Pearl and Houston streets, east of the Bowery, while Jewish immigrants inhabited the Tenth Ward, west of the Bowery. Italians moved into the old Irish sections of the Lower East Side; Jews inherited the old German sector. The new immigrants lived and worked huddled together in tenement houses within easy reach of the garment district, surrounded by peddler stands and shops where language was not a barrier. If all America allowed its immigrants was a few city blocks, the blocks themselves were transformed to meet the needs of their inhabitants.

Caught in the margins between old and new, the neighborhoods were simultaneously an enclave of old-world custom and new-world adaptation, a curious admixture of tradition and change. For the first generation, a great deal of comfort was derived from this partial reconstruction of the old country: they nestled in communities of common language, bound by ties of custom, ritual, and institutions—a world not lost, but rebuilt.

For some old-world children, finding "America" was difficult. Rose Cohen, in her autobiography *Out of the Shadow*, described how it took her almost five years to find the New World:

> For though I was in America, I had lived in practically the same environment which we brought from home. Of course, there was a difference in our joys, in our sorrows, in our hardships, for after all this was a different country; but on the whole we were still in our village in Russia. A child that came to this country and began to go to school had taken the first step into the New World. But the child that was put into the shop remained in the old environment with the old people, held back by the old traditions.[13]

Yet even in old-world neighborhoods there were signs of change, glimpses into the elusive promise of American life. Greenhorns who shopped in the market streets saw bananas for the first time, in addition to new kinds of mops, pots, and kitchenware. Advertisements showed new products: canned food, soap, toothpaste, modern sewing machines, furniture, and clocks of all varieties. For the fact was that industrial urban America was busy transforming material life, substituting machine-made products for those once produced by hand. While Maria Ganz's mother was reproaching her husband with a broken dream, Simon Patten, an American economist, was developing a theory to explain the effects of industrialization on immigrant women. In the Old World, he argued, women had primarily been "mothers and the makers of commodities." In the New, the relationship between women and production changes: here factory-made goods aroused and reinforced the economic motive, and this, Patten believed, would bring about a fundamental change. The immigrant working class would now, through wage labor, "spend its current wealth on commodities as formerly it spent the current wealth of womanhood."[14] Thus, the loss of nature and of home production was a gain for women: for Patten, the progressive apostle of consumption, progress was measured by the access to new modes of life made possible by industry and commerce. It touched women's lives in two decisive ways: industry called women out of the home into the factory, and new factory-made goods transformed the home itself. If the Lower East Side appeared to its inhabitants as the underside of progress, to Patten this was mere appearance; under the surface were social forces that would alter women's lives as they moved from a patriarchal past to a progressive future.

Lazarus Ganz was upset by his wife's reaction to her new home. One day he came home with a sewing machine, a present to his wife that he had bought on the installment plan. According to his daughter:

> The machine he presented to my mother in the hope of making her more contented, for she had never been able to reconcile herself to the American tenement and had spent much time lamenting the more cheerful and comfortable home she had left behind in Galicia. It was a marvelous machine . . . I had never seen my mother so happy and enthusiastic.[15]

Lazarus Ganz had hesitated for a long time, deciding between a sewing machine and a bronze clock for the mantelpiece: in his neighborhood, recently arrived immigrants purchased either one or the other as a sign of their Americanization. Each in its own way was an intervention into the rhythm of daily life. It took, however, eighteen years to pay for the sewing machine, raising questions as to whether Patten's belief in the power of economic arousal was not a condemnation to economic bondage as well.

Leonard Covello's father had preceded his family to America and had spent six years "trying to save enough for a little place to live and money for *l'umburco* [the voyage over]." During those six years he boarded with the Accurso family. As was customary, "it was Carmella, wife of his friend, Vito, who saved his money for him until the needed amounts accumulated. It was Carmella Accurso who made ready the tenement flat and arranged the welcoming party." And when Leonard Covello's mother was upset when she arrived, and cried her way through the party, "it was Mrs. Accurso who put her arm comfortably upon my mother's shoulders and led her away from the party and into the hall and showed her the water faucet. 'Courage! You'll get used to it here. See. Isn't it wonderful how the water comes out.' Through her tears my mother managed to smile." In southern Italy, carrying water was one of the worst domestic chores. Mrs. Accurso offered running water as a miraculous compensation for Mrs. Covello's felt loss. For the first time since her arrival, Mrs. Covello was pleased: "Water, which to my mother was one of the great wonders of America—water with just a twist of the handle and only a few paces from the kitchen. It took her a long time to get used to this luxury. Water and a few other conveniences were the compensation the New World had to offer."[16]

In another variation of this experience, Anna Kuthan recounted her understanding of new possibilities. During World War I she had worked as a domestic servant in the home of a wealthy woman in Vienna where one of her responsibilities had been to pick up the Red Cross packages sent from America. She was impressed with the packaging of Hecker's flour, Nestlé's cocoa, and Carnation evaporated milk: "I saved all the labels, even from the Hecker's flour. I says, oh my God, they must have everything so good if they pack everything so good. If I could only come to this country." Although she was allowed to save the labels, she was not allowed to taste any of the products:

> The lady locked everything up. I wanted to get a taste of the sweet condensed milk. One day she forgot to lock it up. She went into the bathroom. You know what I did? I just put the can in my mouth and it was dripping the milk like honey right in my mouth. And one, two, three, she opened the door. I says it's inside already, you can't get it out of me. I got a taste for it. I never forgot it.

When Anna Kuthan came to the United States right after the war, this experience of denial and theft was constantly in her mind:

> When I came to this country, the first thing I see is those big stores, I said there is the Hecker's flour . . . there is the condensed milk! When I was married . . . one day I was shopping and I came home crying; he says what happened to you. All the things I bought in the stores, what I got in Vienna and I could only dream about, not even taste it. And here I see it on the shelf. I bought everything and I'm gonna go there every day and I'm gonna buy it.[17]

As a domestic servant in Vienna, Anna Kuthan saw the consumer products of American society as magical objects, the fruits of the land sealed mysteriously in shiny vessels, with beautiful painted scenes gracing their outsides. Yet what was magic for her had become for others—those of the Viennese upper classes—part of everyday life. Already, among the elites of Europe, American exports were beginning to make their mark on daily existence. "Luxury" came in cans. For Anna Kuthan, these cans thus took on great significance as concrete embodiments of her own deprivation, and stealing a taste was part of her attempt to break through a world of denial and assert her own needs. Anna Kuthan's self—before she ever set foot in America—intertwined with the brand names and products of a young and burgeoning consumer economy.

In the United States being able to buy Hecker's flour and Carnation evaporated milk symbolized Anna Kuthan's new social position: a "free consumer" in the universal marketplace, where money could free one from the class-bound world of European society. The ability to buy goods in the American marketplace was not simply an act of consumption; it was also an act of transcendence, the realization of a new social status.

If immigrant mothers were consumed by the realities of home life, some of their daughters were quick to notice the new world that swirled around their tenement apartments. The Lower East Side presented an audiovisual montage of possibilities: women dressed in ready-made American clothes, women running to work, billboards and posters graced with women in the latest styles, women carrying schoolbooks under their arms, women in the streets and in restaurants, women speaking openly to men on the street. While the mothers attempted to reassemble the terms of a known life, their daughters were busy decoding the messages, disassembling the old life, stepping into the present.

And the contrast between the greenhorns and the Americans was ever present. As social worker Josephine Roche put it:

> Inevitably, the influence of the new life in which she spends nine hours a day begins to tell on her. Each morning and evening as she covers her head with an old crocheted shawl and walks to and from the factory, she passes the daughters of her Irish and American neighbors in their smart hats, their cheap waists in the latest and smartest style, their tinsel ornaments and their gay hair bows. A part of the pay envelopes goes into the personal expenses of those girls. Nor do they hurry through the streets to their homes after working hours, but linger with a boy companion "making dates" for a movie or an affair.[18]

Through observation and contact, through friends and relatives, immigrant daughters learned the vital importance of shedding their pasts. To be a greenhorn was to inhabit a region on the margins of modern life; to overcome being green was a metamorphosis. Gino Speranza wrote with patriarchal dismay in *Charities* magazine:

> Industrially it is the Italian woman that has suffered most. The Italian daughters or sisters, who in Italy used to work around the house or in the fields, never receiving compensation, sees the "girl on the lower floor" [Irish or American working girl] go out every day and earn good money that gives her, what appears to the newcomer, not only splendid independence, but even the undreamed of joy of wearing Grand Street millinery. The home becomes hateful.[19]

Millinery in Italy was reserved, by custom and class, for the upper classes; the peasants wore shawls on their heads. Yet here Italians saw women of their own class donning hats as an everyday occurrence, an incitement to transgression and transformation.

David Blaustein, writing of the experience of Jews in America, echoed similar sentiments: "The woman finds women in public life. She finds it cheaper to eat in restaurants and to buy ready-made clothing."[20]

Immigrant mothers brought large quantities of clothing with them, "representing sometimes their accumulations for a dowry—heavy linen underwear, thick, heavily lined waists, clumsy shoes and wide, bright skirts. A colored scarf or shawl completes the wardrobe." These costumes were discarded in the United States: "Only some of the older women have the courage to appear at their factories in the garments they brought. The first year in this country frequently means much skimping and saving to get new clothes, especially among the younger women who want to look American."[21]

One of the first acts of initiation was to purchase new clothes. Sophie Abrams, a Jewish garment worker, recreated this experience:

> I was such a greenhorn, you wouldn't believe. My first day in America I went with my aunt to buy some American clothes. She bought me a shirtwaist, you know, a blouse and a skirt, a blue print with red buttons and a hat, such a hat I had never seen. I took my old brown dress and shawl and threw them away! I know it sounds foolish, we being so poor, but I didn't care. I had enough of the old country. When I looked in the mirror, I couldn't get over it. I said, boy, Sophie, look at you now. Just like an American.[22]

In another variation, one young immigrant woman who came to the United States in 1911 had been taken by her relatives for new clothes. She also bought "the wherewithal to fix her hair in an American fashion. When asked why, she responded quite proudly:

'Yes, I'm almost an American. I have a rat for my hair. The essential thing in America is to look stylish.' "[23]

If immigrant and American mothers grew up in an era of home production, where clothing was made to last, their daughters, caught up in the whirl of ready-made clothing, valued it for its symbolic power—style above durability or comfort. Sophinisba Breckenridge, in *New Homes for Old*, captured this change:

> In her [daughter's] main contention that if she is to keep up with the fashions she need not buy clothing that will last more than one season, she is probably right. It is also natural that this method of buying should be distressing to her mother, who has been accustomed to clothes of unchanging fashions which were judged entirely by their quality.[24]

Style was not only alluring; it was also necessary for employment. One woman from Russia explained that in the old country, "the dresses we wore were made out of sack, old sheets or table cloths that did not need much style. It was not a question of style, but of how to cover one's body in those days." What she desired most in Russia was "the leather jacket that came with the Revolution"; the jacket to her was a "symbol of both Revolution and elegance." As soon as she got here she bought a leather jacket, but it brought her a lot of trouble. When she tried to get a job, the door was slammed in her face or she was asked if she belonged to a union. Finally, one employer made clear his understanding of her jacket: "I am sorry, miss, we don't like Bolsheviks." She asked why he thought she was one. He replied: "Never mind. I can see it at once. These leather jackets and bushy hair. I know them well." For a year she endured but, finally, faced with starvation, she decided to get rid of the jacket. "I dressed myself in the latest fashion with lipstick in addition, although it was so hard to get used to at first that I blushed, felt foolish and thought myself vulgar. But I got a job."[25]

Some middle-class moralists were upset at the displays of finery; in their minds, the poor should *look* poor. Home economist Ellen Richardson was shocked to discover that tenement girls were not dressed in rags:

> Did you ever go down to one of the city settlements full of the desire to help and lift up the poor shop girl? There must be some mistake, you thought. These could not be poor girls earning five or six dollars a

week. They looked better dressed than you did. Plumes on their heads, a rustle of silk petticoats, everything about them in the latest style.[26]

Jane Addams had a more realistic approach to the issues involved: "The working girl, whose family lives in a tenement . . ., who has little social standing, knows full well how much habit and style of dress has to do with her position. . . . Her clothes are her background and from them she is largely judged."[27]

The daily press was fond of using the stylish look of working women as a weapon against their claims of poverty. In 1914 Lillian Wald, angered by one such editorial, decided to get to the bottom of the matter. She went to a young acquaintance "whose appearance justified the newspaper description" and discovered that she lived on $5 a week. She kept up her appearance by purchasing

> stockings from pushcart venders, seconds of off-colors but good quality for ten cents; boys' blouses, as they were better and cheaper. These cost twenty-five cents. Hats (peanut straw) cost ten cents. Having very small feet, she was able to take advantage of special sales, when she could buy a good pair of shoes for fifty cents.

Yet even with all this careful planning "there was practically nothing left for carfare, for pleasures, or the many demands made upon the meager purse but she looked good."[28]

Some women made their own clothes. One newspaperman, for instance, reported an encounter with an East Side girl who showed up for their appointment all dressed up. He was taken aback: "One who did not know East Side girls would have said uncharitably that the heartless young woman was spending on clothes the money needed to buy bread for her old mother and small sisters." But then the truth came out:

> The waist, thin and charmingly cool-looking, she had made herself, buying the material from a Hester Street pushcart for twenty cents. Its style came from the really handsome neck arrangement . . . she worked at neckware and the boss allowed her to take the odds and ends from which she fashioned the pretty thing. The skirt, her brother-in-law who works in skirts, made at odd times. Her hats, her chum made. To the uninitiated, the costume represented an outlay of twenty dollars at least, although she had achieved it at an expense of $3.30, and was able to go out without proclaiming to the world the dire poverty of her home.[29]

Most bought their clothes, however, although they could do that on an installment plan:

> To solve the clothing problem many of these women have to steer between the dangers of Scylla and Charybdis. If they buy only what they can pay for it with ready money, without going into debt, they must get the cheapest qualities which give poor wear. Of course, on the other hand, they appreciate the economy of buying a better grade of goods, they must pay the high prices of the installment plan and incur debt to be paid out of future wages.[30]

For greenhorns, the change in dress and hair was an essential part of adaptation. Yet these acts concealed a secret. As Leonard Covello put it: "To all outward appearances I was an American, except that I didn't speak a word of English."[31]

It was a good idea to shop with relatives, since it was a common practice for shopkeepers to take advantage of newcomers unskilled in the practices of the marketplace. Anna Kuthan, for example, described her first attempt to buy new clothes:

> My first expense when I came to this country was paying back money I owed from my trip. Then I decided I had to dress myself a little bit decent. All the stores had signs showing what language was spoken inside. I went into a Czech clothing store and I didn't have experience [bargaining]. I paid whatever was asked. The store owner said: "I have a coat for you, you're going to look like a million dollars." I paid forty dollars for this coat, but I found out the next day it was worth less than eighteen dollars.[32]

The America contained in the Lower East Side did not just define new possibilities in terms of goods and products. It also presented to new immigrants new forms of pleasure and recreation. Greenhorns were often taken out to new forms of entertainment: the nickelodeon, the soda shop, and the candy store.

A common form of introduction, reported by *Survey* magazine, was to be "taken to the nickel show." There the newly arrived Jewish woman hears Yiddish jokes and American popular music and "marvels at the wonders of the motion picture."[33] After being shown this magical new medium, she is taken to an ice cream parlor where she has her first ice cream soda. Magic for the eyes, sweets for the taste, a little piece of unheard-of luxury in the new world of concrete and steel.

Movies, soda shops, and candy stores were luxuries either unavailable or unknown in the older European world. In terms reminiscent of Anna Kuthan, Leonard Covello described his family's ecstatic encounter with an American candy store:

> There was a counter covered with glass and all manner and kinds of sweets such as we had never seen. Candy, my father told us, grinning. This is what we call candy in America. We were even allowed to select the kind we wanted. I selected some little round cream-filled chocolates which tasted like nothing I had ever eaten before. The only candy I knew was confetti, which we had on feast days or from the pocket of my uncle, the priest, on some special occasion.[34]

While certain changes spoke to new possibilities, others widened the gulf between parents and children. The children, more plastic than their parents, often formed the advance guard: they were the first to learn English, the first to demand changes in those old-world cultural practices thought dishonorable by the older generation, the first to incorporate forms of American culture into their daily lives. A Jewish woman whose daughter had come to the United States before her wrote to the *Jewish Daily Forward* in dismay:

> During the few years she was here without us she became a regular Yankee and forgot how to talk Yiddish. . . . She says it is not nice to talk Yiddish and that I am a greenhorn. . . . She wants to make a Christian woman out of me. She does not like me to light the Sabbath candles, to observe the Sabbath. When I light the candles, she blows them out. Once I saw her standing on the stoop with a boy so I went up to her and asked her when she would come up. . . . She did not reply, and later when she came up she screamed at me because I had called her by her Jewish name. But I cannot call her differently. I cannot call her by her new name.[35]

The changing of names was thought of as demeaning by the older generation, robbing the family of its history and honor. Leonard Covello's name had been changed in school from Coviello to Covello—the teacher thought it was easier to pronounce. His parents found this out when he brought home his report card. His father exploded: "In America anything can happen and does happen. But you don't change a family name." Leonard tried to explain. His mother intervened, defining the difference between external and basic change: "A person's life and honor is in his name. *A name is not a shirt or a piece of underwear.* . . . Now that you have become Americanized you understand everything and I understand nothing." The child, upset, fled the house feeling that "somehow or other the joy of childhood had seeped out of his life." An older female friend of the family who had witnessed the scene came up to him, and when he protested that they did not understand, replied: "Maybe some day you will realize that you are the one who doesn't understand."[36]

Immersion in the public schools, in the language and manners of urban America, sometimes made the children carriers of culture and information. Whether by necessity or desire, the children broke through the barriers of language and custom, yet this changed the traditional conventions of the parent/child relationship.

For example, Lawrence Veiller, the noted tenement-house reformer, was working on a project to disseminate tuberculosis information to Italian immigrants. He conceived of a leaflet that combined a picture of an Italian pastoral scene on the top and rules about prevention on the bottom. He first thought to print the rules in Italian, but decided to consult the respected Italian doctor Antonio Stella. Dr. Stella advised him that "the majority of adult Italians do not read any language, either Italian or English. On the other hand, most of the children read English, but few read Italian. If you want your plan to be successful, print your poster in English. The children will then read it and translate it for their parents."[37] Since the majority of immigrant parents did not have enough interaction with American institutions to require knowledge of the English language, the child often "stood between the new life and its strange institutions, he is the interpreter . . . he becomes the authority."[38]

Despite the attractions of the new world of consumerism, many recognized its other side. Israel Friedlander, writing in *Survey* magazine, remarked that the immigrant Jew

> quickly notices those negative features which live on the surface of American life: the hunt after the dollar, the drift towards materialism, and he is forced to the dangerous and cynical conclusion that America—and here I repeat what one may frequently hear from the lips of Jewish immigrants—is the land of bluff, that religion, morality, politics and learning are a sham and the only thing of value in this country is almighty Mammon.[39]

Whatever way one looked at the promise of America, it started and ended with money.

Underneath the consumer marketplace, the myth of money, and the image of the good life was a reality that was not completely different from the experience of life back home. Anna Kuthan spoke to the contradiction between image and reality. When she was seven years old, she had worked in a textile factory in Czechoslovakia. Her job was to unload bales of cotton sent to the factory from Texas. She remembered those cotton bales vividly, for they formed her first impression of America:

Those big plantations they have big beautiful picture [on the bales] from their factories and the plantation and the colored people, you know how they work, and we [the children] always got it off nicely and we decorate everything. Oh my God, we save every picture and I was always saying I wish I could get to this country. I was dreaming already about this country. It's something you can't even picture until I came to this country and worked with the colored people and hear about and read about the history about the slaves and everything. Then I realize that, oh my God, how they have to work on the big plantation in the cotton fields, all those black people and the children almost for nothing . . . you know, like slaves, So you see, this is all real history, no matter where you live, no matter where you come from.[40]

5
◇
AGENTS OF ASSIMILATION

As the new immigrants settled into their neighborhoods and began their search for America, what they found was each other. Their lives were touched by the images and products of the New World, but they came into contact with precious few "Americans"—middle-class America had fled its old neighborhoods, and the new immigrants were more likely to meet working-class Irish or Germans than people who were "native born." There was, however, a small group of Americans—mostly women—who eagerly sought out the immigrants, hoping to influence their attitudes and beliefs about America. These were the social workers; their mission was to bring a message of progress to the tenements.

Starting in the 1880s, settlement houses cropped up in the tenement neighborhoods of most large American cities. Most settlement workers were women from old-stock Protestant families, whose fathers were well-off professionals: teachers, lawyers, civil servants, doctors, or businessmen. The majority grew up in northeastern or midwestern cities in middle-class districts and had had little contact with the working class. Most were young: in 1890 their median age was twenty-five. Nearly 90 percent had gone to college and over 50 percent had gone on to graduate school, in the United States or in Europe. Many were unmarried. Some, like Jane Addams, Mary Simkhovitch, and Lillian Wald, devoted their entire lives to the movement; for others, settlement work was a brief interlude.[1]

Given the advantages of class and background, why did these young people consciously choose to live in a world so different from their own? If so many of their compatriots were fleeing the tenement districts, why were they running the other way, crossing the tenement line in reverse? More specifically, why did some middle-class American women feel it their responsibility to try to cross class and ethnic barriers to become the one group of "real" Americans that the immigrants would encounter? And how were they received?

These questions have a particular relevance to our story because women social workers were the only people in America who had a passionate interest in the lives and problems of immigrant mothers and their daughters. Some were sympathetic, some highly judgmental. Some were intent on remolding immigrant cultures, to adapt them to new American norms; others looked at immigrant women from a more sympathetic perspective and saw themselves as advocates. Together, they left a rich written chronicle, in the form of books, magazines, articles, and newspapers, which gives us a detailed picture of the cultural interaction between two very different groups of women. The social workers had a major influence on the lives of the immigrants, and also played an important role in shaping the ways in which the rest of America perceived immigrant culture. As individuals, they felt challenged by cultures so different from their own, and certain aspects of the immigrants' culture—the role and importance of the family, the relationship between parents and children, the way in which housework should be done and social life conducted, even the basic rhythms of everyday life—became areas of conflict. As the deeply held beliefs of the two groups clashed, the social workers felt it imperative to write about these conflicts, and in the process they have provided us with intimate insights into the lives of the immigrant women, as well as into their own cultural biases and to changing attitudes toward women in general at the time.

A partial, if brief, answer to the question of why these middle-class women went to downtown neighborhoods can be found in the contradictions of American middle-class life in the late nineteenth century. Middle-class daughters were not totally bound to home and family. Progress brought new patterns of consumption into middle-class homes, and they turned out to be both a blessing and a curse. "The old tasks of our mothers have dropped from our hands," social worker Margaret Byington explained, "and we are not always wise enough to find new ones to take their place." Isolated from society, cooped up at home, women were, as Jane Addams put it, "forced to be shut off from the common labor by which they live."[2] Still unable to vote and discouraged from working, even those middle-class daughters who went to college were expected to return home to wait for marriage. Many accepted their fate, but others broke out of the domestic trap to join the suffrage or social work movements.

Jane Addams, in her *Democracy and Social Ethics*, articulated the demands of some of these daughters against what she called the "family claim." Educated daughters, she argued, felt a new calling to service to society. As the parent generation was unable to conceive of any role more important than duty to family, such youthful waywardness was seen as "willful and indulgent." To the daughters, this parental intransigence seemed hypocritical. Their parents had given them an education that taught a sense of social obligation, yet at the same time they were being asked to withdraw from society in favor of the insular life of the home.[3]

Ironically, the solution to this crisis came from the very traditions these women were attempting to escape: charity work. The settlement house was a new institution in the nineteenth-century tradition of moral philanthropy, a domain where women were able to find access to the larger community as the spiritual guardians of morality.

Moral philanthropy perceived poverty as a character flaw, a problem of bad habits or intemperate behavior. Regeneration was possible if the poor would adopt the Protestant ethic: hard work, discipline, order, punctuality, temperance, and "clean Christian living." By the 1880s the Charity Organization Society, the large philanthropic organization, was collecting vast amounts of information on the "moral" character of the urban poor. By 1890 some four thousand "friendly visitors" were visiting individual families to scrutinize character and preach the values of the middle class. One immigrant woman characterized the friendly visits this way:

> She comes to see that we don't overeat ourselves. She learns us how to cook corn meal. By pictures and lectures she show us poor people how we should live without meat, without milk, without butter, and without eggs. Always it's on the tip of my tongue to ask her, can't you yet learn us how to eat without eating?[4]

While the settlement house was built on the traditional link between women and philanthropy, it also broke with that tradition. It was often referred to as the "college dormitory in the slums."[5] For young middle-class women it resolved the conflict between the social claim and the family claim. Not quite as "masculine" as a career, still connected to tradition, settlement activity allowed women to immerse themselves in the urban industrial world and at the same time to carve out a space of their own. The settlement house was then in many ways the product of the "new woman," the enterprising daughter who had broken from her middle-class home. Charity was no longer preached from the Victorian porch, as the settlement worker moved directly into the community she wished to serve. Even more important, if their mothers had seen themselves as missionaries, *to* the poor, the daughters saw themselves as advocates *for* the poor.

Young charity workers like Jane Addams felt increasingly alienated from the old homilies of hard work and character:

> The grandmother of the charity visitor could have done the . . . preaching very well, she did have industrial virtues and housewifely training. In a generation our experience has changed and our views with them. . . . The daintily clad charitable visitor who steps into the little house made untidy by the vigorous efforts of her hostess [the washerwomen] is no longer sure of her superiority to the latter; she recognizes that the hostess after all represents social value and industrial use, as over her own parasitic cleanliness and a social standing attained only through status.[6]

The poor, in Jane Addams' eyes, were the working classes, dignified by their labor—mirror opposites of middle-class daughters, who felt useless and parasitic. If the mother generation saw the people as people to be taught, the daughter generation—separated from a sense of meaning in their lives—saw the poor as people to learn from despite their suffering. If their mothers had been charity visitors, they would self-consciously call themselves social workers, a significant term indicating that they were responsible to the social claim and that this claim was dignified by work. If their mothers had preached to the people, they would study and learn from the people to understand society from their point of view. Caught betweeen identifying with and condescending to the poor, young settlement workers were romantically drawn to the "bigger, more emotional and freer lives of working people."[7]

But could social workers overcome their own class experience—what Jane Addams called "incorrigible bourgeois standards"—to understand working-class immigrant life, or would their experience become a blinder in their work? Would they too attempt to impose the cultural ideals of the middle class on the lives of immigrant people?

They tried not to. Lillian Wald, for example, was initiated into the Lower East Side through what she called a "baptism of fire." Working as a nurse, she was approached one day in 1893 by a young girl whose mother was sick. As they walked the garbage-strewn streets, Wald felt a sudden rush of comprehension; she felt she began to understand "all of the maladjustments of our social and economic relations." She then met the girl's family and desperately tried to judge them using the prevailing philanthropic wisdom. Although the conditions the family lived in were appalling—the family of seven shared their two rooms with boarders, the husband was a cripple, and the sick woman lay on a filthy bed—the people "were not degraded human beings judged by any measure of moral values." Moreover, "it would have been some solace if by any conviction of the moral unworthiness of the family I could have defended myself as part of a society which permitted such conditions to exist."[8] Her passion aroused, she immediately moved to the Lower East Side to found the Henry Street Settlement House.

Mary Kingsbury Simkhovitch, the founder of Greenwich House, went through a different kind of "social baptism." After college and graduate work in Europe, she felt compelled to join the settlement movement. She spent a year as an apprentice at College Settlement on Rivington Street. There she not only witnessed poverty and crime, but learned to appreciate the intelligence, wit, and culture of her Jewish neighbors (no mean feat for a sheltered, provincial New England girl). She learned Yiddish from a young boy in the settlement house, and took great delight in running the Sunday Evening Economics Club, where the members were better versed in the literature than she was. She described her year there as "a new kind of university with the lessons hot from the griddle."

From College Settlement she went on to the Friendly Aid Society, a conventional Unitarian philanthropic organization on Thirty-fourth Street. In her naiveté she assumed that because the society called itself a settlement it was not a charity. But she had a rude awakening. The society was run by Christian gentlemen who practiced a kind of upper-class largesse: they believed that their "enlightened" leadership would bring the masses into the fold. The house was lavishly furnished in the conviction that "the influence of elegance would . . . import respect for property." The neighborhood was poor and rough, and the society had no "roots in the soil." Although the people were all Catholic, the society never felt the "incongruity" of holding Unitarian Sunday evening services. Simkhovitch was mortified to learn that one of the ways they tried to make contact with young people in the neighborhood was to invite them to church on Easter Sunday and ask them to come to the altar one by one "to receive a blossoming geranium plant"! While Simkhovitch attempted to design more realistic programs, she found the society's "ignorance of neighborhood custom" highly embarrassing.

Mary Simkhovitch was forced to ask herself: "Is a charity to be run more or less as a factory is run?" Her answer was a resounding no, and she left to create Greenwich House, which was based on radically different principles:

> The settlement ought to be the matrix of a more adequate understanding of what goes on . . . its permanent value is not so much in the rendering of specific services . . . as in the fruitful knowledge obtained through firsthand contact with the people in the neighborhoods. To voice their wrongs, to understand their problems, to stand by their side in their life struggles, to welcome their leadership, to reveal to others who had not had the opportunity of direct contact . . . is the primary task.[9]

To accomplish this last purpose—the broadcasting of information to other middle-class Americans—settlement workers developed an idealistic regard for the power of what they called the "facts." To the children of middle-class America, sheltered from working-class life, the revelation of economic and social conditions—in a sense, the context of characters—acted like time bombs in their minds. As Lillian Wald put it, "It seemed certain that conditions such as these were allowed to exist because people did not *know* and for me there was the challenge to know and to tell."[10] The facts, recorded over and over again in *Survey* magazine, the *Pittsburgh Survey*, and numerous books, magazine articles, and, most importantly, photographs, were the weapons of the settlement movement. Social workers used facts as their mothers had used morality. For Mary Simkhovitch there was "something majestic about a fact. Contact with facts, forcibly perceived made a never-to-be-forgotten dent on our plastic minds."[11]

The gathering, disseminating, and use of facts revealed crucial gender differences within the social work movement. Male social workers were more interested in improving the technological aspects of tenement living, like increasing the amount of cubic feet of air space, and used impersonal statistics to press their cases. They were also more likely to be involved in city commissions and investigations, and interested in the statistical and scientific aspects of change.

Victorian conventions tended to bar women from participation in this aspect of social work. For example, in 1894 Lillian Wald was nominated for membership in the Tenement House Commission for the City of New York. The chairman declined to accept her nomination: the male members believed that "a woman would be a disadvantage in hot weather, the gentlemen members obviously could not take off their coats in hot weather at meetings if a lady was present. Besides, there might be things in the tenements a lady ought not to see." Such a prudish "gentlemanly" sensibility seemed ridiculously inappropriate; Lillian Wald had seen more jacketless men and naked bodies than all the male members of the commission put together. In addition, she was frequently asked to accompany male doctors into tenements with dangerous or lewd reputations; the doctors felt safe if they entered the buildings with her at their side.[12]

Women in general were more humanistic in their approach to their work, feeling that statistics without a sense of the lived experience would produce little change. Women, as social worker Madge Hadley put it, "looked at the tenements with the eyes of a woman and as a possible home."[13] When Lillian Wald was asked to give a speech on the findings of the Tenement House Commission, she decided to humanize its content. With fervor, she demanded that her audience

> read each figure a human being. Read that every wretched unlighted tenement described is a home for people—men and women, old and young, with the strengths and weaknesses, the good and bad, the appetites and wants that are common to us all. . . . Reading these things must bring a sense of fairness outraged, the disquieting feeling that something is wrong, and turning to your own contract, you must feel a responsibility for the how and why. Say to yourself, Is there a wrong in our midst, what can I do? Do I owe reparation?[14]

A division of labor gradually developed. In the housing reform movement, for example, this division was clear: by 1912 the movement "had attended to all of the structural and scientific points of tenement living so that the men who started it no longer made inspections, only speeches, and turned the field work over to women."[15]

Women, because of their experience, often knew more than the more academic or political men. Women were more active in making contact and developing relationships with their neighbors, shaping the everyday activities of settlement life. For example, a group of male sociologists from Columbia University was interested in how working-class families spent their money, but had no means of finding it out. They contacted Greenwich House, where Louise Bolard More, a worker who ran a popular evening women's club, decided to undertake the project. "She took her women's club members into her confidence and asked for their assistance. They were so fond of her that they gladly entered into her confidence and kept painstaking records over a period of several weeks."[16] Her study, *Wage Earners' Budgets in New York,* was a pioneering work on the standard of living that quickly became a classic. The idea itself was innovative—a kind of participatory scholarship.

Making contact, however, was not always that easy. Immigrants were often puzzled by social workers, unable to understand why wealthy, educated Americans were moving into their neighborhoods, wanting to share their lives. The ideal of the settlement house was to make contact between equals, but class barriers were always there. When Lillian Wald and Mary Brewster moved to the Lower East Side they wanted to identify themselves with the neighborhood but immediately revealed themselves as being different. First of all, in looking for a place to live they "clung to the civilization of the bathroom," even though there were reportedly only two bathrooms in tenements below Fourteenth Street at that time. They found one of the two, but it was in the hall. Second, they had to appease their families' anxiety about two young women living alone in slum areas as they took with them good mahogany furniture and a Baltimore heater, unheard-of luxuries in that neighborhood. They invited the son of the Irish janitress to share their first meal, and the mother came up later to find out what he had eaten. The boy "had rushed down with his eyes bulging and had reported that 'them ladies live like the Queen of England and eat off solid gold plates.' "[17]

Female social workers tried to overcome the social barriers by making the settlement house into a "home." A first step was to establish neighborly relations. A curious and suspicious crowd watched Mary and Vladimir Simkhovitch move their furniture into Greenwich House, but when Mary's father appeared with her new-born baby, the suspicion turned to approval. The baby "set us right with the neighbors. After all, it was a family that was coming."[18] Both Mary Simkhovitch and Lillian Wald were invited to weddings, christenings, bar mitzvahs, funerals, and an occasional supper, the greatest honor, "for meals are expensive; in general, tenement house parties were in the evening and not at meal hours."[19]

By participating in these rituals and befriending women and children, the social workers tried to become part of the daily life of the neighborhood. They wanted the settlement house to become a center for neighborhood activity, problem solving, and the development of broad social programs. Both Henry Street and Greenwich House offered their rooms for meetings, discussions, and social events, and also developed some of their own.

The programs they developed were of two kinds. On the one hand, with an optimistic faith in the power of industrial change, they advocated programs to solve the disequilibrium between the "social surplus and social misery."[20] Believing that the United States had bridged an economic frontier, moving from an economy of scarcity to one of abundance, they argued that society had a responsibility to provide a decent standard of living for all. They therefore worked hard for housing reform, health programs, trade union rights, the abolition of child labor and industrial homework, social security, unemployment compensation, and equal access to technological improvements.

At the same time, social workers saw themselves as advocates of a new Progressive ideology. At the heart of this "progressivism" lay a belief in the ability to apply the scientific method to the amelioration of social ills. True to the temper of the machine age, society was seen as a complex mechanism in need of good-willed social technicians, a mechanism that could be improved through rational analysis combined with the right "technical adjustments." While some argued that this scientific modernity was but a new version of middle-class Protestant values that were being imposed on the immigrant poor, many social workers felt that it was their responsibility to bring the immigrant up to date.

These social workers took pride in being the apostles of progress to "the thousands of foreign women who have come to us for the most part illiterate, ignorant and without any training, whatsoever, doing what their mothers and grandmothers did before them." They had firm "scientific" ideas about proper infant care, family life, parent-child relationships, diet, and hygiene. As one social worker put it, "Old standards must be changed if we are sincere in our desire to attain a higher form of civilization. The strangers from across the water must be taught to discard un-American habits and conventions, to accept new ideals."[21]

This did not mean that their ideas were not met with resistance, however. The basic arena of contention revolved around the changing nature of family life. Social workers argued, with echoes resounding from their own past, that the traditional preindustrial family subordinated the interests of the individual family member to the economic and social priorities of the family as a whole, while the new industrial order created the possibility of a reversal in the customary relations between parents and children. The New World demanded that children, instead of serving their parents, be served by them. As Margaret Byington argued: "In looking back on primitive life, we perceive a great reversal in the relations of parents to children. Aside from the feelings of personal affection, children were then consciously desired mainly for service to their parents; now parents center their efforts and ideals on the future of their children."[22] The old society was patriarchal; the new society was child centered. The struggle to liberate the child from the industrial or primitive family thus became one of the most important goals of modern social work, and the settlement house became the institution through which this was to be accomplished. Edward Devine, one of the founders of social work, contended that the goal of settlement work was "to bring forward the individual to insist that living human beings shall not be sacrificed to a tradition of family solidarity."[23]

Social workers found strong family cohesion and unity in the neighborhoods, but misunderstood their role and power. As social worker Eva White put it:

A native in this country [America] is often not in close enough touch with European family standards to realize fully how very important it is to go back continuously to the family relationship. Two extremes are often found in immigrant situations: the instances where persons have no relatives in this country and so are free from family restraints, and the instances where family dominance is so strong as to completely submerge the individual and create an almost insuperable obstacle to necessary freedom of action.[24]

While social workers saw the issue as one of total freedom or total domination, for the immigrants these two poles of family life were aspects of family obligation: single men and women working to bring their families over, and family groups evolving their own sense of responsibility within an American context. Social workers were continually amazed to find well-worked-out systems of neighborly support and solidarity in the new communities—forms of assistance unthinkable in their own lives, where economic stability and privacy were barriers to a vibrant community life. For instance, Jane Addams found that

there was the greatest willingness to lend or borrow anything, and all the residents of a given tenement house knew the most intimate family affairs of all the others. The fact that the economic condition of all is on the most precarious level makes the ready outflow of sympathy and material assistance the most natural thing in the world. There are numberless instances of self-sacrifice quite unknown in circles where greater economic advantage makes that kind of intimate knowledge of one's neighbors impossible.[25]

Lillian Wald thought that it had "almost become trite to speak of the kindness of the poor to each other, yet from the beginning we were much touched by manifestations of it." She noted many acts of mutual assistance, including "a Jewish woman, exhausted by her long day's scrubbing of office floors who walked many extra blocks to get us to get a priest for her Roman Catholic neighbor whose child was dying."[26]

Some social workers saw that for immigrants sharing was a way of life, and that in this women took the lead. Mollie Linker explained the tenement ethos:

If somebody needed something, she was there. . . . It's the women that got together, collected food. When they saw a woman in the butcher shop not buying enough and they knew how many children she had, my mother would go to a few neighbors, collect money and bring food, put it under the doorway and walk away. Somebody came in, they wanted to eat, or a beggar, you sat him down at the table, you made coffee. If you had bread and butter or a piece of herring, whatever you had, you offered it.[27]

They also understood that the material life of the immigrants was necessarily dominated by the need for money to sustain the family and that the work of many family members—not just the father—was essential to the family economy.

Yet middle-class principles demanded that the husband work to provide a home for his leisured wife and children. Middle-class social workers universalized their own particular relationship to society by asserting this principle as an unshakable moral good, and faulted immigrant families for accepting conditions in which both women and children worked. In the pages of *Survey* magazine and elsewhere, they etched out the cultural "superiority" of their position:

> The social and moral life of a smaller family where the father earns enough to support wife and children, and where the mother can devote her time to the care of them, and where neither she nor the children go out and help in the support of the family, is superior to that of a family with a large number of children where the wife and often the older children must slave.[28]

Some social workers, however, whether through investigation or sympathy, took issue with the dominant middle-class view of family life. Mary Simkhovitch looked at immigrant families with admiration rather than contempt:

> The family pattern had a conservative cut, but on the whole it worked. The position of the mother was a strong one, much stronger than often obtains in families of a higher economic level. She paid not only the rent, insurance and food, but also bought the family's clothing and gave the husband and children enough for carfare and lunches. This built up a solid family life where each was dependent on the other. Clash and conflict were necessary corollaries of this closeness, but there was something loving about such a home life in which no individual could live for himself alone. It made of sacrifice not a beautiful thought, but a common custom.[29]

Some social workers tried to modify these family patterns through contact with the children. If the parents were perceived as determined to maintain their own cultures, the children were thought to be more malleable. The public school and the settlement house were both wedges in the cultural battle for modernization. Charles Bernheimer, the assistant head of University Settlement House on the Lower East Side, argued:

> A number of the immigrant population . . . are unable to look after their children properly because of strange language and habits, the necessity of employment and the lack of knowledge of our institutions. Private social agencies such as the settlement as well as public educational agencies assist the child. It is true that the authority of the parents is weakened by those influences with which the younger generation comes into contact but that is inevitable. The youth in gaining knowledge in the public schools, in following his life vocation, undoubtedly breaks the shackles of parental control.[30]

The school and the settlement taught children to substitute American manners and morals for those of their parents. Social worker David Blaustein, for instance, argued that for Jewish children "the most important changes are those of his industrial and religious life and education. The child attends the public school, and within a few months may come to despise that which he formerly held sacred. He sees no further use of Hebrew and laughs at his father for his pride in the knowledge of it."[31] The first generation often reacted with horror: "A godless country, America. All the wrong side up. The children are fathers to their fathers. The fathers, children to their children."[32] Certain practices of American life were incomprehensible and even insulting. For example, Leonard Covello went to a Charity School:

> Once at the school, I remember the teacher gave each child a bag of oatmeal to take home. This food was supposed to make you big and strong. You ate it for breakfast. My father examined the stuff, tested it with his fingers. To him, it was the kind of bran that we gave to pigs in Avigliano. "What kind of a school is this?" he shouted. "They give us the food of animals to eat and sent it home to us with our children."[33]

Italian parents also frequently complained that American schools took their children away from them. The children, on the other hand, affected by these Americanizing influences, sometimes tried to force American customs on their parents. The social workers encouraged the children, as this report from Reed House in Philadelphia makes clear:

> By having the children with us constantly, we are able to further our plan of teaching them American manners and customs. The reaction, at times, has been irritating to the child, for it is really difficult to bridge from the peasantry to City life. Parents are being criticized as to their mode of cooking and eating, until one desperate mother sent word to me to please tell her where to buy an American cookbook.[34]

Events like these caused the radical Emma Goldman to derisively exclaim that settlement work "was teaching the poor to eat with a fork."[35]

Sometimes the zeal and concern social workers felt for their new neighbors backfired. Looking back, Mary Simkhovitch recalled "how much there was to learn about family life in our early days." One young social worker, "indignant to learn about wifebeating and hearing screams from the window, called the police and secured an arrest. But she was reproved by the wife, who said, 'Sure I'm going back to my husband. She ain't got any, and she don't know.'"[36]

Sometimes there was open confrontation. Cecilia Razovski, for example, taught English to immigrant men in night school. Fired up by a suffrage demonstration she had just attended, she tried to think up a lesson that would contain "a feminist moral." She chose sewing and asked a student, Mr. Contilli, for a sentence with the word "button." He answered, "I make my wife sew a button on my coat." Cecilia Razovski, describing this incident in an article entitled "The Eternal Masculine," continued: "Teacher, who is still under the influence of the parade, is in no mood to accept the word 'make,' and proceeds to explain, 'You do not make your wife sew the button on your coat. . . . You ask her. You say please . . . and if she is too busy with the baby, you sew it on yourself.'"

This prompted a lively discussion. Mr. Contilli answered that if his wife refused, he would beat her. The teacher then decided to give the class their first lesson in the history of the women's movement in simple English, "the old, old story of the industrial revolution which forced women out of the home and into public work, winding up in an eloquent eulogy to the men in America . . . who permitted women to be educated as men are." Just as she was finishing the principal walked in with a man from the immigration service who explained to the class how to obtain citizenship. Mr. Contilli, "the eternal masculine in him still harboring slight resentment . . . suddenly awakes to a staggering realization":

> Teacher, shouts Mr. Contilli, you say American men—they treat ladies just like men. Yes, says Teacher. . . . If I take out papers I can vote? Yes, says Teacher, still not sensing his drift. Teacher, bawls Mr. Contilli loudly and triumphantly, standing up at his desk. If American men are so good, why we can vote and *you* can't?[37]

Sometimes social workers learned new ideas from immigrants—ideas the immigrants thought were a part of the American tradition. Lillian Wald, for example, was much impressed with one of the daughters who lived in her tenement. The young woman worked long hours, carried books about with her, and kept a "tidy appearance." One evening the daughter stopped to see them: "Our pleasure was mixed with consternation to learn that she wished aid in organizing a trade union. Even the term was unknown to me. It was evident that she came to me because of her faith that one who spoke English so easily would know how to organize in the 'American way.' "[38]

Lillian Wald was so concerned about her own ignorance that she went to the library the next day to read up on trade unionism. But "that evening in a basement . . . I listened to the broken English of a cigarmaker who was trying to help the girls, and it was interesting to find that what he gave them was neither more nor less than the philosophic argument of the book I consulted—that collective power might be employed to insure justice for the individual, himself powerless."[39]

Both Lillian Wald and Mary Simkhovitch were interested in the effects of trade unionism and socialism on Lower East Side women. If Progressive education had changed the lives of middle-class daughters, labor unions and socialist politics provided an education for those of the working class. As Mary Simkhovitch said, "The real university of the Lower East Side was Marx's *Capital*. Read like a Bible with faith, it formed the taste and moulded the minds of its readers. Socialism as an economic theory is one thing; as an education it is another. It is what we are excited about that educates us. What the East Side was excited about was socialism."[40]

Yet at the same time that Lillian Wald was involved in trade unions, she was also bringing the cultural conventions of the upper class to the settlement house. She regularly held "coming out" parties for members of her young women's clubs when they reached the age of eighteen, an annual ball at which they were formally introduced and promoted to the senior group.[41]

Ultimately, social work was based on the assumptions of a Protestant middle class in transition, whose values and ideals social workers held out to immigrants as beacons of the new way. American charity work, whether in its nineteenth-century or Progressive variety, emanated from the presumed moral, cultural, and economic superiority of one group over another. In this tradition charity was for the other, never the self. A significant number of social workers managed to overcome this attitude and let themselves be drawn into the spirit of the immigrant community, but most simply attempted to modify it to fit American patterns. An ironic contradiction developed between a society that, in the name of individualism, tried to standardize immigrant cultures to fit new American norms, and old-world cultures, which in the name of cultural tradition preferred to be left alone.

6

◇

OUR DAILY BREAD

I F THE CHILDREN OF IMMIGRANTS RECEIVED A DAILY DOSE OF NEW American values at school and in the factory, their mothers were the least drawn into the new public world. Their lives posed a visible dichotomy: they seemed to have little direct contact with American institutions, but they had the most contact with their families and the ethnic community.

Social workers focused on mothers precisely because of this. They were concerned because these women were not subject to a daily infusion of American values, and feared their influence on the first generation of "real" Americans, the children. Caught in the margins between old and new, immigrant mothers posed a threat to assimilation.

Within the changed context of daily life, this space away from the dominant culture allowed mothers to live according to their own sense of economy and order, their own values and beliefs. While it also meant isolation, it nevertheless created a social environment in which the old culture could be adapted to the new.

The experience of the Grimaldi family was typical. Grace Grimaldi, who narrates her own story, came to the United States in 1911 at the age of fourteen. She grew up in Sicily, but her family first migrated to Tunisia, where they lived in the Italian colony. Her father was a shoemaker, her mother a housewife with four children. Her mother did not work outside the home in the old country because, according to Grace, "there was no means for women to work there." When Grace was a schoolgirl, her education was supplemented at home, where she learned to sew. Urged by relatives, the family moved to New York:

When we first came, we expected a struggle. For the first year or so, it was a struggle to put up a home; to transplant the family, it's very hard. In any family that transplanted itself from one country to another, you've got to expect drastic change. My father, my mother and myself went to work, the other three went to school. My mother hadn't worked before. She didn't like it, of course, but we knew that. We were prepared to face that. When I first came, I didn't expect to work. I had been a schoolgirl before. Here, I went to work. I resented this because at my age I wanted to go to school. But the situation was such that I had to go to work; there were six people and the earning was very little.

Grace's father found work in a shoe factory. This assembly-line production deeply offended his artisanal sensibilities, but he "couldn't find a place of work that let him make the whole shoe." Finally, a friend got him a job as a presser in a men's clothing factory. Grace and her mother found work in the needle trades:

My two aunts took my mother and myself to the shop they worked in and we were hired. My mother found this adjustment hard. Both Jewish and Italian worked there. Both groups were fresh immigrants and couldn't speak English. I only heard English from my brothers and sisters when they came home from school. I was quite miserable for the first few years. I couldn't speak English. I didn't like the work or the surroundings. My mother was more miserable. She found this situation too difficult. I didn't find it as difficult because I was a child. It was something of an adventure for me.

While her mother was working she established a division of labor at home:

The children had to take care of themselves. My brother was twelve, my sisters eight and six. We were a very close family. My mother told her son what to buy at the butcher's and the market when he came home from school. He always shopped the day before it would be prepared for a meal. She told her two daughters how to prepare meals from food. We all cleaned the house. My father didn't help with family and domestic matters though. Forget that. That was out. He was a man. My mother trained us all in how to work things out. After she quit, we still did a lot of work but it was nicer to come home at night when the whole family sat down together and we could be in harmony again.

After three years, her mother stopped working in the factory and took work home from a garment shop around the corner: "The children used to pitch in and help her. After a while she quit that—we earned enough money which we always turned over to her. The work was too much. A woman should go to work and have a house to take care of—it's not pleasant, believe me."[1]

The first-generation immigrant mother had very little formal contact with the dominant value system of American life: her immediate context determined her energy, organization skills, and familial responsibilities. While she was the main actor in her own home, to outsiders she appeared passive and estranged. In the language of social work, the situation of the Grimaldi family, which was common among such immigrant families, was rendered in these terms:

> The non-English speaking mother, with her large groups of small children, labors under the most serious disadvantages. A stranger to the language of the public schools—the new language spoken by her children—the mother, all unconscious of what is happening, soon loses control of her children and their respect. She cannot keep up with them: she is too busy with home life and family adjustments in a new land.[2]

Social workers believed that immigrant mothers led an isolated existence in a world apart from their husbands and children and therefore had no communication with American culture. As one social worker remarked in the pages of *Survey* magazine: "The Italians are a domestic people; their women rarely leave their homes and so come into contact with American ideas much less than the men do."[3]

From the perspective of the Grimaldi family, these statements seem absurd. In Grace's eyes, her mother was quite conscious of what was happening and certainly had the respect of her children. Maternal authority was not weakened; rather, the bonds between mother and children were strengthened: they were all deeply involved in home life and in the family's adjustment to a new land. In any case, American ideas did not stop at the front door. The ideology of nineteenth-century middle-class life may have separated the home from the outside world, but in immigrant families, although work and home were now physically divided, they were still intimately connected.

At the same time that mothers were perceived as losing control over their children, they were also criticized for being too intensely involved with them. "The fact is," one social workers complained, "that the Italian mother is as much a child as her children and plays with them, quarrels with them, and loves them just as another child would."[4] Immigrant women were considered incapable of transmitting the social and cultural values of American middle-class family life. Consequently, they were seen as children, "infantilized" in relation to their own kin, incapable of rational judgment and proper adult behavior. Since reason in a Protestant society was linked to adulthood, immigrant mothers, socialized in a different cultural context, did not have the right training to differentiate themselves from the world of childhood. Intimacy, love, and playfulness were not considered adult forms of behavior and were therefore grounds for criticism.

But the organization of immigrant families was in fact reconstructed to meet the demands of American life. Mary Simkhovitch tried to define these changes: "The lack of contact with the world, opened only to the privileged . . . throws the industrial family back upon itself and gives it a kind of fierce unity and mutual interdependence unknown in circles where avenues of mutual escape are at every hand. No intermediary comes between mother and child." For the middle class, access to money, servants, and education provided individual options, but immigrant families still had to depend on each other for survival and affection. In this world, so unlike that of most middle-class social workers, "the older children care for the younger. The girls sleep together and find it strange and dismal to sleep alone if it is their lot. . . . Members of the family fight it out, but they love it out as well."[5] The active center of this interdependent world was the mother, whom Mary Simkhovitch contrasted favorably to a middle-class wife:

> It is the mother around whom the whole machinery of the family revolves. The family economy depends on her interests, skills and sense of order. Her economic importance is far greater than that of her wealthier sisters for as income increases, the amount of it controlled by the wife diminishes. . . . But in her humble status, her position is thoroughly dignified. She is recognized as a co-worker on an equal plane with the up-building of her family.[6]

Working-class and immigrant parents were also criticized for using too much discipline and authority over their children. Jane Addams, for instance, once witnessed the head of a kindergarten training class addressing a club of working women on the issue of "parental despotism." The speaker denounced what she termed "the determination to break the child's will," and instead called for "the ideal relationship based on love and confidence." But the women present measured their children by a different standard. Afterward, some came up to Addams and said:

> If you don't keep control over them from the time they are little, you would never get their wages when they are grown up. Another one said, "Ah, of course, she [the speaker] doesn't have to depend on her children's wages. She can afford to be lax with them, because if they don't give money to her, she can get along without it."[7]

In these families, cooperation and discipline went hand in hand: "Those who require the unopened pay envelope do it partly as a matter of family discipline." A frequent refrain on the part of the mother was, "I'd like to see a child of mine that would open their own pay envelope."[8]

However, the mother who was the strictest in demanding her children's wages would return part of them in the form of gifts:

> The mother who is often the most rigorous in maintaining her maternal authority is often the most open-handed toward the boy or girl after the letter of the rule has been observed. She pays out more than the family income warrants in order to give her daughter a becoming dress or hat or her son . . . an extra bite between meals.[9]

Since the wage was the most important component for satisfying needs, maternal control was a necessity, but part of the family income included gift-giving as a mark of love. This demanded self-sacrifice on the part of the mother, who rarely allocated money for herself. One woman summed up this attitude when she said, "I can wear anything myself, but my daughter must have a new suit."[10]

The concept of childhood was also in question. Childhood ended early in the old country: "People got older faster." By the age of seven, "children somehow knew without being taught that they should help the family." Both Italians and Jews thought American children were much younger than immigrant children, who were "a little more advanced—not babies like they are here. We couldn't depend on anybody waiting on us."[11]

For example, Zappira Blondi's father left his village near Naples to look for work in America. He had trouble finding a job and wrote back to his wife and children of his failure. Zappira, twelve at the time, and her mother were very disappointed:

The two put their heads together and laid a plan where they could earn their passage. The mother borrowed a sum of money sufficient to stock a small store in the village. This she and Zappira proceeded to conduct so successfully that at the end of the year the small debt had been repaid and the passage money laid aside. Their venture had been kept a secret from the father, and when they were all ready to make the journey they wrote him. They took two small rooms on Mott Street, and for a year mother and daughter worked in a factory, eking out a living. The girl was now sixteen, old enough to be married. . . . . Although so young, Zappira had, through years of close partnership with her mother, already acquired many of the sober qualities of middle age.

Adolescence was a foreign concept. A middle-class American adolescence, an extended childhood marked by schooling and leisure, made little sense to immigrant parents and children brought up in the logic of family obligation and work. Social worker Josephine Roche, attending an Italian wedding, captured this cultural difference:

> One could not help but reflect that if he [the groom] had been living in Gramercy Park instead of the West Side he might now be receiving his high school diploma instead of assuming the burden and responsibility of a family. And the little bride might be heading the freshman basketball team with years of carefree development ahead of her, instead of facing the imminent trials of child-bearing with the probable addition of factory labor.[12]

One of the common themes expressed by immigrant daughters was that they never had a childhood in the sense of leisure and play. Grace Grimaldi argued that "girls matured much more quickly then." Yetta Adelman, a Polish Jewish garment worker who had come to the United States when she was twelve years old and saved money to bring her family over, put it this way: "When I was here I knew I had to go to work. I didn't come here for pleasure, you know. I was twelve years old but I wasn't. Compared to a child here in the United States I was twenty."[13]

Adolescence was a time of work, responsibility, and cooperation. Judith Weissman, a garment worker from Bessarabia, recalled: "Everyone contributed to the home. There was no such thing as moving out on your own. It was easier for the parents. The parents couldn't wait until their children were old enough to go out to work as it eased their burden."[14] Josephine Roche was impressed by "the eagerness of most Italian parents for the arrival of the girl's fourteenth birthday . . . the girl herself is as eager to go to work as her parents are to have her. She takes it for granted that she should help in the family income."[15]

Lenore Kosloff, a Lithuanian Jew, migrated to the United States in 1901. She started her work life at the age of thirteen in the garment industry because it was her "obligation." Her father was sick with asthma, a disease he developed working in a coat factory, and there were four children to support:

> I accepted my responsibility to help support my family even though this meant I wouldn't go to high school. I wanted to go to school, but I knew this was not possible. I was willing to help my mother because I had a sense of togetherness. I felt as if the younger children were mine as well as my mother's. My whole salary went to the family. If there wasn't enough, I did without.[16]

What did it mean to be thirteen years old and think that the children were as much your own as your mother's? To give up your own education to serve the needs of "your" children? Child or no, Lenore saw the situation with her mother's eyes; she assumed the maternal burden, and put aside her own needs to meet the needs of others. In extreme cases, daughters accepted an overwhelming number of duties. Social worker Elizabeth Dutcher observed:

> The case of Sarah R., for instance. She was seventeen years old and lived with her widowed stepmother and two little brothers in a five-story double tenement. Her stepmother had rent free in exchange for janitress work which she was too feeble to do. So night times, after coming home from the factory and in the early morning, Sarah did all the cleaning of the great building and made all the clothes for the family, even the little boys' suits. No wonder her best friend said of her sorrowfully: Sarah was a fine girl, but no one knew her; she was too busy. *Do you know any man whose families are dependent on him to the same extent?*[17]

Fabbia Orzo's father worked in the building trades, making very little. When she went to work at age thirteen, her mother "used to say why should she leave any of the work, the housework or cleaning, for us to do? We're working. She would do it. By the time we got home she had the cleaning done . . . she was very good . . . what you would call a mother." Fabbia worked for wages; her mother did the housework. She gave her money to her mother as part of this relationship.

During the depression of the 1930s, Fabbia's family lived on her salary alone—a point of pride in her life: "I was able to take care of my parents and the other children. They used to live on my salary. My parents, my two brothers, and my two sisters."[18] Fabbia never married. She took care of her family for most of her life.

The sense of responsibility especially affected older daughters. Jennie Matyras was the oldest daughter in her family of Russian Jews: "My ambition in life was to get to be a good worker because being the oldest daughter, it was my job to do the dressmaking for the family." She went to work at fourteen as a "learner" in the needles trades, and worked her way to the point where "I thought I'd try for a job on my own, to make the whole garment." Her mother was concerned about her working at such a complicated job, but Jennie kept praying that it would bring in at least $8 a week. Instead, she got $11:

> I almost ran home. I was worried all the way home. What if I told my mother I was getting so much and she began to count on it and plan a higher standard of living. I knew I couldn't hold a job that paid so well and I didn't want to get her prepared for a standard I was afraid I couldn't live up to. Finally when I got home mother said, "How much are you going to get" And I said quickly, "well, I'm-getting-$11-a-week-but-don't-count-on-it. It's-sure-not-to-last."[19]

Maybe it was this sense of family contribution that some social workers, themselves brought up in the logic of childhood dependency, found difficult to understand.

In the old culture, the social labor of women had converted raw materials into household goods; in the New World, these same women had to secure these goods in the marketplace—and since the wife was the center of the household, it was her responsibility to manage the conversion of wages into necessities. To some immigrant groups—Ukrainian, for instance—this was a distinct change: "Whereas in the old country, the men kept complete control of the little money that came in, here they generally turn it over to their wives . . . when asked some of the men laughed and said, 'America was a woman's country.' "[20] For Jewish and Italian women, this was a continuation of a previous tradition, but one that had become increasingly important. While most married Italian and Jewish women did not in fact work for wages outside the home, their economic activity *within* the home was a vital component of the family economy.[21] The divorce between production and consumption and the reliance on wages as the sole means for survival made money, as novelist Mario Puzo put it, "the new homeland."[22] Immigrant families, by necessity, had to create a composite income based on the wages of the father and older children, income from boarders, and the earnings of women from work done at home. Louise More, in her study of wage-earning budgets in New York City in 1909, made a crucial observation about the family economy of immigrant and working-class families:

> The number of families entirely dependent on the earnings of one person is small when compared with the number whose incomes include the earnings of the husband, wife, several children, some boarders . . . gifts from relatives, aid from charitable societies, insurance money in the case of death—several or all of these resources may enter into the total resources of that family in a year. Perhaps this income should more accurately be called the household income, for it represents the amount which comes into the family purse and of which the mother usually has the disbursement.[23]

In most working-class families, it was common practice for the husband to turn over his wages to his wife. "In many cases the mother is the cashier and receives her husband's wages once a week, allowing him out of it a fixed sum, say $1 or $2, for his pocket money out of which he pays for his carfare, lunches and whatnot."[24] The turning over of wages was a constant source of tension. The "good man" turned his wages over to his wife and accepted the fixed allowance he received for his own needs. Mary Simkhovitch saw this practice as a form of economic independence for the woman. It allowed her to be "intimately connected with her children and economically independent of her husband; if he is a good man, the woman of the industrial family has a kind of primitive economic importance."[25] Married women were vitally important to the maintenance of the economic structure of working-class family life.

The tension arose when the husband would turn over only some of his wages, keeping some for himself. "In these cases the wife could only estimate what he brought home to her—the rest having been spent by the man himself without adding to the family's comfort or resources."[26] One Italian woman, explaining her problems with her household budget, exclaimed, "Of course, they don't give you all they make. They're men and you never know their ways." The wife, however, felt "fully entitled to her husband's paycheck, and it is one of her grievances that he does not hand over enough of his pay."[27]

Anna Kuthan had a running battle with her husband over the family income. After describing how she met her husband and set up house, she went on to say:

> Things were very expensive, so I started counting the money always. But I was not always experienced like everybody else. I put the money in the drawer like and my husband came home to eat lunch. And he used to take the money from the drawer and then when I went to pay the rent . . . ! So then I said, oh my God, what happened to the money. I said, did you take the money? He says no. I says listen don't lie. So a coupla times it happened like that and I says wait a minute, oh it wouldn't work with me. I says, I'm gonna give you so much spending money every week because you have everything at home. That's how I have to start at the beginning, because we wouldn't have anything if I didn't.[28]

Withholding wages was one way the husband could exercise power over his wife and family. Sometimes a neighbor would then attempt to intervene. According to one study,

> a carpenter who earned $20 a week regularly gave his wife $10 and kept $10 for his personal wants. Out of her share she was to pay the rent and provide for a family of five children. A neighbor undertook to remonstrate him, but he insisted that her allowance was sufficient for most of the neighbors' wives had to do with less.[29]

Sometimes husbands made it impossible for the wife to sustain the family—either through gambling, drinking, stubbornness, or, finally, desertion. A social worker observed a case in which a man "gave his wife $5 on a Saturday night and when she said, 'Is that all?' he put the $5 back in his pocket."[30]

Nevertheless, women recognized the needs of their husbands for male companionship outside the home, and allotted them spending money for these purposes. Fabbia Orzo, an Italian garment worker, recalled that her father went out every night to "play cards for money" in a bar owned by a distant relative on Prince Street. Her mother "didn't really like it," but put up with it nonetheless. She did not think the "family suffered because my father gambled. One night he would be lucky, one night, he wouldn't." Tobacco, drink money, card playing, haircuts, trade union dues, and lodge money were included in the husband's spending money. This gave the men the ability to participate in the larger community. Yet women seldom gave themselves same privileges. If Fabbia Orzo's father went out every night, her "mother never went anywhere . . . she had friends but my mother was the type . . . not to go out. If one of her friends would be sick, she would go and help them out, but otherwise she would stay at home."[31] And social worker Louise More noticed the same pattern:

> The men have the saloons, political clubs, trade unions or barber shops, the young people have an occasional ball to go to or a cheap theater . . . while the mothers have almost no recreation at all, only a dreary round of work day after day with an occasional doorstep gossip to vary the monotony of their lives.[32]

If the husband was *expected* to turn over his wages, the older children were *required* to do so. It was "the general custom for all boys and girls to bring their pay envelopes unopened and [the mother] had the entire disbursement of their wages, giving them 25¢ to one dollar a week spending money according to the prosperity of the family."[33] The unopened pay envelope was a sign of responsibility and respect for the work of the mother. Amalia Morandi, an Italian garment worker, restated this pervasive theme: "I gave my pay envelope to my mother . . . I wouldn't dare open it up . . . I'd give it to my mother because I knew that she worked hard for us and I thought this was her compensation." Mollie Linker articulated another aspect of this relationship: "I gave it all to my mother. It was the respect to bring and give your mother the money."[34]

In the Old World, daughters were expected to support the work of their mothers in the home. But in America, to do this they had to leave the house and go into the factories. Yet mothers expected their daughters to respect the economic priorities of the household, and the sealed pay envelope was a new form of an old responsibility. What was striking about this relationship was its sense of commitment. While to outside observers there seemed to be a major division between the home and the factory, for these women the division was external—the logic of work was family inspired.

Italian and Jewish women also saved their money to bring the rest of the family from the Old Country. Yetta Adelman came to the United States from Poland when she was twelve. Her goal was to make enough money to bring over the rest of her family. She sent back her wages to her mother and kept "money for carfare and a dollar to spare every week. I bought material for two blouses and a skirt and wore that for some time." Since she was so young she was a "helper"; she had to be "hidden in the bathroom when the child labor inspector came around." She took these risks because she "only wanted to make a living for mother and the kids." Asked how she did this, she said, "When you're born in a poor depressed place, you get smart, you have to."[35] Agnes Santucci had a similar story. She migrated to the United States in 1911, when she was seventeen. Her sister lent her money for her passage, and she had to pay her back out of her wages in a garment factory. "And once in a while when I had extra money I used to get $10 and send it to my mother." When she married, "I had $5 of my own."[36]

These mothers and daughters haunt the literature of social work. Mysterious and incomprehensible, they battled well-intentioned social workers who desperately tried to understand them. Addams, for example, was impressed by the vast numbers of daughters who handed over their weekly wages uncomplainingly to their mothers and asked for little in return. She asked a key question:

> Is it habit or virtue which holds her steady in this course? If love and tenderness had been substituted for parental despotism, would the mother have had enough affection, enough power of expression, to hold her daughter's sense of money obligation all these years? The girl who spends her paltry two cents on chewing gum and goes plainly clad in clothes of her mother's choosing, while many of her friends spend their entire wages on these clothes which factory girls love so well, must be held by a powerful force.[37]

Social workers were constantly struck by the fact that the young immigrant woman went to work not just "because she feels the need of self-support . . . but because she feels so strongly the sense of family obligation." Even though young daughters worked in factories, "going to work does not achieve that economic independence which is often thought to be the chief motive impelling the modern woman to take up a gainful occupation."[38]

The sense of obligation was strong among daughters, but what about sons? Boy children were allowed greater access to social life outside the domain of family life. In Jewish families, it was common to find young men attending Hebrew school or keeping money for themselves for outside activities.[39] In a study of Italian working-class life, a social worker observed that it was assumed that the girl's pay envelope should be turned over to the mother because "it wouldn't look nice to pay board to the mother who raised you," but the question as to whether brothers should also contribute everything received the answer, "Oh no, he's a boy."[40]

Nevertheless, a similar tension was inherent in the mother-daughter relationship. In America, the wage-earning power of daughters shaped their lives in ways that were critically different from the more homebound experience of their mothers. For Italian women, "probably the chief evidence of Americanization . . . appears when the daughters begin wage earning." Instead of joining the ranks of mothers doing piece work at home, the daughters went into the factory: a union organizer in the needle trades made the following observation: "Only those who are familiar with the submissive way in which Old World Italian women endure industrial exploitation can understand what a stride towards independence the Italian girl has made by simply working in a factory instead of at home."[41] Factory work was to them a step forward.

And if most daughters took for granted their mothers' claim to their pay envelopes, some did not. Wage earning was a heady power; if women worked like men, should they not also be allowed some male prerogatives and keep some of their wages for themselves? The change from homebound status to industrial work led some to a change in consciousness and a redefinition of goals. Abraham Bisno, a long-time labor organizer for the International Ladies' Garment Workers' Union (ILGWU) was impressed by this:

> While the majority of them turned their money over to the family chest, there was quite a significant minority who would themselves be holders of their earnings, pay regular board to their families, and either save or spend money for themselves. This change in their lives which allowed them the right to do whatever they pleased with their own money, and gave them standing and authority because of their earnings and contributions, was for them a very significant item in their lives. They acquired the *right to a personality* which they had not ever possessed in the old country.[42]

This "right to personality" was encouraged by the new urban social life. American culture increasingly identified adolescence with a social world outside the family. Access to that world was dependent on having money to spend on oneself. A generational conflict began to develop within immigrant families: some sons and daughters wanted to control their own wages so that they could go to the dance halls, or to play the nickelodeon, visit the candy store, and hang out in the street. Girls began to feel the need for proper clothing, new hair styles, and the economic independence necessary to enter the new world of their peers.

Social workers linked the struggle for adolescent independence not only to the control of wages, but to the relaxation of conventions regarding association between young people of opposite sexes.[43] Sexual independence was always closely associated with economic independence: access to money defined the ability of young women to present themselves to the New World on its own terms.

This brought them into conflict with the family ethic, which conceived of luxury and pleasure as part of the family economy in which the whole family participated. The development in America of separate recreational activities for parents and children assumed that families, while cooperating on necessities, did not cooperate on luxuries and pleasures.[44] An Italian mother perceptively analyzed this change on the part of daughters: "It is my money, they assert, and therein lies the greatest change."[45] The daughter's new needs put pressure on the mother, who had to manage a meager household income and who found outside adolescent life threatening to both the family economy and cultural values. This led some daughters to subterfuge. Josephine Roche, in her investigations of Italian life, noted the example of

> Filomena Moresco, whose calm investment of $25 in a pretty party dress, a beaver hat and a willowed plume was reported as little less than the act of a brigand. If she had withheld twenty cents out of her pay envelope a week from her mother she probably would have been beaten; as it was she appropriated $25 and her high-handedness was her protection.[46]

Another strategy for withholding income, less dramatic but more risky, consisted of sneaking money out of the envelope before it was turned over. Sophie Abrams, a Jewish garment worker, devised this scheme:

> I always needed money. There was a long list of things I wanted to do. My mother always made me give over my envelope unopened. I was miserable. One day an Irish girl told me at work that she steamed open

her envelope and took some out for herself. The amount was written in pencil. After she steamed it open, she would erase the real amount and write in the amount minus what she took. I decided to do the same thing. Boy, was I scared. But, it worked. I lived in fear my mother would catch me, that she would find out I was cheating. I didn't think I was cheating. I was just taking some of what was mine.[47]

Covert strategies ran the risk of exposure; some daughters preferred a more direct route. Becky Brier, a rebel from Poland, said that "in the beginning of my work life, I gave every cent to my mother and got spending money. After a while, I put my foot down and gave $10 a week and kept the rest."[48] Paying board was a compromise. Sometimes a daughter's demand to pay board resulted in the intervention of her father. Judith Weissman, the oldest of five, earned $6 a week:

> I gave my mother the pay envelope and she gave me 10¢ a day. One day I wanted a more expensive blouse than my mother would allow. My father came in on this argument and settled the dispute. He said to my mother, I should be my own boss and pay a certain amount into the household. This way I could take care of myself and buy what I wanted. I used the money for clothes for myself, my sisters, fancy curtains and other goodies, even though my mother complained.[49]

Even here, Judith did not use her money just for herself, but spent it on things for the family.

Only in rare cases did young women move out to live and manage their own. This option was open only to the few who were engaged in either political or artistic work—intellectuals or bohemians. One example was Fania Horvitz, who had come to the United States to live with her older sister in 1906: She remembered that

> in the beginning, I gave my money to my sister. But she was old-fashioned and wanted me to be in at night and I had no money to buy myself new clothes. I left my sister to live with friends. I wanted to have my own life and my own money. In those days, you had no savings, you lived from day to day, especially people like myself. I was active then, a little bit here, a little bit there and I didn't believe—who has to save money? If you were out of work for two or three weeks you felt it, but it wasn't too bad. After all, I was on my own.

Living as a single woman gave her a new attitude, in strong contrast to the general experience. On the other hand, after she married and had six children her consciousness changed. She described some of the economic differences between being a single woman and the mother of six when she compared the depression of 1908 with the depression of the 1930s:

> In 1908 we had a depression here. But I was alone. And if I didn't have enough, I didn't have enough; but in the thirties when it hit my family and my children, that was worse, because one person can help herself a little bit—but I had six children at the time and we were eight people. And it takes a lot to feed eight people, even if you don't feed them as well as you would like.[50]

What, in the end, can we say about the immigrant mother? Was she as isolated from American life as some social workers claimed? She certainly was not isolated from the economic facts of the New World: she was daily engaged in battle with this reality. Her position in the family made it necessary for her to learn about it and to develop the ability to navigate. She relied on old-world ties to support her; she depended on her children's sense of responsibility to the home to satisfy essential needs. But she also reckoned with the reality that, in America, sons and daughters went out of the home in order to support it. This was risky, but she took that risk and accepted most of its consequences. That the majority of daughters internalized their responsibilities to the home was the most striking testimony to the power and strength of their mothers' ability to adapt their own families to new needs in a strange environment. If men had split allegiances between work and home, women were the marrow of family life, or as Mollie Linker put it, "The father went out to earn a living. The mother was the backbone of everything."[51]

7
◇
How Many Tears
This America Costs

I F THE NEW WORLD TRIED TO FEED IMMIGRANT FAMILIES WITH
dreams and visions, reality attested to constant sorrow. The
America experienced by first-generation immigrant mothers
made insistent economic demands, demands that had to be balanced
against the obligations of the past and the requirements of the
present. Americanization impinged on the world of immigrant
women economically and culturally. While there was a constant
interplay between these two, the economic was primary and shaped
the contours of family life and the role of women in it. Yet the
domestic experience of immigrant women, from the payment of
rent to the bearing of children, was affected, in subtle ways, by the
interplay between economics and culture.

Although the average working-class family in New York City
earned between $600 and $700 a year in the first decade of this
century, immigrant families had particular obligations that limited
the use of their income.[1] Recently arrived families had prior debts:
"Before the immigrant can realize any return from his labor in the
form of American wages, he must first incur the following expense
of indebtedness, for even if all the costs [of passage] are prepaid for
him by relatives or friends . . . he eventually pays them all by
deduction from his wages."[2]

Another obligation was to send money back to Europe to help
out those family members left behind. According to the Immigration Commission in 1909, monies saved to send back to Europe
were "an important factor in promoting the general economic wel-
fare of several European countries."[3] It was estimated that Italians
sent back "$100,000 as savings, partly into home investments, partly
to support dependent parents and other relatives, and partly to
bring relatives here."[4] For Eastern European Jews, the continuing
survival of shtetl life depended on assistance from the United States,
either for remaining relatives or to bring over those left behind.[5]

This often meant "the most humiliating deprivation of the bare necessities of life: the money they send being the result of sorrow and drudgery and every dollar remitted representing a lack of food and lodging."[6] Traditions of family obligation and collective aid made sacrifice a necessity. But "emigrants were well aware of this and of the suffering with which they had paid and they were proud; they [Italians] stated as much in the bittersweetness of their songs: 'How many tears this America costs.' "[7]

The popular press depicted immigrants as interested only in money, accepting low standards of living in order to send money back home. Both anti-Semitic and anti-Italian stereotypes depicted Italians and Jews as hoarders and misers.[8] In a consumer society "American" meant spending money in the marketplace, and not on "old-fashioned" forms of family commitment.

In fact, even after money was sent back to the Old County new immigrants used their meager savings in different ways from native workers. One report that compared the standard of living of native-born and immigrant families indicated that "native families considered it necessary or expedient to spend more for recreation, trade unions, papers, spending money for husband and children and for domestic service, while the foreign born preferred to spend more for gifts or loans to relatives and friends."[9]

Another restraint on spending for pleasure was the need to spend on burial insurance, lodges, mutual-benefit societies, and aid for sick or unemployed relatives or friends. Jewish immigrants used their savings for lodges and mutual-benefit societies; Italians used both benefit societies and the family system to provide for burials and funerals, sickness and unemployment. *Landsmanshaft* societies (organizations of people coming from the same town or district in Eastern Europe) provided burial plots, paid expenses in case of death, and helped the sick or needy.[10] For Italians it was common "for a group of relatives or friends to contribute four or five dollars for funerals," or for people from the same town to organize mutual-benefit societies.[11]

Immigrants preferred to create their own forms of insurance rather than to buy the life insurance offered by American companies. Most American insurance plans paid only cash benefits at death, while fraternal organizations provided both death benefits and medical care.[12] Mutual-benefit and *landsmanshaft* societies used the immigrant's savings for their collective benefit rather than for the profit of the large Protestant-controlled insurance companies.

Hutchins Hapgood, in his book *The Spirit of the Ghetto*, captured the cultural adaptability of these organizations: "These societies curiously express at once the old Jewish customs and the conditions of the new world. They are mutual insurance companies formed to support sick members. . . . Mutual insurance societies are American enough and visiting the sick is prescribed by the Talmud."[13] In addition, these societies provided experience in collective organization and mutual problem solving. They were usually organized by men, although the money paid in was saved by the women. Rose Cohen, in her autobiography *Out of the Shadow*, left a vivid account of her father's participation in such an organization:

> Father belonged to a society in which he was an active member. The men often came to our house to talk things over and he felt important. Before they opened the meeting they always assured mother that they would not keep us up later than ten o'clock. But when the time came they were always so deep in discussion that they never even heard the clock strike the hour. Always it was a piece of burial ground that was the subject of discussion and when a member or anyone belonging to his family died, whether the members should contribute an extra dollar and whether as a society they should or should not employ a doctor out of the fund.[14]

When the meeting was over, they still had not settled these questions.

Anna Scott belonged to one of the oldest and best established Jewish organizations, the Workman's Circle. Part of her dues paid for a burial plot in a New Jersey cemetery. When she died, the funeral procession passed by a variety of resting places: closest to the gate were large stately mausoleums; next came broad headstones, casting their shadows across roomy "suburban" plots; finally there was the "neighborhood" where Anna was to be buried, next to her husband. The stones were narrow and not quite straight, with dense Hebrew inscriptions. Each stone stood inches from the next, creating the visual impression of a tenement community. It seemed fitting that she was buried in a place so like the one she had lived in.

A family's contribution to a mutual-benefit society or ethnic lodge obviously cut into the amount of money available for everday needs. But death and sickness were common events on the ravaged

Lower East Side, while "the desire to have a decent burial and an abhorrence of pauper burial created an obligation which must be paid before any other. A family is frequently willing to go without food, clothing or fuel in order to keep up on insurance."[15] A common saying among New York's working class was "Insurance keeps us poor."[16] For new immigrants, it made sense to keep saving for emergencies, sickness, and death within the collective group or family system. While American, German, Irish, and black working-class families often carried insurance from the big companies on every person from the age of two on, Jewish immigrants carried such insurance on property alone and Italians carried practically none at all.[17]

Social workers who worked with Italians were often surprised to visit families who endured long bouts of sickness but did not appear financially incapacitated:

In times of hard luck, the temporary deficit of the family will be met by relatives and friends. This was the expected form of behavior because in Italy "everybody helps everybody else." If the head of the household falls ill, the neighbors drop in daily to see how he is, and rarely does one leave without slipping into the sick man's hand a nickel, dime, or quarter. Not the slightest thought of charity is entailed by the act, either in the giver's mind or the receiver's. It is understood, however, that an act of kindness will be reciprocated when the occasion arises.[18]

However, the higher funeral and sickness costs in the United States sometimes forced these families to buy insurance from the large companies. One mother insured her entire family after she lost a nine-month-old baby whose life was not insured: "I had to pay $95 for the funeral; with the drinks it came to $115. It took us some time to pay it up. I thought it was bad enough to lose the child without having to do without insurance money, so since then I have had insurance."[19]

While the past made definite incursions into the family economy, immigrant women were also caught up in the dynamics of American life. When they arrived, they were generally unfamiliar with the use of American money or how it would convert into goods. A common experience was to compute the dollar in the home money: "They thought they were rich until they had to pay rent, buy groceries, clothes and shoes. Then they knew they were poor."[20] For example, Rose Cohen's family at first boarded with a woman friend. They were impressed that the husband made $12 as a presser, and could not understand why the woman, Mrs. Felesberg, spent her days "finishing pants which she brought in big bundles from the shop, while she rocked her smallest child in the cradle." They asked her why she had to work so hard when her husband was earning such a high wage. She explained the situation this way:

> Life here is not all that it appears to a greenhorn. No doubt $12 would be [a lot of money] . . . where you used to live. You had your own house and most of the food came from the garden. Here you have to pay for every potato, every grain of barley. Would that [$12] be too much for my family of five. We had to admit it would not. And even from these she said, I have to rent one [room] out.[21]

Rent was the biggest single item in a working-class family's budget. The average rent for a three-room apartment on the Lower East Side was $13.50 a month. In the 1900-1920 period, the average yearly income of immigrant families was approximately $600. Work was often seasonal or irregular, so that each month the rent loomed large.

For Italians, paying rent every month was a cultural readjustment. One tailor explained that in Italy, "it takes not much money to live. We pay the rent once a year, only little money."[22] Phyllis Williams, a student of southern Italian folkways, explained that "Italians adjust themselves with difficulty to the regular payment of rent in cash. . . . They learn but slowly the need of putting aside each week's wages for that purpose here."[23] The mother was responsible for collecting and dispensing the family income, and she was the one who had to discipline herself to save on a weekly basis to be sure to make the rent at the end of the month. This was difficult, and "in many households, the week the rent is paid the allowance for food is cut down."[24]

Yet even though there was cheaper housing to be had in Brooklyn or in the other outlying boroughs, the close proximity to the workplace made the Lower East Side the best place to live. If the family lived in an outlying borough they would have to pay in carfare what they would have otherwise paid in rent.

Landlords were viewed as exploiters, and "jumping the rent" was not considered dishonorable by people who otherwise felt an obligation to pay their debts.[25] Jumping the rent by moving was a common practice on the Lower East Side, a strategy for dealing with the high cost of housing. In *Breadgivers* (and in other stories), Anzia Yezierska explored the feelings of new immigrants toward the landlord.[26] The common refrain was hatred: the landlord was "worse than the pawnbroker," a washerwoman complained. "Every month of your life, whether you're working or not, whether you're sick or dying, you've got to squeeze out so much blood to give the leeches for black walls that walk away, alive with bedbugs, leeches and mice."[27]

In another story, "The Lost Beautifulness," Yezierska chronicled a washerwoman's struggle with her landlord. Her son was serving in the army and she decided to paint her kitchen as a present for him when he returned. The landlord refused to give her money for paint, and so she took in extra washing to pay for it herself. Her husband, a pushcart peddler, thought her extravagant, but she had earned the money herself, there was nothing he could do. When attacked, she defended herself by saying, "What do I get from living if I can't allow a little beautifulness in my life. I don't allow myself the ten cents to go to a moving picture I'm crazy to see. I never treated myself to an ice cream soda. Shine up the house . . . is my only pleasure." The contradiction, however, was made clear by her husband: "But it ain't your house. It's the landlords'."

The woman in the story identified this need for beauty as American: "I'm sick of living like a pig with my nose to the earth, all the time only pinching and saving for bread and rent. So long as my Aby [her son] is with America, I want to make myself an American." After she painted, she went into her butcher shop—the neighborhood center—and brought all her neighbors to her new kitchen, glowing with pride. The neighbors described the kitchen as "gold shining in every corner." She then showed it to the landlord, who in true Benjamin Franklin fashion said, "I got no time, the minutes is money."

Two weeks later he sent her a note raising her rent. When she confronted him, he told her that he did not care that she had used her blood money to fix up the apartment. Now it was worth more: "If you can't pay it someone else will. In America everybody looks out for himself." She went back to the butcher shop with a heart-piercing wail: "the dogs, the blood-sucking landlords. They are the new Czars in America."

Two weeks later she got still another rent increase, went to court, lost the case, and was faced with eviction. In a blind, passionate rage and armed with the thought that "someone who got nothing but only money will come in here and get the pleasure from all this beautifulness that cost me the blood from my heart," she murderously hacked her kitchen into bits and peces, destroying her own work. Her son came home to find his mother in a familiar situation on the Lower East Side, huddled outside her apartment building surrounded by a heap of household things, having just been evicted.[28]

If the landlord or his agent was a member of the same ethnic group as the tenant, the sting was especially severe. The money collected for the rent was often a passage out of the ghetto for the landlord or his agents. The "allrightnick"—a term used by Jewish immigrants to describe people who got rich off of other people's sufferings—made his living from the rents paid to him by his own people. Still, he did not set the rents. The costs of city living made high rents a fact of urban life, a monthly reminder of the new forms of discipline and denial in the New World.

Eviction was common on the Lower East Side. It was not unusual to find a dispossessed woman standing in front of her old building looking at "the disorderly array of household goods . . . the wreck of her home." According to Maria Ganz, eviction was an old story in the ghetto, and the sight of an evicted woman brought the nightmare home: what happened to evicted women was "what we had escaped many times, and that sooner or later luck might turn against us in our struggle to meet Mr. Zalkin's [the landlord] demands and we should see our own things strewn just as these were helter-skelter on the walk."[29]

Maria Ganz was intrigued by the eviction process, the remnants of the home now strewn all over the street:

The evicted woman kept staring at the litter of cheap things in which she must have taken no end of pleasure and pride while she had been gathering them one by one in the making of her home, now left in pieces on the street, a symbol of eviction and destitution. Occasionally, she would make the last sacrifice—her pride. She brought out a china plate from the folds of her dress and placed it on one of the chairs. People would drop pennies perhaps even nickels and dimes into that plate—enough to save her from being wholly destitute.[30]

Yet even here the women would help each other out in such times of economic distress. Mike Gold, in his memoir of Lower East Side life, remembered how his mother would go from house to house, begging for pennies to aid evicted women:

> How often have I seen my mother help families who were evicted because they could not pay the rent. She wrapped herself in her old shawl, and went begging through the tenements for pennies. Puffing with bronchitis, she dragged herself up and down the steep landings of a hundred tenements, telling the sad tale with new emotion each time and begging for pennies.

His mother did this out of sense of community and tradition: "But this is an old custom on the East Side: whenever a family is to be evicted, the neighborhood mothers put on their shawls and beg from door to door."[31]

Taking in boarders was one way to meet the rent. The daily press created stereotypes of new immigrants filling their small apartments with boarders in order to have more money to send back home. Boarding was also supposed to be common and even act as a spur to sexual immorality.[32] But E. A. Goldenweisser, an immigrant expert who worked on an inquiry into the conditions of immigrants living in cities for the U.S. Immigration Commission, reached a different conclusion:

> Another current belief is that all foreigners in poorer sections keep large numbers of boarders . . . and sacrifice comfort and decency in order to presumably return home and live on what they earned in America. I shall only point out that the study of immigrant homes has shown that only about one out of every four keeps boarders, so that three-fourths of the households consist of what my be called the natural family.[33]

Boarding was often one stage in a family's life cycle: "In general, as the family increases in size the income increases. In families where there are small children, boarders or lodgers may swell the income, until large families of six or seven are reached, when some of the children are of working age and contribute to the family income."[34]

Other studies emphasized that both native and immigrant families, from all income levels, took in boarders as a means of supplementing income, getting better accommodations, or adding to the family's savings.[35] Certain situations—the death of the husband or prolonged illness, for instance—served as a catalyst to taking in boarders.

Boarding also met certain social needs: single men or women often came over before the rest of their families in order to save for the family voyage. Boarding with a family from the same ethnic group was preferable to living alone or in a boarding house: immigrant men, according to social worker Sophinisba Breckenridge, "almost without exception preferred living with a family group if possible. This perference is easily understood as it meant less work for the men who in cooperative groups had to do women's work as well as their own."[36] Women boarders usually did housework and domestic chores for the family they boarded with, in addition to contributing to the rent: "Frequently the woman helped with the general housework or sewing or even the washing and ironing."[37]

Although boarders absorbed part of the cost of the rent, the presence of a boarder often meant great discomfort for the rest of the family: the boarder was given the best accommodations in the house and the family crowded into whatever was left. The social cost of boarding was thus crowded conditions for all, and increased household labor for the women. Evelyn Vogelman, a Lithuanian immigrant who came to the United States in 1905, succinctly summed up the effect that boarders had on a household: "When you have roomers in your home, it's not your home. They take it over."[38]

Judith Weissman grew up on the Lower East Side "in a fifth floor railroad flat with windows only in the kitchen and living room." Two men who worked at the same factory as her father shared a bedroom, while she slept on the couch with her brother—until her father thought she was too old for this. Her brother then moved into the kitchen, where his bed consisted of two chairs placed close together. Even when the family moved to a better apartment (which cost $17 a month), they had three boarders who, in addition to rent, paid thirty-five cents a month for a big dinner every day.[39]

Boarding with relatives was also common, although kinship relationships sometimes got in the way of the economic principles of the boarding situation. Louise Odencrantz, who studied Italian women, observed:

> In some cases, the relatives with whom the women were living admitted that the cost did not cover expenses. For instance, two sisters, living with an aunt who provided them sleeping space and three meals a day gave her only $1.50 a week each so that they might send money to Italy. Others were similarly subsidized by relatives, even friends,

who undercharged them or kept them without payment when they were out of work.[40]

Boarding was also a way in which widowed women made ends meet. Maria Ganz's mother lost her husband to the workingman's disease—tuberculosis—and eviction and starvation looked her in the face. Although she was helped by relatives and neighbors, she knew that this would be only temporary. Suddenly a potential boarder appeared and "she fairly rushed at him. With both hands she clutched to make sure he was real and not a vision that might fade away into nothing." Her boarder payed one-third of the rent and was vital to the household economy: "Sure, we want a boarder. Just look at what you get for four dollars. All the comforts of home you shall have. A real folding bed, with blankets and sheets on and a pillow. Oh such a pillow! Never a bad dream you would have with such a pillow." His contribution was essential to the Ganz family, whose weekly income at the time was about "five dollars besides the four a month the boarder paid. The money from the boarder was set aside to make up the rent, besides about two dollars a week from our earnings. The remaining three dollars had to meet all our expenses. As a matter of fact, it was only enough to pay for food." The boarder moved in with a few possessions, mainly a bank book and a large bag of money:

> I was often awakened by a jingling sound in the still late hours to discover him in the adjoining room with all his money spread out before him on the table. I knew no banana peddler could possibly make so much money. Most of the money in the bag he must have been saving for a long time and it was plain that a good deal of the counting must be due to the fact that this was his way of amusing himself for he never went anywhere, seldom talked . . . never had any pleasure except this solemn poring over his coins.

Upset that he might be a miser, Maria discovered one day why his only pleasure seemed to be handling his money: "For two years he had been saving in the hope of having enough some day to be able to send for his wife and children whom he had left in Galicia."[41]

Another way of supplementing the rent was to take in work: as in the Old Country, the home was once again a workshop but of a critically different kind.

"Homework," as it was called, was rampant in New York's

tenement districts between 1880 and 1919. The garment industry was organized along gender lines. Immigrant men were employed as cutters and pressers; immigrant daughters were operatives in small shops and factories; married women were at the bottom of the ladder, doing finishing work at home.

In 1902 the New York City Bureau of Labor Statistics estimated that there were between 25,000 and 30,000 homeworkers. The bureau also stressed the sexual dimensions of this work: "Seven-ninths of all licensed homeworkers in New York City are women, and six-sevenths of these women work on clothing, nearly all of whom are home finishers."[42] Studies by social workers discovered that over 13,000 New York tenement houses were licensed by the Bureau of Factory Inspection of the State Department of Labor as places where work given out by manufacturers and contractors could be made or finished, "where the labor of all the members of the family can be utilized without reference to age or factory law."[43] There were many unlicensed tenement houses as well. Although reform legislation and the evolution of the factory system made a dent in the amount of finishing work available, the practice of homework continued well into the 1920s.

At first homeworkers were primarily Jewish, but by 1900 they were mainly Italian. Of 842 women interviewed by the New York State Bureau of Labor Statistics, 487 were Italian and lived on the Lower East Side. The other large group was Germans living in Brooklyn.[44] John R. Commons, who participated in the bureau's investigation, observed that one branch of the garment industry, that of finishing and hand sewing on coats and trousers, "had within the past ten years fallen into the hands of Italian women who work in tenement houses."[45] By the turn of the century the Jewish community discouraged the paid work of women in the home, although widowed or deserted women still took work in. Italian families accepted it, perhaps because the lower-paid and highly irregular labor and construction jobs available to Italian men made this necessary.[46] Mary Van Kleeck, a social worker who carried out extensive investigations of the children of homeworkers in the garment and artificial flower trades, found that "with few exceptions the children who were visited in the year 1906–07 were of foreign parentage. Of 210, 195 were children of Italian parents, nine were Russian Jews and two, Irish."[47]

Homework, from the point of view of married women, was a

means of supplementing the family income without leaving the home. It was a way of finding work that did not involve learning English or confronting strange American institutions.

Small-scale manufacture and homework was centered in the Lower East Side. Aside from garment work there was also a brisk trade in artificial flowers, although such work was also done in such parts of the city as East Harlem and parts of Brooklyn. Social workers who walked the streets of the Lower East Side argued that "so general is the custom of homework in this district that as one mounts the stairs in any one of these houses one finds on every floor and almost every apartment, families of flower makers."[48] Lawrence Veiller, a tenement house reformer, maintained that "today such goods clutter living rooms throughout the city, especially in the neighborhood of Mulberry, Mott, Elizabeth and Chrystie Streets [that] make tenements over into . . . factories." Homework was so common in this part of the city that "in the thickly populated districts of New York City, especially south of 14th St., little children are often seen carrying large bundles of unfinished garments or boxes containing materials for making artificial flowers."[49] This aspect of homework has been immortalized in the photographs of Lewis Hines and Jacob Riis.

Garment contractors and manufacturers used homeworkers as cheap labor. Mary Van Kleeck argued that the evils of the homework system were "intense competition between unskilled workers in crowded districts, low wages, unrestricted hours of work, irregularity of employment and utilization of child labor." These were, in fact, "the very conditions which make the system possible and profitable to employers."[50] The contractor saved the cost of rent, heat, and light, while the low wages further increased his profit margin.

The contractor often lived near the workers, frequently spoke their language, and his shop was close by. According to Commons, the most capable contractor was the man "who was well acquainted with his neighbors, [was] able to speak the language of several classes of immigrants and who can easily persuade them or their wives and children to work for him."[51] In this sense, homework exploited ethnic family patterns: the contractor used ethnic ties to his own advantage. Mary Van Kleeck summed up this situation: "Homework was a regular means of supplementing the father's irregular earnings, and it was the habit of the family to take work as often as possible from the contractor whose shop was within a block of their homes."[52]

The contractor argued that homework was not exploitation, but rather provided needed pin money. A New York garment contractor who testified before the Commission of Industrial Relations maintained that "most of the women had husbands at work so what they made at finishing was extra money in their pockets."[53] Most social work investigations disproved the contractor's claims and demonstrated that homework was necessary for maintaining a minimal standard of living:

> The average wage for husbands whose wives were homemakers was under $500 a year. A visit to 515 families of homeworkers showed that all the women worked "out of dire necessity." The average weekly income from the men's work was $3.81. The average monthly was $10. The average family size was four and a half. As it required more than two weeks wages to pay for one month's rent, it is very evident that these women must work or the family goes hungry.[54]

Since seasonal or day labor was common and food had to be bought on a daily basis, homework was a way of maintaining a small but steady inflow of cash. Even when husbands worked in skilled jobs like bricklaying or rock drilling, the irregular nature of the work and changing weather conditions were constant factors. An artificial-flower maker who worked on willowed plumes complained: "Everybody, all people, they willow the plumes. It hurts the eyes, too bad, bad. How can we help it? The man he no works two days, three days maybe in one week, two weeks. Sunday no work, no money. Well, what can we do? My girl we maka da feathers. The children must have to eat."[55] Fabbia Orzo explained the logic of homework:

> It was pretty hard to make a living at that time. Everybody was pretty much in the same shape. My father worked in the building line—his work was seasonal—he didn't work much in the winter. Women who couldn't go out to work took in home sewing. Women who could go out did factory work. Women with young children couldn't go out to work, there was no one to take care of their children.[56]

Homework was usually done in the kitchen. The women had to work constantly to earn a small amount of money—few earned more than $100 a year. The typical Italian homeworker was thirty-four years old, and most were between the ages of twenty-one and forty-five, prime childbearing years.[57] She was, during the same period, giving birth to and raising small children, caring for the house, and doing finishing work as well. Some of this burden was relieved when the children were old enough to take factory jobs, but most families had children of many ages. Even when the older children were out working, the mother still had to work at home and care for the smaller children. These mothers bore the most severe burden; while the husband and older children provided money from a single job, the mother's workload was doubled by the raising and care of her family as she worked in the home to ensure their survival.

The home system was a breeding ground for child labor:

> Given the fact that the tenement industries, in which the largest number of children have been found, are those trades which form the bulk of the homework system and that they consist of processes so unskilled that the labor of children may be utilized to advantage . . . the conclusion seems inevitable that in New York City there is an alarmingly extensive employment of children.[58]

Girl children pulled out basting threads, sewed on buttons, and separated artificial flower petals. They prepared the work for their mothers to finish. Older children could do the same work as their mothers, before and after school. Children carried bundles of clothing and boxes of flowers back and forth from the contractor to their homes.

Children also helped their mothers taking care of younger children and the house. In some homes, social workers observed that "the children take entire care of the smaller children and carry on the work of household." There were children who did no homework but "cared for the younger children or did housework while the mother sews or makes flowers."[59]

The division of labor within the household was vital for the maintenance of family life. Cooperation was essential because the hours of work were so long and the pay so low. Sometimes unemployed husbands and brothers would help with the housework so that the women could continue their homework. For example, the following case was reported by social worker Christina Merriman:

> Mrs. Minora was an Italian woman of fifteen. She had been married for two years and had a six-month-old-baby. She had worked with her mother at finishing since she was ten. She lived with her husband,

child, father, mother and brother, in a three-room tenement apartment. She and her mother worked from eight in the morning until nine at night at a fast pace; she earned sixty cents a day, her mother eighty. Their rent was $19.50 a month. On the combined earnings of these two live the six members of the family, for the father and husband have been out of work for the past nine months. They take turns at housework in between looking for jobs so the women need lose no time from their work.[60]

Jane Robbins, who investigated homework among women from the Czechoslovakian province of Bohemia, also noted that "several times I have come into a home and found the strong young husband washing [the dishes] and not at all embarrassed to be caught at the washtub."[61] Although the evidence of this point remains fragmentary, it suggests that some immigrant families modified the conventional sexual division of labor and the organization of household tasks to meet their needs.

There were times, however, when all these expedients failed to make ends meet. During the depression of 1907–1908 there were more than one hundred thousand unemployed men and women on the Lower East Side. At the same time, the price of housing went up, with apartments that were renting for $12 in 1902 renting for $14 in 1908.[62] At this point the women of the Lower East Side exploded into activity:

Toward the end of January, during a cataclysmic spell of snow, ice and iron frost, the pipes burst, and for weeks everyone suffered for lack of water; the babies, old people, the sick ones. The neighbors were indignant. They gathered in the hall and held wild conversations. Mrs. Cracauer suggested that someone send in a complaint to the Board of Health. Mrs. Shuman said it would be useless. . . . "Let's all move out together!" she shrieked. "Let's get axes and hack out the walls and smash the windows and then move out!" Then and now, on the East Side, there have been rent strikes of tenants against their landlords. East Side tenants, I am sure, have always been the most obstreperous that ever gave the landlords sleepless nights and indigestion. My mother suggested a rent strike. The neighbors agreed with enthusiasm.[63]

In the winter of 1907, six hundred women banded together and went house to house organizing a rent strike. After the first few days, two thousand names appeared on the rent strike rolls. Each tenement building organized and held house meetings, while some landlords were hung in effigy. Tenants gathered on their stoops to protect the strike and the women were armed with household weapons—brooms, ashcans, and dusters—to keep the landlords and police away. By the second week, according to *Survey* magazine, the rent strike had "grown to astonishing proportions and sympathetic movements are reported in the upper East and West sides in Manhattan and the Williamsburg district in Brooklyn."[64]

There were mass meetings, and occasional violence. One meeting was broken up by the police: "The only real violence recorded thus far was on Sunday Jan. 5, in clashes resulting from attempts by police and landlords to compel the removal of red strike flags. Injuries were reported on both sides."[65] Although the local community claimed the right to peaceful assembly, Police Commissioner Stephan Bingham countered with his version of Americanization: "If you don't like your rents, get out. If you are not satisfied with our system of rents, go back where you came from."[66]

The strike met with varied success, with some landlords agreeing to a rent reduction and others resisting. Nevertheless, the strike demonstrated the organizational power of women in the community, and it was the most far-reaching and well-organized strike of that period. By 1919 rent strikes had become an ongoing form of consumer resistance: "Strikes of tenants are no longer a novelty in New York. There was one a year ago, and now several have broken out spontaneously in the Bronx and other respectable neighborhoods."[67]

Plagued by the constant need to add dollars to the family chest, immigrant women seized every possible option, even though these choices often meant deprivation and sacrifice. For these women, the home was not a "haven" from the outside world; instead it showed the imprint of the economic universe that structured its reality. Struggling to meet the rent, taking in boarders and homework, immigrant women worked at making a life that kept family and kin together. And even if economic disaster was only a heartbeat away, women still had each other to complain to, to share with, talk to, or to go on strike with. They were capable of enduring hardship. They were, as Mario Puzo put it, urban "pioneers."[68]

8

◇

In Sickness and in Health

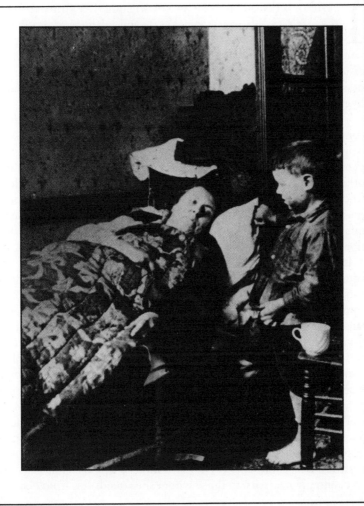

I N THE OLD COUNTRY MEDICAL KNOWLEDGE WAS RUDIMENTARY, doctors rare, life expectancy short, and infant mortality high. Women, to the best of their ability, delivered babies, nursed young children, ministered to the sick, and, through the application of folk medicine, intervened against the ravages of nature. In sickness and in health, women depended on each other: health and hygiene, childbirth, and infant care were in their hands.

The urban environment challenged this culture in many, often contradictory, ways. On the one hand, women were plunged into neighborhoods that were dirty, unsanitary, and disease ridden. For people of all ages, death was as common here as back home. On the other hand, American doctors and social workers preached a scientific, medical "enlightenment" to women that may have been progressive but was also disruptive. These messengers brought useful information and genuine concern in ways that often denied traditional community practices.

In Jewish and Italian culture women relied on midwives. In addition to aiding in childbirth, midwives acted as surrogate doctors, taking care of the sick, administering herbal medicines, and sometimes performing abortions. Knowledge about pregnancy, infant care, health, and illness was passed down across the generations, but the midwife was consulted for special advice. Midwives were also neighbors and friends, living in the same community, speaking the same language, and living the same kind of life. As they went from house to house, midwives passed on information and news, helping to tie the community of women together.

The practice of midwifery on the Lower East Side was common. Social workers were surprised to find that "the large immigrant population in America clings through custom and deeply rooted tradition to the midwife."[1] They also noticed that the "midwife was an economic necessity to those whom she attends for, from her, the patient is able to secure both medical attention and nursery care at a cost which does not exceed a doctor's fee for medical attention alone."[2] The midwife not only charged less than the doctor, but performed services the doctor did not: "The midwife acts not only as a visiting nurse, but as a general adviser and women's friend, neither of which functions are usually expected of the doctor."[3] Doctors were thought of as strangers and were treated with suspicion, but the midwife was known and familiar, a part of the past as well as the present. F. Elizabeth Croswell, who studied midwives for the Public Health Committee of the Association of Neighborhood Workers, concluded: "Midwifery was a custom which had been sanctioned by usage for thousands of years and was in complete accord with the deepest, most sensitive prejudices. . . . Through it, women of the masses in their hour of travail have demanded aid from their sister women and received it."[4] One of these prejudices, which was observed by Elsa Herzfeld, a social worker at Greenwich House, was that only the female sex may be present at a birth;[5] therefore, immigrant women also preferred midwives because it was culturally taboo for men to be present at the act of birth. This taboo was extended to doctors who were male—as most doctors were: by definition they had no place at a childbirth.

The reliance on midwifery was closely connected to attitudes about the home: the home was known, the hospital was feared. Even if a pregnant woman wanted to go to the hospital, her husband or women friends would say that it was only "for them that don't know better."[6] Hospitals were thought of as places where people either died or were experimented on—the antithesis of birth. Adriana Valenti, an Italian garment worker, noted that her mother had all of her thirteen children at home with a midwife. She recalled bitterly that her mother would have been alive if she had gone to the hospital for her last child, but her father did not want her to go: "They feared it so much, that if you go to the hospital you die; many babies would die."[7] And although hygienic conditions were hard to come by on New York's Lower East Side, midwives were generally clean, as were their houses.[8] Users distinguished between good and bad midwives: each midwife had a reputation that was known to the community of women she served.

In 1905 Elizabeth Croswell went through birth certificates in Manhattan and found that "42 percent of the total number of births reported in Manhattan in 1905 were attended by midwives." Adriana Valenti suggested that the number may have been even greater: "There were so many children born that sometimes midwives forgot to register them. They forgot me, for example."[9]

The cost of a midwife was far lower than that of a doctor. The regular charge of a "pay doctor" was $10, while the midwife received between $1 and $5 and she "washes the baby and cleans up besides."[10] In addition, midwives would often stay in the house, or check up on the mother for a week or two after the birth, helping with the housework and attending to medical and emotional needs. Since new immigrant mothers were usually without the help of their own mothers, this aid was crucial. Adriana Valenti's mother was so conscious of the fact that when she delivered her children she had no help from her own mother that she was determined to make up for this loss with her own daughters: "When we would give birth, for one month she would make us do nothing. She would say, 'I didn't have anyone, you have me to help, now you will have your health when you get old.' "[11] Even so, many new mothers lost their health through childbirth and the burden of the housework that followed.

It was common not only for the midwife but for the mother (if present), aunts, and mother-in-law to help the new mother during the act of childbirth and the first months afterward. The women of the family and the midwife acted as doctor and nurse, friend and housekeeper to the woman giving birth. Letitia Serpe, an Italian woman from Bari, described the birth of her first child:

> I got my midwife through my mother-in-law. The midwife and I got acquainted a month before I delivered. When it was time, my mother-in-law, the midwife, my aunt, and I were all together in the bedroom. The midwife was lovely—clean—she was like a she-doctor today—that's what she was. I had a beautiful nine-pound baby and the midwife wrapped her in swaddling so her legs would grow long and straight. My husband didn't sleep in the house for a week. My aunt slept with me and took care of everything.[12]

About half of the midwives interviewed in the Croswell study were between the ages of thirty-five and fifty-five and most had become midwives to supplement the family economy. The husbands of midwives held the diverse jobs common to immigrant communities, as carpenters, day laborers, street cleaners, tailors, and peddlers. The occupation of midwife was an acceptable means for a married woman to contribute to her family economy.[13]

The medical practice of midwives included abortion, and it was variously estimated that there were about 100,000 abortions performed every year in New York City alone, although it is impossible to gather reliable figures on this point.[14] It was common knowledge that midwives performed abortions, but the price was high and many women asked to pay in weekly installments.[15] This fact horrified Margaret Sanger, who worked for a while as a midwife on the Lower East Side, and propelled her to agitate for a more adequate and safe method of birth control.[16]

Both Jewish and Italian culture stressed procreation. Adriana Valenti, for instance, recalled that large numbers of children were a point of pride with Italian men: "When my father's friends would come to visit us, you know, the *paisanos*, they would say, 'How many children you have?' And if one had six, my father would say I have eight. Another would say ten. The larger the family, the better; they were so proud of big families."[17] For the women, however, an additional child was often less a blessing than a "curse of God." In a world in which there was no adequate means of birth control, and where procreation was hailed as a virtue, many immigrant women went to incredible lengths to secure an abortion. Even so, the average number of children for Italian and Jewish immigrant families was about five.[18] Emma Goldman, who also worked for a while as a midwife on the Lower East Side, was impressed by what she called "the fierce struggle of the women of the poor against frequent pregnancies."[19]

Many women asked her to perform abortions "for the sake of the little ones already here":

> Most women lived in continual dread of conception; the great mass of married women submitted helplessly and when they found themselves pregnant, their alarm and worry would result in the determination to get rid of their expected offspring; it was incredible what fantastic methods despair could invent; jumping off tables, rolling on the floor, massaging the stomach, drinking nauseating concoctions, and using blunt instruments.[20]

In July 1916, Margaret Sanger organized a birth control clinic in the Brownsville section of Brooklyn, a poor community of Jews and Italians. With two other women, she rented an apartment in the neighborhood and distributed handbills describing the work of the clinic in Yiddish, Italian, and English—despite the fact that disseminating birth control information was illegal in the United States.

One Italian woman, when asked if she would tell her priest at confession that she had come to the clinic, exclaimed, "It's none of his business. . . . My husband has a weak heart and works only four days. He gets twelve dollars [a week] and we can barely live on it now. We have enough children."[21] The eagerness of immigrant women to have access to birth control information was demonstrated by the fact that in the *first day* of operation the clinic had 464 visitors.

Unfortunately, these women's case histories were confiscated by the police when, several days later, they closed down the clinic, destroyed the files and equipment, and arrested Margaret Sanger and her helpers. Carlo Tresca, the well-known editor of the Italian anarchist paper *Il Matello,* was arrested at about the same time for advertising a book called *L'arte di non fare i Figli* (The Art of Not Making Children), an attempt to disseminate birth control information to Italian immigrants.[22]

Despite their knowledge, and the respect they had in the community, midwives aroused the wrath of the medical establishment. Lillian Wald argued that American attitudes toward midwifery demonstrated a real contempt for immigrant culture:

> Perhaps nothing indicates more impressively our contempt for alien customs than the general attitude taken toward the midwife. In other lands she holds a place of respect, but in this country there seems to be a general determination on the part of physicians and departments of health to ignore her existence and leave her free to practice without fit preparation despite the fact that her services are extensively used.[23]

Midwives were depicted by the medical profession as a remnant from the age of barbarism, and high rates of infant mortality were often blamed on the midwife's "ignorance" and filthy living conditions rather than on conditions of the Lower East Side itself. It was believed that "Americanization" would mean the end of a need for the midwife's services, and her replacement by a trained doctor in a hospital setting.

Many social workers had a different image, however. On the

insistence of social workers and nursing organizations that recognized that the use of midwives was not just a barbaric remnant of another culture but the established preference of immigrant women, the Bureau of Child Hygiene in 1906 assigned its nurses the task of inspecting the bags of licensed midwives to make sure of the quality of their instruments, and to give them medicine to wipe out *opthalmia neonatorum,* a disease that led to blindness in newborns.[24]

If social workers and nursing organizations looked for ways of improving the viability of midwifery, doctors and hospitals were preparing to take the entire birth process out of traditional hands. The promise of painless childbirth through the use of narcotics was the medical profession's answer to midwifery: "Just as the village barber no longer performs operations, the untrained midwife of the neighborhood will pass out of existence under the effective competition of . . . painless wards."[25] The doctor/hospital was eventually successful in routing the midwife from her customary position, and by the 1930s most women were having their children in hospitals under the direct supervision of male doctors. While narcotics may have killed their labor pains, and the hospitalization of birth made a dent in infant mortality rates, one of the most significant aspects of this change was that the act of birth was isolated from the community of women.

But this was not entirely due to the medical profession. As immigrant women became more familiar with American culture, they began to prefer the services of the doctor. Emma Goldman noticed that immigrant women who "had risen in the scale of material Americanism" soon began to turn to doctors.[26] Adriana Valenti's childbirth experience was a cross between two cultures: she had her children at home, but used the services of a doctor instead of a midwife. And in recalling her mother's extensive experience with childbirth, she felt that the high cost of hospital birth and doctors' fees was to blame for the decline in large families. Exaggerating the facts to make a point, she said, "When I was born the midwife got $5. Now I heard someone say that today when the wife gives birth, the doctor charged $4,000. You know how many babies my mother would have had for $4,000? None!"[27]

Another cultural confrontation occurred over the issue of nursing and infant care. Immigrant mothers nursed their babies on demand. In addition, lactation was believed to be a form of birth control, so babies were nursed for a considerable length of time, sometimes up to eighteen months. In the Jewish tradition, intercourse with nursing women was forbidden by law and Jewish women often used nursing to avoid pregnancy. As a Yiddish proverb put it: "It the wife is afraid of getting pregnant, she lets her husband think she's still nursing."[28]

The turn-of-the-century American apostles of "scientific motherhood," obsessed with what they called "good habits," were appalled by the irregularity of immigrant nursing habits. Elsa Herzfeld put it this way:

> The babies were nursed irregularly. If the mother was working or "goes out for the day," she nurses the baby at meal times and during the night. Irregular artificial feedings supplement the nursing. In the case of the non-wage-earning mother, the nursings are equally irregular. The child is nursed when it cries or whenever the mother thinks it necessary, day or night. The clock is not consulted.[29]

Good habits were thought to be the crucible of character, and mothers were trained to inculcate these habits in their infants from birth. Nursing on demand was perceived as irregular, contrary to notions of a proper upbringing that created people capable of adapting themselves to the machine age. Social workers applied these standards to immigrant mothers; clock time was a gauge used to determine the level of assimilation. The popular *Infant Care*, a manual, published in 1914 and widely distributed to middle- and working-class mothers' clubs, stressed that the "baby should be nursed regularly, by the clock, from the very first, and should have nothing between meals, save water, to drink."[30] In the interests of standardization, mother and child were expected to suffer through long bouts of crying; endurance was the key to success. Yet luckily for the children, the mothers preferred to feed them on demand, despite the criticisms of proponents of scientific mothering.

Even so, working conditions, undernourishment, long hours of work at home, and excessive stress created difficult nursing situations. The mother's milk was often inadequate to meet the needs of the infant, and artificial bottle feedings were used as a supplement. The lack of nourishment during pregnancy and nursing often affected the supply and quality of the mother's milk. In the Old World mothers had poor but simple diets, but here mothers were "so poorly nourished before the baby arrives that it comes into the world half-starved: the mother must often do work, the bottle is much simpler and frequently she does not have enough milk to properly feed the child."[31] A study of bottle-fed babies stated: "In Manhattan, 12,500 mothers of the poorer classes are forced to rely upon bottle feeding for their infants—two main reasons for this material impotency are physical disability due to improper nourishment and disease, and industrial employment due to abject poverty."[32]

An additional problem was contaminated milk. Milk in New York City was graded according to quality: the higher grades were more expensive and sold in bottles, while the cheaper grades were sold as "loose milk," taken from large open buckets in grocery stores and carried home in pails and glasses. The stores had little refrigeration and the milk was contaminated with bacteria that could cause illness and death in young children. John Spargo, in an article on the milk question for *Survey* magazine, argued that high rates of infant mortality were linked to dirty milk: "One-third of all babies die before five years old of diseases chiefly connected with the digestive tract and a considerable percent of diseases are definitely known to be caused by milk."[33] Yet in the end it was a question of money: the higher and more sanitary grades of milk were simply too expensive for most women to buy.

In 1908, in a response to this situation, social workers set up clean milk depots in poor neighborhoods where bottled milk, free from bacteria, was sold at reasonable prices. It was a constant struggle to maintain the milk depots: year after year, "Baby Week" campaigns were run to raise money for them. In 1911, after much pressure, New York City authorized "the municipalization of fifteen milk stations and so satisfactory were the results that the next year the appropriation permitted more than a trebling of this number."[34] Lillian Wald argued that in the neighborhoods where there were milk depots there was a sharp decrease in the infant mortality rate. Yet there were still not enough depots to satisfy the need for clean milk.

In any case, the milk stations were only a partial solution. The responsibility for unbottled, dirty milk was ultimately in the hands of the commercial dairies. *Survey* reported that a long fight with the dairy industry had resulted in the establishment of new standards for the production and pasteurization of milk that recognized pasteurization to be of primary importance if milk was to be safe.

Nevertheless, pasteurization was being abused by dealers who "poured dirty milk into the machines."[35]

The problem was complicated by the lack of adequate refrigeration at home. Even if milk was bought in bottles, there was no way to keep it cold—in the summer it would go bad by mid-morning.[36] Most immigrant mothers had small iceboxes that had to be supplied with ice bought daily from the iceman. Since a small amount of ice cost between five and ten cents, few women could afford to buy more than small quantities.

The social workers who established milk depots included mothers' clubs and classes as part of their program. Although the classes at first focused on the milk question, they quickly turned into a general program for teaching immigrant women scientific motherhood: "When breast feeding has been found impossible, they [mothers] have been taught the value of many other things: of keeping the milk cold; of feeding the babies regularly; of throwing away the deadly pacifier; of peeling off the long red bands which swathe and infest the little baby."[37] In the campaign to change immigrant mothering, pacifiers and swaddling clothes became bones of contention. Social workers and child care "experts" thought that pacifiers represented "an extremely bad habit," a habit for which "someone else is entirely responsible. The baby does not teach himself this disgusting habit."[38]

Anzia Yezierska fictionalized this tension in a story called "The Free Vacation House," which was about a poor Jewish mother desperately trying to go on vacation with her children in the country. She applied to a charity organization, which sent a social worker to investigate her case:

> I hear a knock on the door and a lady comes in. She had a white starched dress like a nurse and carried a black satchel in her hand. I am from the Social Betterment Society, she tells me. You want to go to the country. Before I could say something she goes over to the baby and pulled the rubber nipple from her mouth and to me she say you must not get this child used to this; this is very unsanitary. Gott in Himmel, I beg the lady. Please don't begin with that child or she'll holler her head off. She must have that nipple.[39]

Enrico Sartorio observed the same conflict between immigrant mothers and social workers in Italian communities:

Italian families complain about the blunt, aggressive way in which some social workers burst into their homes and upset the usual nature of their lives, undressing children, giving orders not to eat this or that, not to wrap up babies in swaddling clothes and so forth. The mother of five and six children may be inclined to think with some reason, that she knows a little more about how to bring up children than the young looking damsel who insists upon trying to do it.[40]

The confrontation over the pacifier, swaddling clothes, irregular feeding habits, and so on, was an area of cultural collision in which customary motherhood was confronted by the new techniques of scientific mothering. The tension between immigrant women and the representatives of industrial culture was not over the need to change the external conditions of motherhood in an urban slum environment, but over how and what knowledge was to be incorporated into the rhythm and patterns of daily life. These difficult conditions often led to extreme frustration, as exhibited by the mother in "The Free Vacation House":

Then I looked around me in the kitchen. On one side was a big washtub of clothes waiting for me to wash. On the table was a big pile of breakfast dishes yet. The baby was beginning to cry for the bottle. Aby [one of the six children] was hollering and pulling me to take him to kindergarten. I felt that if I didn't get away from here for a little while, I could land in the crazy house, jump from the window or go to the country with the charities.[41]

If one set of diseases devastated the lives of young children, another set—like tuberculosis and scarlet fever—ravaged the adults. Immigrants called tuberculosis the "workingman's disease" or the "tailor's disease." It was, as Lillian Wald noted, "pre-eminently a disease of poverty" created by "underlying economic causes, bad housing, bad workshops, undernourishment and so on."[42]

The garment industry was particularly responsible for its spread. Small factories with no light or air, small apartments with no windows or ventilation, the homework system, and industrial dust, dirt, and grime made the Lower East Side a breeding ground for a disease that caused prolonged illness and death, and upset the precarious economy of many immigrant families. It was also responsible for acute suffering within the family. One immigrant father who had been tubercular for years wrote a poignant letter to the "Bintel Brief" column of the *Jewish Daily Forward:*

> I am the father of a three year old girl, a clever, pretty child who attracts everyone's attention. All who know my child hug and kiss her. I may not. . . . Every time I kiss the child I feel my wife's eyes on me, as if she wanted to shout "murderer"! but she doesn't utter a word— only her face reddens. I feel that a battle is going on within her: she compresses her lips and keeps silent. She tries to keep the child away from me though she doesn't want to hurt me. My wife's suffering deepens my pain.[43]

Disease was also spread by the continuation of traditional customs in an environment that made no provision for them. For example, Jewish women, as part of their religious duties, were required to take *mikveh* baths:

> Women are required to use the pools regularly within seven days of menstruation. The Hebrew law is very strict regarding the method of using these baths and states that after a thorough cleansing, the person should immerse herself in a purified plunge filled with uncontaminated water or water that has not been polluted by human beings.[44]

On the Lower East Side, *mikveh* baths were usually located in the basements of tenements in congested areas where it was impossible to change the water, which was used by hundreds of people and became a breeding ground for disease. The bath cost five cents, and it was five cents more for a shower. Since people usually did not have the extra nickel, the showers were not used. Despite the fact that the Lower East Side *mikveh* bath did not comply with the standards of "the Mosaic laws," their abolition was strongly opposed by the Jewish people who bathed there.[45]

The attempt to find clean air and water encountered the same obstacles. Immigrant women knew about the value of fresh air and clean water, but it cost money to get to the country, or even to parks in the city. The parks had been built for the middle and upper classes and were far away from the Lower East Side. In a story for *Survey* magazine, Annie O'Hagan reconstructed the attempts of a tenement house mother trying to give her youngest child the benefits of fresh air:

> In pursuance of her resolution to procure sunlight and fresh air for Tobias without paying for it by separation from him or the rest of her tribe, her life was very strenuous. She got up at dawn to push her baby

carriage through garbage-laden streets. There wasn't a park available to her. All day, as she did her own and other people's wash, she tried to get the baby out in the fresh air, but there was little fresh air to be found.[46]

Most adult diseases were treated at home. Social workers did a house-to-house canvas in 1904–1905 and discovered that "in the East Side district, 90 percent of sickness is cared for at home. Even such grave diseases as typhoid and tuberculosis are nursed at home. Ancient prejudices against going to the hospital persist in these districts." At the same time, social workers recognized that the hospitals were "ignorant of the home conditions from which their patients come and their patients distrust dispensaries and hospitals."[47]

Immigrant women, lacking adequate medical advice, occasionally used folk medicine in an attempt to eradicate illness. One Jewish woman remembered that when she was very sick as a child her mother adopted her own medical practice: "My mother had me urinate and rubbed it on my forehead and my fever subsided. Another time I had fever so my mother ripped the top of my ear and let the blood flow and the fever subsided, too."[48] Another woman remembered a cure for burns:

My mother was very badly burned by hot water. So the grandma took some lima beans and put them in a pan on the gas stove and practically burned them. She then chopped them and put them through a sieve. It looked like powder. She put it on the burned area and it coated and cleaned the burn. The burn never showed.[49]

The women also resorted to prayer. Fabbia Orzo's mother claimed to be cured by a miracle:

St. Anthony was her favorite saint and she had reasons to believe in St. Anthony. My mother was crippled before her youngest son was born. She couldn't walk. Three months after she gave birth she couldn't walk until she prayed to St. Anthony. One day a parade for St. Anthony went past her window. My mother prayed that she be able to walk to the window and see the parade for St. Anthony walk by. She said if this happened she would go to church no matter where it was to pray for the saint, and pay her respects. She did walk those few steps to the window and from then on she regained her health.[50]

Mike Gold, in his autobiographical novel *Jews Without Money*, told of another form of folk healing. During the summer months it was common to find children sleeping in the streets outside their apartment buildings. One such night, a Fourth of July, Gold was falling asleep in his bedding on the street when someone threw a lighted firecracker that exploded on his pillow and burned him. He then became subject to recurrent nightmares and lost weight, and the family consulted doctors whose cures proved to be of little help. His mother took the advice of a neighbor and called in "the Speaker-Woman, Baba-Sima":

> There were many such old women on the East Side. They were held in great respect. . . . Baba Sima called one summer night as I lay pale and exhausted by the dark mental shadows. She was a humpbacked old crone in kerchief and apron with red rheumy eyes and protruding belly. . . . She turned me on my stomach and with a blunt knife graced magic designs on my back, mumbling over and over in singsong. . . . I was left irritable and skeptical. This foreign hocus pocus did not appeal to me, an American boy. . . . "My dear," said my mother, "this is a famous Speaker. . . . She knows more than many doctors. . . . She is sure to make you well."[51]

Through the use of spells, incantations, and rituals, he was cured of his nightmares. The Speaker-Woman practiced a kind of primitive ritualistic psychiatry:

> The East Side worshipped doctors, but in nervous cases or in mishaps of the personal life, it sometimes reverted to medievalism. Lovers sought philters of the old Babas, to win victory over a rival in love. Deserted wives paid these women money to model little wax figures of their wandering husbands and torture them until the false one returned. . . . That greedy, dirty, foolish old woman knew some deep secrets, evidently. She had cured me.[52]

Money and time were components of that "ancient" prejudice and distrust of hospitals. Hospitals were not located within walking distance, and finding carfare was a problem. Time was also a problem: immigrants could not afford to stay away from work for even short amounts of time. Further, the hospitals cost money and sickness could easily absorb a family's entire meager savings, even with the aid of a mutual-benefit society; prolonged illness sometimes forced a family to apply for relief.

Even public clinics and dispensaries took enormous amounts of time, and provided little relief:

Most immigrants were unwilling to go to public dispensaries. Crowded rooms, hasty examinations and prescriptions that gave no relief were some reasons for that feeling. Some people had to wait half a day before their prescriptions were filled and could not afford the time to go again; others found to have contagious diseases had merely been told to go away.[53]

Dispensing personnel frequently told people that the dispensary could not cure the disease and that they should go to a doctor's private office at a high price per visit.[54]

Sometimes doctors came into the neighborhoods, brought either by the public schools or the Board of Health, to vaccinate children and perform minor operations. Vaccination was a yearly event, yet its purpose was never explained to the community: both agencies and doctors assumed that its value would be intuitively understood, and neglected to communicate the medical meaning clearly. Deeply suspicious, many immigrant parents believed that vaccination was poison, and, according to one newspaper account, "vaccination is always accompanied only by force in the Lower East Side."[55]

On one occasion, in 1908, neglect and suspicion erupted into violence. The doctors descended on the schools to vaccinate and, this time, to surgically remove the children's adenoids, since it was believed that this would prevent illnesses. Although parental consent was required, most parents misunderstood what they had signed. Word spread. As the *New York Tribune* reported: "Rioting women and children, by the thousands, swept into a senseless panic by an absurd story that children's throats were being cut by physicians in various East Side schools, swarmed down on these buildings . . . in great mobs . . . intent on rescuing their children and companions."[56] The women, described by the *Tribune* as "voluble Yiddish women of luxuriant flesh," cried out that "their children were being murdered and buried in the school yard . . . [and] stoned the school houses, smashed windows and door panes." The *Tribune* attributed this riot to "ignorant, excitable Jews, fearing Russian massacres here, knowing nothing of American sanitary ideas." Events like this did little to improve the condescending attitude of the medical profession, or the ability of the women to understand the value of American medicine.

Given this lack of communication, and the immigrants' resistance to hospitals in general, social workers began to establish health care centers and visiting nurse services to help care for the sick in their homes. In this case, social workers recognized cultural practices while doctors did not:

> In the home, the largest proportion of sickness has been and will be cared for. . . . If the municipality assumes the obligation to adequately care for sickness and to prevent it when possible, measures must be taken to render service in the home. It is idle to argue that if the city provided hospitals, the people, when sick, would go to these hospitals.[57]

They also instigated antituberculosis campaigns, argued for more sanitary working conditions in the garment industry, and agitated for new tenement house legislation that would require better ventilation and more air space.

In the final analysis, however, most of the diseases of the Lower East Side were produced by industrial conditions, and their cure was therefore dependent on better conditions and access to money. Immigrants, through lodges, mutual-benefit societies, and local unions, employed doctors who spoke the same language and whose fees were considerably lower than those of American doctors. But there were never enough of these to deal with the enormous amount of sickness. A group of concerned Lower East Side doctors confronted this situation directly when they organized a free medical visiting service during the garment strike of 1916:

> We have seen babies die because their parents had no money for a doctor and our volunteer service came too late. We have seen men suffer because they had no carfare to go to the hospital. We doctors don't complain for ourselves. These are our people. We are glad to give them our medical services freely in their great need. But hunger is a disease we cannot cure. Money is the only medicine that can save them.[58]

If social workers and official public agencies experienced great difficulty curing the health problems of the immigrants, there was another group of "medicine men" who had few scruples about taking advantage of the health problems of the ethnic communities. Beginning in 1911, under the truth-in-advertising legislation, quack doctors and salesmen of fake and patent medicine were driven out of national magazines and high-class metropolitan dailies and found "refuge in the small town papers and especially the foreign press.

The foreign-language press, it was estimated, derived 36% of their advertisements from quack practitioners and patent medicine interests."[59] Disreputable doctors advertised in these papers, relying on the fact that most immigrants trusted their own newspapers.

The advertising consisted of all kinds of quick cures for immigrant illnesses. The ads appealed to ethnicity as the basis of trust. In 1920, *Survey* reported that the same doctor, writing ads in several papers, appealed to "my Rumanian brothers," or to "my sick Lithuanian brothers"—the nationality changed with the language of the paper—or, in a message to the Italians, "Sick Italians, don't be discouraged. Thousands of your countrymen have found health and happiness by going to see Dr. Landis." Or they appealed to a common language, "You can hold a conversation with me in your own tongue. . . . Here we speak Hungarian." The *Survey* article claimed that "the type of appeal is more vivid and dramatic in Italian, Hungarian and Polish papers, while in Swedish, Lithuanian or German, more matter of fact."[60]

Those responsible for the ads were quick to spot what the hospitals and doctors missed: that ethnic groups preferred to rely on their own people when sick. Quack doctors made use of community interdependence for their own pecuniary benefit, while the foreign press acquiesced in return for needed revenues. The same study reported:

> The foreign language press cannot afford to give up bad types of advertising unless they can get something remunerative to replace it. One small foreign language paper refused quack patent ads to an amount of $1500 a month because its people were being exploited and victimized. As a result, it could barely pay expenses but the editor declared he felt at peace without stained money. It has, however, gradually resumed much of what it had once refused.[61]

The remedies offered by quack doctors and patent medicine men offered little relief to those who lived in the beleaguered tenement districts, and instead compounded the problem of finding reasonable medical care from doctors who shared a common language. Few professional Italian or Jewish doctors had emigrated and the American medical profession was largely unsympathetic to the health needs of the new immigrants. This situation helps explain the desire of Jewish and Italian parents to have their sons enter the

9

◇

HOUSE AND HOME

I MMIGRANT WOMEN COMING TO THE UNITED STATES LEFT BEHIND
a world to which they were accustomed, one they took for
granted and felt comfortable with. Both Jewish and Italian
women had the benefits of household training, of mothers, aunts,
and grandmothers who passed down a known system of housework
and home production. But the costs of migration usually prohibited
bringing the entire family group, and it was particularly grandmothers and unmarried aunts, who traditionally had shared the
housework, who were left behind. Mothers were subjected to a
strange and unknown domestic world without the assistance of the
women they had customarily relied on. Even though aunts and
sisters did, to some degree, find their way over, the grandmother
was the person most missed.[1]

American household culture was itself in the process of transformation. As Susan Strasser points out in her book *Never Done,* most
late-nineteenth-century urban American women were no longer
producing the basic necessities in the home, and this applied to
immigrant women as well: "In this country, the housewife no
longer spins and weaves or even as a rule makes the cloth into
clothing. She does not work in the fields or care for the garden or
the farm—all of which she was expected to do in the old country."[2]
The mass production of clothing, the evolution of such food industries as meat packing and canning along with changing food standards, the availability of household decoration and mass-produced
furniture, all altered the nature of the home:

> In Italy, the peasants lived mainly in the open air. Their houses had
> large rooms with stone floors which required no scrubbing. The
> washing of the clothes was done at nearby streams. . . . There were no
> stoves which required care. When the peasants immigrated here, they
> naturally settled near their friends and relatives who lived for the most
> part in already crowded areas. These sunshine-loving people were

forced to live more or less in dark rooms; small ill-smelling tubs replaced their outdoor creeks; pulley lines their fresh green grass; wooden floors which require scrubbing, their hard stone floors. Housekeeping here required the use of tools of which they had no knowledge. The writer has come into contact with many immigrant women who had never seen a scrubbing brush. When to these new experiences is added the strangeness of the new country, strange language, and the evils which necessarily accompany congestion, and poverty and the upbringing of American-born children, the wonder is that they adjust at all.[3]

Both living and cooking in the old country were done in simple quarters. The houses were usually two rooms with a fireplace for cooking and the floors were made out of stone. While the walls were whitewashed occasionally and feather beds restuffed and aired, housework was relatively simple. Maintaining a household in the United States demanded more work and care than in Europe, in part because the evolution of new standards of living and new household acquisitions made housework more complex. As a Polish woman put it, "Housework is much more difficult in this country, with the cleaning of the woodwork, washing windows, care of curtains, carpets and dishes and more elaborate cooking."[4] And a Sicilian woman exclaimed: "We had no blinds, no curtains and the floors were all made of stone. You have no idea how simple life is over there. Here one must wash two or three times a week; over there once a month."[5]

Even such a seemingly simple matter as bedding was more work. Mattresses in the old country, when used, were generally made out of straw, and in cold weather feather bedding was common. In the United States beds came with mattresses that required sheets and blankets; these needed washing and airing on a weekly basis.

The art of cooking, as practiced in the old country, was done with pots and ovens not available in the United States, where kitchenware was designed for English-style cooking and a diet that used canned fruits and vegetables to supplement the meat. Soup, stews, and sauces were meals that took "two or three hours to prepare in the old country, while here all the emphasis is on foods that can be prepared in twenty or thirty minutes."[6] It was therefore not always easy to transplant native cooking to the new environment: "The Italian women, for example, cannot bake their own bread in the ovens of the stoves they make here."[7] Economist Robert Chapin discovered that "the dependence on the baker was a universal; the Italian custom is to mix one's own bread and take it to a baker to be baked for ten dollars a week."[8]

Laundry was also done in the home. Middle- and upper-class American women had labor-saving devices, commercial laundries, or domestic servants to perform this hated job; immigrant women washed clothes by hand in small apartments. Urban grime and ready-made clothing increased both the dirt and the amount of clothing. In the old country, washing was done about once a month by groups of women who took their clothing to the nearest lake. Italian women quickly learned that laundry had to be done inside the house. Carrying the wash in baskets to the East River was a sign of being a greenhorn, and women who tried it occasionally became targets of violence. One Italian woman explained: "When first the Italian people came from the old country, they used to carry baskets of wash on their heads. They were beaten up for doing this, they stoned us."[9] While marveling at having running water, they had to accommodate to the fact that in America the laundry was done in the kitchen—a multipurpose room where "we used to take baths in a basin or in the tub where my mother washed clothes."[10] In tenement apartments, Monday was laundry day, and the entire household was turned upside down: the clothes were washed in big tubs filled with water boiled on the stove, then put out to dry on the famous clotheslines of the Lower East Side. As one perceptive observer put it, "In Italy washing is a social function; here it is a task for each individual woman."[11]

The tenements provided very inadequate homes for newly arrived immigrants. While the Italians mainly occupied two- to three-room apartments in small tenement buildings, Jews inhabited "dumbbell tenements." Dumbbell tenements, named after their shape, were generally six to seven stories high and had four three- and four-room apartments per floor. Only one room in each apartment received light or air; the airshafts between the buildings accumulated garbage and bred disease. The toilets and bathtubs (if any) were usually located in the hall and were shared by three or four families. The three rooms were a combined sitting room, parlor, and workroom; a kitchen; and a dark bedroom. At night large families and families with boarders converted the entire space into a bedroom, spreading out mattresses on the parlor floor. In the summer, the roofs and fire escapes provided cooler places to sleep. If the family bathed at home, they did so in the kitchen (on a Saturday night) in a large tub of hot water placed in the middle of the room. More often people used the public baths.

Ruth Mishkin, who migrated to New York City from eastern Galicia in 1917, was terribly disappointed when she arrived at her aunt's apartment:

> In Europe I showed the address to a cousin who had been in the United States a few years as a governess with very swell Jewish people. The address on the piece of paper I had was 5 Avenue C. She looked at it and said, "Oh, you're going to be very rich if your aunt lives there." She thought it said 5th Avenue. 5th Avenue. It still makes me laugh. She had a small railroad apartment. I slept on the chairs on a straw sack in the kitchen. It was very miserable.[12]

No matter how often one moved, all the apartments were similar. Becky Brier migrated to the United States from Poland. There were five in her family and they lived in a three-room apartment: "We moved every year to better ourselves, for cheaper rent or a better apartment. But we never found more than three rooms."[13] When Yetta Adelman's mother arrived she was enchanted by the hot water and the sink, exclaiming, "If you find a woman in here that is not clean, you have to kill her." Their apartment was three rooms, but "it was always open. We had ten girls sleeping on the floor." Yetta did not mind. She felt that "whatever we had it was wonderful then and we shared whatever we had. Nowadays people want more but then whatever it was, it was wonderful."[14]

Fabbia Orzo recalled her mother's apartment: "We had three rooms in our apartment, a kitchen and two bedrooms. The boys slept in the kitchen where there was a big Murphy bed. The bathroom was in the hallway and it only had a toilet. We didn't have a shower or a bathtub."[15]

Carmella Caruso migrated to the United States in 1911 and lived with her father's sister, to whom she paid board: "That time the people used to sleep four, five, and six to a room, you know, and they used to pay board like $3 a week. And the owner of the house, she used to give you your meals and a place to sleep but there was no bathtub or anything like that."[16] Louis Lefkowitz recalled the tolerance in tenement apartments, where the kitchen served as bathroom, kitchen, and visiting room simultaneously: "We had nothing like showers. We had a big galvanized tub in the kitchen

which was just inside the front door. We'd wash our clothes then take a bath. It was nothing to be taking a bath while my mother was having a friend in for a visit."[17]

Some of the newer tenement buildings included an "inside bathroom." Shirley Levy recalled her amazement at finding a three-room apartment that included a bathroom: "It even had hot water running, a white sink and a white tub. Can you imagine? But it had no steam heat or electric light."[18] Lenore Kosloff also had the good fortune to find a three-room apartment with hot water as well as an inside bathroom. However, her family had so many boarders and relatives living with them that "the visitors from Europe always used the bathroom—so much that the family rarely had a chance to use it."[19]

Since a steam-fitted apartment in New York City in 1909 cost $360 a year, only those with incomes of at least $1,500 a year could afford it—and they were few. And since only the well-to-do could afford electricity, kerosene was used for light and coal for cooking. Gas cost twenty-five cents per hour by meter and was used only on special occasions. Heat was the responsibility of the tenant: apartments were kept warm by a stove in the kitchen, which was the warmest and most used room. Coal was a major but necessary expense, costing twenty-five cents a bushel. Even with very careful management, the family usually required between one and three bushels a week. In cost-of-living surveys, social workers discovered the grim facts of the family economy in the tenement districts: it was estimated that immigrant families spent 30 percent of their earnings on rent, 40 percent on food, and 30 percent on everything else—clothing, washing materials, fuel, light, recreation, medical services, and insurance.[20]

Both foreign and native-born working-class families tried to offset the expense of heat by utilizing the "city forest": wood from abandoned construction sites, industrial debris, and pieces of coal from the railroad tracks, dock areas, or fallen from the coal delivery truck. Although some writers referred to this as the workers "claiming the old rights of the peasant,"[21] the city forest in working-class neighborhoods showed its industrial origins. The children "usually gathered all the wood necessary for kindling and frequently for fuel also from buildings in the process of erection or being torn down."[22] Construction was abundant on the Lower East Side and the market streets provided fertile ground for collectors of broken crates and boxes. Although the city considered these activities socially disreputable and defined them as illegal, they were nevertheless encouraged at home. "Johnnie is a good boy," said one mother frankly. "He keeps the coal and wood box full nearly all the time. I don't have to buy none." In an analysis of arrests of young boys in 1909, petty thievery of wood and coal led the list.[23]

In fact, a large part of the minimum necessary to support life could be picked up on the streets by boys and girls whose hunting instincts have been sharpened by necessity. Boys especially developed these instincts:

> Boys were brought up to consider it part of the daily routine; the winter cold drives home his family's need for heat and yet the family income is too slender to allow the purchase of coal. His mother sends him out to get the coal and he knows that somewhere he must find it. . . . It is natural and easy to fall in with the parental fiction that the fuel which reaches the tenement has miraculously dropped from heaven.[24]

Robert Chapin discovered that most families with incomes of between $500 and $1,000 reported gathering wood and coal from the city streets.[25] Even an "illustrious" immigrant like Louis Lefkowitz, former attorney general of the state of New York, remembered collecting coal: "Most of us had coal stoves and we had ice boxes. Of course, there was no money for coal, so what we'd do is make a "truck" out of a fruit crate on wheels. We'd follow the coal delivery trucks and pick up the pieces as they fell off the truck. It was yours for the taking."[26] And if a family could not gather wood, "they frequently went to bed to keep warm."[27]

Clothing was another arena in which the family income was supplemented, in this case with gifts and hand-me-downs. Since immigrant women were no longer responsible for the production of clothing, they had to purchase it, particularly since the clothing they had brought from Europe marked them as greenhorns. Italian and Jewish immigrant families had to spend more on clothing than did American, Irish, or black families of a similar class position, at least until a system of gifts and hand-me-downs was established. A large family could absorb a tremendous amount of handed-down clothing and gave a large amount away to relatives and neighbors when it was no longer needed.[28]

Those family members who had connections to outside institutions required more presentable clothing than those whose lives were centered primarily in the home and community. The father and older and school-age children needed more clothing than the mother: "While the father's clothing costs more (35.6 percent of the clothing budget) . . . the mother's percentage remains nearly constant; even in families with incomes over $1000, hardly a case was reported in which the women spent as much as the man or the boys and girls together."[29] As the family income increased, more money was allotted for clothing but the mother's share remained the same—one-fifth of the clothing budget.

In Italian families "the custom is for even the older working children to turn over all their earnings into a common purse and the mother buys clothing for them all. Even the father rarely asks for enough spending money to clothe himself."[30] The mother bought the family's clothing from peddlers and second-hand clothing stores, often on an installment plan. While it was unusual for immigrant mothers to make clothing, it was made to last by mending and patching or by making over the clothes of the older children for the younger ones.

Another way of lessening the pressure on the family economy was to move. Life in the tenement districts was described as "nomadic; they move from tenement to tenement, drifting from poorer to better quarters and back again, according to the rises and falls in their fortunes."[31] May Day was the traditional moving day, an industrial adaptation of the meaning of the preindustrial holiday. The reasons for moving were numerous: eviction for failure to pay the rent, the desire to live closer to relatives, the search for better apartments with "stationary tubs" or inside toilets, mean landlords, bad housekeepers and superintendents, or a change in the place of work.

The reputation of a tenement house was dependent on several things: how the landlord kept the building, the rent, and the way in which the tenement housekeeper, usually a woman, kept the hallways and toilets:

The housekeeper's influence is very great, and depending upon her neatness, authority, character, and ability, the house earns the reputation for a good or bad class of tenants. She is the criterion by which the house is rated [by the community] and, in fact, the house is generally called by her name in the neighborhood rather than by its street number.[32]

If a family did not get along with the housekeeper or she was cross with the children, they would move into apartments with house-keepers with better reputations. The job of housekeeper was generally given to a woman who lived in the building and exchanged work for rent: "The women dislike the 'rough work' such as keeping the cellar and the water closets clean. Besides the general duties of keeping the house, halls, yard, etc., clean, she has to see that the house is full."[33] Sometimes the rent was paid directly to the housekeeper rather than a paid agent of the landlord. In that case, when a family was ready to move the housekeeper might "beg off" the rent, intervening with the landlord and enabling the family to stay another month rent free.[34]

Tenement living made American standards of cleanliness difficult to achieve. Judith Weissman recalled that in school "everybody was examined for cleanliness, handkerchief, clean nails, and for proper hair combs."[35] Adriana Valenti felt that the most important lesson she learned in school was that "no matter how poor you are, soap costs four cents, and you can keep yourself presentable. I never forgot that."[36] But parents found it hard to meet the new American standards on a daily basis: clean and different clothing every day, good shoes, and daily baths were out of reach. In addition, parents had problems incorporating the new standards into their own lives. As one sympathetic social worker stated, "The teacher has said, for instance, that clean hands, clean clothing and a toothbrush are essential. But the father, and the mother at her household tasks, though they may not oppose these ideals, yet they hardly exemplify them."[37]

The technological limitations of tenement-house living were class defined. Only the rich had hot and cold running water in their bathrooms, bathtubs, toilets, electricity, and such pioneering labor-saving devices as washing machines and vacuum cleaners.[38] These "millionaire things" were clearly out of the reach of immigrant families. One woman who worked as a domestic servant for rich people uptown reported to her East Side family that

> rich people had marble bathtubs in their own houses, with running hot and cold water all day and night long so they could take a bath any time they felt like it, instead of having to stand in line before the public bath house as we had to do when we wanted a bath for the holidays. But these millionaire things were so far over our heads that they were like fairy tales.[39]

Even model tenements were not much better. Despite structural reforms, these buildings were still using kitchen appliances from the nineteenth century. Social worker Madge Hadley, for example, investigated the new tenements, built with more air space and proper fire escapes, and found that the women still complained about housework and, in particular, backaches caused by their sinks. Armed with these facts, she singlehandedly set out to change the technology:

> Madge Hadley saw that the sink of the model tenement in the twentieth century is as low as the ancestral sink of the nineteenth over which she had leaned and ached. The tenement women confessed to her that their backs ached in spite of the cubic air space. She went to a sink manufacturer to find out why sinks were so low to the ground. He didn't know and confessed to her that he had been making sinks the same way for years and had never questioned the construction. The low wooden sink, he discovered, was made at a time when there was no running water and dishwashing was done in low buckets and tubs over fire. Porcelain and metal sinks were built with the same idea with no consideration for advancing technology. By the time he had figured all this out, the sink man was so interested that he designed a new sink, a sort of sink on stilts and daddy long-legs, and in no time it will be on the market for the use and easement of women. All of which is to the everlasting credit of Mrs. Hadley.[40]

Nevertheless, despite the small cramped quarters and the endless fight against dirt and grime, immigrant women kept their houses clean. The U.S. Immigration Commission reported:

> In connection to the prevailing opinion about filth which is supposed to be the natural element of the immigrant, it is an interesting fact that while perhaps five-sixths of the blocks studied justified this belief so far as the outward appearance of the street was concerned, five-sixths of the interiors of the homes were immaculate. When this is considered in connection with the frequently inadequate water supply, the dark halls, and the large number of families living in close proximity, the responsibility for uncleanliness and unsanitary conditions is largely shifted from immigrants to landlord and municipal authorities.[41]

In her daily rounds, Lillian Wald was often struck by the "scrupulously kept rooms, plants by the windows, happiness and a real home." For Wald, East Side women rose to "real heroism scrubbing rotten floors and polishing brass in rooms which could never catch the light of the sun."[42]

Italian and Jewish mothers, in a valiant struggle against unsanitary and filthy conditions, taught their daughters the value of a clean, attractive house:

> Mothers so inculcate orderliness and cleanliness into each Italian girl that American visitors are constantly filled with admiration at the neatness and attractiveness of small apartments. However dingy the outsides of the blocks may appear . . . brightly colored linoleum covers the floor, light curtains cover the windows and beds have spotless counterpanes. If there is a sitting room, it is commonly furnished with a three piece suite of cheap pattern but with highly polished wood and well brushed cloth surfaces.[43]

The kitchen was often decorated with colorful fabrics to hide the unsightly pots and pans. Paint, pictures, and calendars brightened the walls. Leonard Covello humorously described his mother's kitchen table, "which was covered by an oilcloth with a picture of Columbus setting foot on American soil. More than once my father glared at this oilcloth and poured a malediction on Columbus and his great discovery."[44]

Household ornamentation, bric-a-brac, and new furniture were used to make a warm environment that served as a personal statement against the filth of the outside world. Mabel Kittredge, a leader of the scientific housekeeping movement, was upset about the furnishings that immigrant women used in their fight against the ugliness of tenement living, but even she had to admit that these women were concerned about their homes:

> Look at the energy and thought she puts into furnishing her home . . . the hemming and the hanging of ruffles over every door, around every shelf and even around the tubs. Look at the tartelan festooned around the chandelier and over the pictures; see the dozens of calendars collected and pinned on the walls. Isn't this a reaching out with all the power that is in a woman to express to her family and her neighbors what, in her ignorance, she believes to be a home.[45]

Kittredge wanted to tear down all the home decorations in immigrant households and replace them with "scientific knowledge regarding food, air, sun, and cleanliness."[46] To do this, she established what she called "model tenement apartments," decorated in austere style along the lines of a hospital room where immigrant women were given demonstrations of clean, uncluttered "scientific" living. Mary Simkhovitch was more sensitive to aesthetic needs: "It takes a very specialized taste to prefer the bareness of the hospital or convent to the comfort of home. The average woman wants the satisfaction of her own ideas rather than suit the point of view of anybody else, no matter how worthy, how sanitary, how progressive that other point of view might be."[47] She also understood the social importance of the apartment's interior to immigrant women and the desire to remake these small rooms: "In many three-room apartments, families tried to make one room into a sitting room, at least during the daytime. Often the parlor contained a gay carpet . . . the much craved easy payment furniture, lacy curtains and the wall pictures of fruit and fish."[48] Peddlers and secondhand stores sold furniture and decorations on installment. Poor families could obtain beds, chairs, and tables from the local market, while slightly better-off immigrants bought rugs, oilcloths, mirrors, clocks, and sewing machines, all in great demand. Occasionally a family might buy a piano on installment, although this was considered a display of great wealth. A standardized furniture industry grew, leading Simon Patten to exclaim in the pages of *Survey:* "Houses, parlors, food and dress are the same for millions of people."[49]

If many middle-class social reformers attacked immigrant taste as garish, Simkhovitch saw that the decision to create a parlor "indicated the emergence of a differentiated existence and with it, an ideal of leisure." The parlor, she argued, "as it is the depository for strange ornamentation and unmeaning isolation, is no more garish in tenement homes than it is in the more prosperous homes, the parlor set, the phonograph, the colored chromo, the . . . bric-a-brac are not a whit more hideous than their more expensive counterparts."[50]

In addition, many families decorated their parlors with objects of personal significance: "On the parlor wall hang the marriage certificate . . . and the enlarged photograph of the father and mother when married."[51] Decorations transformed ugly walls into ornamental collages, with calendars depicting natural scenes, pictures of fruit, fish, and forests, all a way of keeping in touch with a remembered past: immigrant families created their parlors as shrines to a family culture.

The addition of bric-a-brac, mirrors, and so on, often cost the family a day's meal. A choice was constantly being made between food, rent, and the aesthetic pleasure derived from furniture or household objects. If a new chair or a piece of oilcloth was needed or desired, the family cut down on other expenses for the week. Installment buying alleviated some of the monetary pressure, and weekly payments were often skipped and paid later. The amount of furniture was an indication of social status, while taking furniture to the pawnshop was a sign of unemployment, illness, or financial difficulties.

For example, Maria Ganz's neighbor, Mrs. Zulinsky, was regarded as a "woman of wealth" by neighbors. Her husband had recently died and left her his small grocery store, which she sold for $600:

> Six hundred dollars. A fortune on our block. Everybody envied her. She kept the six hundred dollars in a stocking under her mattress, for her distrust of banks was great and was not without reason, considering the frequency with which such institutions went to smash in the ghetto. One day the stocking disappeared. Too many people shared the secret of its hiding place. That was why Mrs. Zulinksy became a furniture dealer.

She had three children to support, including a son she considered a genius at the piano: "She disposed of all the chairs, the two beds and the table. . . . Even the marble clock surmounted by a bronze horseman armed with a spear had been pawned." Eventually the family was "reduced to sitting on boxes and sleeping on the floor," but she kept her piano. When the Bureau of Charities wanted her to sell it, she fought bitterly and hard for a compromise; finally, she was given some money and her son agreed to find a job during the day and play the piano only at night. Mrs. Zulinsky was jubilant: "They had almost starved, their home was stripped bare and the future uncertain, but she had saved the piano."[52]

The care of the home demanded a great deal of attention. To some social workers the routines established by immigrant mothers were old-fashioned, chaotic, and unregulated. Declaring their intention to make housework more scientific, social workers charged that immigrant women were task- rather than time-oriented. They argued that "the old way of doing housework made every act an end in itself. Now every act is simply a means to an end, every move important, the way the dishes are washed, the beds made and the cooking done may win or lose the game."[53]

Mabel Kittredge, an apostle of "scientific housekeeping" and a leader of the model-tenement movement, posed industrial science as the necessary successor to traditional housekeeping: "Our school children, whether foreign or American, do come from homes where the mothers are good housekeepers according to their light: but the last generation cannot teach the coming one everything. . . . The accumulated experience of the ages is the grandmother and yet she is an authority no longer; since her day, science has stepped in."[54]

Scientific housekeeping contained the possibility of remodeling the home along factory lines. Kittredge argued that the basic problem with "old-fashioned" housework was that it was too dependent on old customs where "the sense of time, so important to the highly civilized, does not exist" and "home life [is] too dependent upon the work of one woman [so that it] cannot attain anything like a strict sense of regularity." The time had come for both women and educators to realize that "the whole housekeeping question is dependent on scientific management, efficiency, skilled labor and effective tools."[55] Industry and its advocates promised a utopian future, technology that would alleviate the major burden of housework, freeing women from domestic drudgery.

The program of the model-tenement movement was based on an analysis of tenement living that saw "the internal anarchy and disorder of too many a tenement house [as] its curse." The program advocated bringing "order out of disorder, to establish a system by which the everyday acts of life (sleeping, eating, cleaning) would be reorganized,"[56] to instill a clock-like regularity and discipline to tenement living through the re-education of the mother. The imposition of the clock would enable women to develop a daily schedule, consistent repetition would inculcate habits that would promote order and efficiency; by adopting an assembly-line approach, mothers could become model workers.

Yet immigrant women could not organize their days according to such principles of so-called efficiency. Immigrant families arose around six o'clock. Breakfast, usually coffee and rolls, was bought in the morning and was not a sit-down meal: family members took their own breakfast while the mother cleaned up. Ice and milk had to be bought every day. The schoolchildren, as well as the older working children and sometimes the father, came home for lunch, which was bought and prepared on the same day. The babies were nursed all day long. Families usually had one sit-down meal together—supper—which also had to be bought and cooked every day.

Immigrant women did a tremendous amount of daily housework, but they did it at their own pace. While social workers thought that there was no system in the way immigrant women kept house, and often criticized mothers for not having regular sit-down meals three times a day, or for not scrubbing the breakfast dishes immediately, what was at issue was a different definition of housework. Mabel Kittredge was upset about what she considered the disorder, yet she nevertheless saw a pattern:

> Scrubbing in this typical tenement house is done when someone has the time: it may be at eleven at night or it may be in the morning. If the older boy wants to study, he must do it, perhaps while his sister sweeps. There is no hour for going to bed, the baby has been given tea to keep her quiet, is awake until eleven. The older children play on the street until midnight.[57]

The work got done, the houses were kept clean, the children fed—but it was not done in the same order every day. Immigrant women decided for themselves what tasks to do at what time of day. They followed their own sense of order and defined their own rhythms.

The congested tenement living lent an aura of sociability to women's labor in the home that offered some respite from the newly imposed discipline of individualized housework. Elsie Clews Parsons, the well-known contemporary anthropologist, was taken with this seeming contradiction. In comparing the tenement liver with the middle-class urban dweller "who may himself have lived for years behind a brownstone front without learning the wishes of his right or left hand neighbors," she observed:

> One of the most noticeable traits of the life of the average tenement house dweller to the eyes . . . of the private visitor . . . is the more or less intimate and friendly intercourse of the families of the house. Washtubs and cooking dishes are borrowed from one another at any hour of the day: a mother leaves her child with a friend across the hall when she goes shopping; a child runs in to learn the time of day from a neighbor whose clock is standard; a kindly soul sits up at night with a sick child, [yet] in spite of all the little individual acts of service, the whole round of economic activity is entirely independent of every other family.[58]

Borrowing tools and lending or exchanging services created a community within the tenements, even though the industrial organization of the home demanded that each family perform its daily work as a separate unit.

Newly arrived immigrant women joined relatives and friends from whom they learned how to cope with the new facts of daily life. Fabbia Orzo's mother's experience was typical. She recalled that "in the beginning, my mother missed Italy a lot. She missed her parents." But some of her mother's friends from Italy had also migrated to the United States and they settled in the same area: "They would go out with each other shopping. If one needed the other, if they were sick or needed help, they would go over. There was *something* about my mother and the friends she had."[59]

The community of women compensated for the family left behind and acted collectively as an agency of adaptation to the rules of the new culture. They taught each other where to shop, the new definitions of housework, how to wash clothes, what kinds of pots to buy, and so on.

The exteme gregariousness of the Lower East Side was well known and tenement-house living was a shared experience. Judith Weissman, who grew up on the Lower East Side, recalled:

> Families were close. You just got up and visited. You knocked on the door. They opened it and you were one of the family. If someone got sick, the neighbor took care of them. My mother went for an operation and the neighbor took the younger children. They would shop and cook. Neighbors gathered in the halls, brought out their chairs, and chatted. If someone was bad off, they made a collection.[60]

And Josephine Roche observed that "sympathy is the keynote of the Italian community. It binds together not only members of the same family, but relatives of all degrees, friends, fellow tenants and speakers of the same dialect."[61]

Sometimes this community crossed ethnic barriers. Adriana Valenti had vivid memories of how her mother "would speak with the Jewish women because we lived amongst the Jewish and Irish people. And they would exchange the way they knew. And then the heart would speak, they would understand each other—they all had large families and they all were housewives."[62] As Anna Kuthan put it, "Everyone knew who we was because we talked so loud, and we laughed so loud, we was so glad that we met each other."[63]

For greenhorns especially, this community was an important antidote to the alienation and loneliness associated with the first months in the new place. Anna Kuthan explained her joy at meeting people from her own background a few days after her first arrival in America:

One day I went on the street. And I heard some girls with baby carriages (they turned out to be Czech). . . . We were talking about what country, what part of country we came from. The first thing everybody asks you, no matter what nationality—what country you came from? How long you're here? How do you get in here? Many people don't realize how important it is, when you meet somebody and you could speak to them you don't feel lost anymore and lonely, you say, oh I'm gonna meet them again and we gonna be friends.[64]

In a strange country, immigrant women created a world within their own community. Barred from access to the larger culture by reason of language, class, custom, and gender barriers, immigrant women on the Lower East Side depended on each other. This created a web of personal, social, and familial relationships that mediated the world of culture left behind and the alien culture they had stepped into.

10
◇
THE LAND OF DOLLARS

T HE PACE OF LIFE TOOK WOMEN OUT OF THEIR HOUSES INTO the streets, markets, and other gathering places in their neighborhoods. The streets of the Lower East Side were constantly filled with women shopping, running errands, and exchanging news and gossip. To some social workers, who had no street life of their own, this appeared to be idle activity:

> In the woman this apathy shows in an air of leisure. It might be thought that the care of four or five children, and the maintenance of a home in three rooms, would furnish the average woman with occupation for most of her hours. But there are always women to be seen gazing out of the window, sitting on the steps, and standing on street corners engaged in no more fruitful activity than the interchange of ideas. Even the holding of the baby is apt to be delegated to one of the older children.[1]

Apathy, however, was not the issue; immigrant women saw these activities as social involvement. For them neighborhood life was a way of guarding the streets, comparing prices, being informed about who was sick, out of work, evicted, or deserted. Within the comfort of their own language, they could shop, watch young children, and socialize at the same time. Marie Concistre commented, "Those immigrants who settle in homogeneous communities where the mother tongue is spoken have no immediate problem. The Italian immigrant may shop contentedly in Little Italy without the use of one English word."[2] People congregated on the street with others from their old villages, towns, or shtetl communities. They were often identified by where they came from: "Thus it comes to pass that while a man may be known as an Italian, he is far better known as a Neapolitano, Calabreses, Veneziano, etc."[3] And once settled in a homogeneous community, the first generation saw little sense in moving away: "It is expensive to move; it is sometimes hard to find a position in a new environment, or to pay carfare, or even to be deprived of coming home to lunch. Furthermore, friendly relations, kinship, language, religious affiliations, dietary laws and preferences . . . tend to keep the families where they once settled."[4] When Jewish and Italian families did move, it was to similar ethnic neighborhoods in the outlying boroughs.

One way of making a living in the neighborhood was to set up little shops or engage in peddling activities that catered to particular ethnic populations. Peddling and small shopkeeping were occupations that both Jewish and Italian people became involved in. They offered the possibility of maintaining customs (like the Jewish injunction against work on the Sabbath) and at the same time dealing with one's own people and making a little money.

In 1913, the peak population year on the Lower East Side, a survey showed that in the 57 blocks of the Jewish community, there were 112 candy stores and ice cream parlors, 70 saloons, 78 barbers, 93 butcher shops, and 43 bakeries.[5] While butcher shops, barbers, bakeries, and saloons were a part of the village economy in the old country, candy stores and ice cream parlors were adoptions of American institutions. Ida Shapiro, who migrated from Minsk in 1910 at the age of fifteen, recalled her initiation, as a greenhorn, into this new experience:

> Right when I arrived, my brother took me to Grand Street for an ice cream soda. I was ashamed to say that I didn't know what it was. But I was lively not dumb. I was willing to try new things. He asked me if I wanted chocolate or pineapple. He was the greenhorn, he should have known that I didn't have that in my shtetl. He should have explained to me. I didn't even know what to do with the straw—so I just watched other people.[6]

Being a small shopkeeper was difficult, but one advantage was that the family could help in the store:

> From the dark coal and ice cellars, the cluttered tailor and cobbler shops, the grocery and candy stores, at the fruit stands and in the saloons, all members of the family take a hand and help bring in the common income. The mother is almost always on duty, delegating the housekeeping and tending of the babies to the daughter at home.[7]

Often husbands and wives both worked. Ethel Adelson, for example, worked in the garment trade, while her husband ran a dry goods store. She quit her work when her husband became ill since she had to help him in the store. In the store itself, there was "an equal division of responsibility. He did the buying, I did the selling." They shared in decision making, and Ethel sometimes helped with the buying. However, she thought that "the woman would not be equal with the man in a commonly run store"—it depended on the character of the husband.[8]

Peddlers came in two varieties: some serviced the home directly while others had stalls on the street. They all sold practically everything, but there was a distinction between those who sold food, clothes, and household goods on a cash basis, and installment men who sold on time, sometimes waiting for years before complete payment was made. As Judith Weissman put it: "Custom peddlers went from door to door. People paid twenty-five to fifty cents a week on credit. You could buy anything from pushcarts. Rivington Street was the shopping center with all the pushcarts."[9] And Maria Ganz, whose father was a peddler, noted the occupational hazards of both types of peddling:

> The collecting of money earned was often the hardest part of making one's living in our neighborhood. How fortunate that my father was in a strictly cash business. Surely we would have starved if it had been necessary to extend credit for part of the ten or twelve dollars a week that he earned. That might be some small consolation for this poorly paid twelve-hour workday, though the clock and sewing machine agents, who sometimes had to spend fifteen years to collect an account, made better incomes than the pushcart peddlers.[10]

Peddling was demanding work, with long hours and low pay. Although few peddlers amassed enough capital to establish themselves in business, there was always that possibility. Peddling was also a way of avoiding the discipline of factory labor. Many orthodox Jewish men became peddlers because it allowed time for study and was a way to avoid breaking the Sabbath taboo on work. But many were women. For some it was a part of a family economy: the 1906 Mayor's Pushcart Commission found that many men had "other occupations regularly and let their wives and children attend to the pushcarts."[11] For others, it was an alternative to the sweatshop. In 1907, a reporter from *Cosmopolitan* magazine interviewed a group of women who had worked in the shops. One had been fired for demanding better working conditions and was now supported by her sister, a peddler. The other women who were being interviewed contrasted the sister's work with their own, and concluded that the sister would "have many rivals soon, because boss peddlers have not yet sprung into existence, so that in selling pretzels and shoelaces we need not support the contractor and the other go-betweens, as we have to do now."[12]

Sigmund Schwartz, a representative of the U.S. Peddling Commission of Greater New York, explained the advantages of the peddling system over the neighborhood store:

> The peddler sells cheaper. He doesn't pay a cent of rent, but the people who go to the carts could not go into a store and get one cent worth of stuff, but they can go to the market and come home with a basket of stuff for fifty cents. A pushcart man gets his goods at wholesale and he sells more than a storekeeper; in a day he sells more than a shopkeeper in a week.[13]

Even so, peddlers were caught between wholesale prices, the need to make a profit, and the bargaining skills of their customers. The Pushcart Commission asked one peddler if it was true that peddlers asked the highest price possible. He responded, "Yes sir, if we ask a woman for half a dollar, she gives you fifteen cents, and if you ask for fifteen cents, she gives you three."[14]

Bargaining was the lifeblood of the marketplace. In his book *Blood of My Blood*, Richard Gambino described a bargaining session between his grandmother and a local merchant:

> My grandmother would walk into a store or shop, ignore the proprietor—in our area virtually always Italian—and peruse the shop's merchandise with the most casual, haphazard manner she could affect. In the custom of the old land it was her role not to seem terribly interested in buying and certainly not to tip what she was after. And it was the merchant's role to guess exactly what she wanted. After a while, my grandmother would begin to ask the prices of items she fingered suspiciously, indicating that they were obviously inferior. In response to his replies, she would immediately unhand the item in question, her every facial and bodily nuance saying it was repulsive in quality and its price a moral outrage. After these unhurried preliminaries, bargaining would begin in earnest over the real object of her interest . . . starting at outlandish extremes, she and the merchant would bark out final prices.[15]

"The Fat of the Land," a story by Anzia Yezierska, depicted a bargaining scene between a fish peddler and a woman:

> A fish peddler held up a large carp in his black hairy hand and waved it dramatically, "Woman, woman! Fourteen cents a pound!!" "How much?" she asked, pointing to the fattest carp. "Fifteen cents, lady," smirking as he raised the price. "Swindler! Didn't I hear you call fourteen cents?" shrieked Hanna Breineh exultingly, the spirit of the penny chase surging in her blood. Diplomatically, Hanna turned as if to go and the fisherman seized her basket. . . . "I should live. I'm losing money on the fish," and he sold it to her for thirteen cents.[16]

The installment plan was a practical solution for immigrants too poor to pay cash on the line but willing to take on long-term debts to satisfy their needs. Installment men specialized in particular neighborhoods and often became intimate with many of "their" families. Maria Ganz's family gained a frequent visitor to their house when they bought a sewing machine on time:

> Every week thereafter Mr. Lefkowitz called for his twenty-five cent installment. Sometimes he got it, more often he didn't. But he was a polite and agreeable man. He was always willing to wait another week for payment. He had the patience of Job. Years passed: he was still coming for his installments and had become an old friend. There were tears in his eyes when he received his last twenty-five cents (after eighteen years) and as he realized that after so long an intimacy, his weekly calls had come to an end.

Mr. Lefkowitz was a neighborhood fixture, performing a variety of services as he put together his income:

> He spread all the news and gossip of the neighborhood from home to home. Good news he brought with a smiling face, and he was as funereal as an undertaker when he told of family troubles. There was not an owner of a sewing machine within a wide radius whose joys and griefs he did not share. If somebody managed to exert political influence to get a job as a street cleaner, Mr. Lefkowitz would report the matter without fail and would be likely to suggest the job-getter as a likely match for the daughter of one of the families on his list. He would advertise the virtues of a girl who had saved a hundred dollars from her earnings, and would try to find a desirable husband for her. He not only sold sewing machines: he supplied wine and whiskey by the gallon for family celebrations, he bought back cloth for those who must go into mourning; he sold lottery tickets; and yet with all these irons in the fire, he was almost as poor as any of us.[17]

In good times women tried to patronize those peddlers and small businessmen known to have fair reputations and decent credit policies. Berel Ginsberg, the local shoemaker in Maria Ganz's neighborhood, explained some of the distinctions: "There goes Fineman, the grocer. . . . A *gozlin* [robber]. The whole block is making poor while he is getting rich with health and money. A pound of sugar by him is eight cents. Next day he will sneak in before the people and eight is eighteen. A wonder that people wear diamonds and we wear rags." Compare this with the description of Lechinsky, the butcher: "I can tell him from his heels. He wears them out in the back. Such a man stands on his own and takes from nobody. That is why he is a poor man."[18]

The local market was an important institution in ethnic neighborhoods. It provided people with employment and gave them a place to shop within the context of their own language and culture. The local markets of New York City were the place where ethnic needs and the growing domestic and international economy met. Banana peddling was a good example of this: here Jewish men sold a fruit unheard of in the old country, picked by workers in Central America, brought to New York by the United Fruit Company, and unloaded at the docks by Italian longshoremen. Goods such as coffee, bananas, and sugar were the material fruits of the growing international market, and were made available to new immigrants through the local market. At the same time, goods not generally available in the United States but associated with the immigrants' culture formed an important part of market activities.

Immigrant women had daily encounters with the market. They bought food, furniture, and clothing from the small neighborhood shops, stands, and pushcarts, finding those stores that specialized in the foods that formed the basis of their culture.[19] Jewish women patronized kosher butchers, and the kosher meat industry was a substantial local industry, closely linked to the tenement district. As in Eastern Europe, Friday was the busiest day in the Jewish marketplace.

Pasta-making was a thriving industry among Italians: "Pasta was made in every block of the Italian neighborhoods of New York. In many streets you will find three or four little shops in one block of tenements with the macaroni drying in the doorways and windows, the front room is the shop, the family living in the middle and rear rooms."[20]

Skilled housekeepers were at first perplexed by the need for daily marketing. The tenement house offered no place for storage, so food had to be bought in small quantities on a daily basis:

> At home they [immigrant women] were used to storing vegetables in quantities: potatoes in caves, beets and cabbage by a process of fermentation, other fruits and vegetables by drying. In the United States this sort of thing is not done. There is, in the first place, no place for storage and the initial cost of vegetables is high, the quality poor and the women know nothing of the modern processes of canning.[21]

In addition, Italians, who were used to making tomato paste by drying the tomatoes in the open air, found this practice difficult to maintain in dirty city streets. Further, poor families could not afford to stock up on food. The daily round was necessary; little storage space and many mouths to feed made a constant incursion into the marketplace part of the texture of daily life.

Jewish and Italian women demanded the foods that were essential to their diets. They bought fresh meat and poultry, fresh vegetables and fruit, herring, black bread and pasta: the staples of their own cultures and identities. Italians relied on their own cuisine and criticized American ways of preparing food: "Here, as in Italy, the peasant wants his food as fresh as possible. While he approves of home canning, he believes that the commercial method removes all the goodness from food and a minimum of processes should intervene between harvesting and consumption."[22] Even peddlers selling vegetables and fruit, who bought from wholesale markets, would claim that it was fresh from their own farms. Keeping goats and chickens in the tenements, although outlawed in 1901 for hygienic reasons, was part of a pattern of not trusting food unless it was fresh.

There were some modifications of the old-country diet, however. Meat, largely unavailable to poor people in Europe, was now available in cheap cuts, and the social meaning of the new standard of life was measured by the increased availability of this precious commodity. For poor Jewish immigrants, concerned about where the next meal was coming from, meat seemed an unbelievable privilege: "The sight of the roast sputtering with hot grease filled me with ecstasy. . . . In the old home I never had enough meat. . . . Now fat meat was mine for the asking."[23]

Rachel Rabinowitz explained that when meat was too expensive she bought "lungs and bones and you could use it for three meals." In a somewhat mystical fashion, she articulated her ability to conjure up enough food for her family on a small budget: "When I look at the pot, it gets afraid of me and gives me a meal. I never throw away leftovers."[24]

Italians, whose diet was composed mostly of pasta, beans, and sauce, nevertheless took advantage of the availability of meat for the Sunday dinner. As Louise Odencrantz put it, "It was a poor family indeed that did not scrape together enough for a chicken or a roast to add to the daily fare of macaroni, vegetables, and soups."[25] Caroline Caroli, a Sicilian garment worker, explained the difference between the United States and Italy: "At least [here] you could go out and buy a piece of meat, butter; over there the only thing you would have is maybe a little vegetable soup left over from the night before, maybe a piece of cheese. Here—as much as we struggle and work hard—at least we always have a good meal."[26]

The other major additions to the diet were coffee and sugar. Real coffee was a luxury of the privileged in Europe and the peasantry drank a hot beverage called *caffe*, made from herbs and roots. In the United States coffee became an essential part of the new diet, even when it too "contained barley and other cheap ingredients."[27]

One Polish woman, when asked if her diet had been altered in the United States, answered, "Naturally, at home everyone had soup for breakfast and here everyone has coffee and bread."[28] In Italy, the typical breakfast consisted of bread, cheese, and water; in Eastern Europe, it was a little soup and tea. But in the United States, the availability of coffee and sugar turned breakfast into a meal of coffee and sweet rolls. In Italy the per capita consumption of sugar was one of the lowest in Europe, while the average intake in the United States was one of the highest in the world.[29] Italian mothers felt that "milk, like many other American foods such as oatmeal, [was] insipid, but coffee, especially when sweetened with sugar, had a definite flavor."[30] Children were given coffee-flavored milk in the morning.

Sugar, and foods made with sugar, were an important modification to the European diet. Sugar could be bought from the grocer, but it was usually "sugar fairly clogged with flour."[31] Candy, doughnuts, sweet rolls, cookies, ice cream, soda, and cake represented a new way of eating. Some social workers were appalled by it: "The intemperate use of sugar represents the most harmful modification of Italian food habits."[32] Others, such as consumer advocate Simon Patten, thought that sugar's low retail price "places a satisfactory diet within the means of everyone."[33] And while immigrants responded positively and incorporated these new foods into their diets, such sweetened foods were also part of the growth and expansion of American industry and the transformation of American culture, where they played a key role as stimulants and quick energy builders.

Hospitality and neighborliness demanded that even if there was no food in the house, a jar of jelly or "a special piece of eating" be saved for company or taken when visiting. Accepting a cup of sweet Italian coffee or a little jam with tea was a part of any visit. In Italian families, "the rule of not refusing such offerings under any pretext whatsoever holds rigorously in this country and many a well-meaning social worker has ruined her prospect of making a good contact in the family by refusing the strong, sweet, Italian coffee."[34] On the other hand, "if the family does not offer refreshment, one may be sure that the process of Americanization has rapidly advanced."[35]

Food was also used as a form of emotional communication between women. Offering food to comfort neighborhood women in financial or emotional distress was a sign of friendship and caring. In Yezierska's story "The Fat of the Land," Hanneh Breineh, a Jewish mother with many children, walked into her friend's apartment, upset and wailing over her daily worries, how to feed her many children on a small income. Her friend Mrs. Peltz, involved in cooking her family's dinner, offered Hannah a piece of gefilte fish on a spoon, apologizing that she did not hand it to her on a plate. " 'What am I, a stranger, you should have to serve me on a plate yet,' cried Hannah. 'Oi Veh! How it melts through the bones,' she exclaimed, brightening as she ate. 'A taste of gravy lifts me to heaven.' "[36] This offering made her forget her immediate problems: she roundly cursed the landlord, wished her troubles on the czar, and felt renewed.

Simultaneously, the loss of culture was identified with American eating patterns. In the same story Hanneh Breineh's children made good in American terms and moved their mother to a fancy apartment on Riverside Drive. While the mother was proud of her children's success, her own life and vitality, molded by her experience as a tenement mother downtown on the East Side, was lost.

Her children demanded that she eat in a public dining room that specialized in American food. It was a painful experience:

I am starved for a piece of real eating. In that swell restaurant [the dining hall] is nothing but napkins and forks and lettuce leaves. There are a dozen plates to every bit of food. And it looks so fancy on the plate, but it's nothing but straw in the mouth. I'm starving, but I can't swallow down their American eating.[37]

When families had no money for food, they resorted to the practice of make-believe. Leonard Covello recounted how in his native village, as well as in America, if the family had no food "we bolted the door and rattled the kitchen utensils and dishes to give the impression to our close neighbors that the noonday meal was going on as usual."[38]

Lillian Wald found a similar practice among Jewish immigrants:

On Sabbath eve, I entered his [unemployed cigarmaker] tenement to find the two rooms scrubbed and clean and the mother and the children preparing for the Holy Night. Over a brisk fire fed by bits of wood picked up by the children two covered pots were set as if supper was being prepared. But under the lids it was only water that bubbled. The proud mother could not bear to expose her poverty to the gossip of the neighbors, the humiliation being the greater because she was obliged to violate the sacred custom of preparing a ceremonious meal for the united family on Friday night.[39]

Culturally, then, food became an arena of contention between immigrant women and American society. Eating American food was seen as an indication of Americanization, both by the immigrants themselves and by the social workers who sought to change them. There were constant campaigns to promote the eating of American food in order to transform ethnic culture. Ideas of "nutrition" and "food value" were scientific euphemisms that degraded ethnic cooking and sought to replace it with Anglo-American tastes. An organizer of one of these campaigns defined them as the attempt to homogenize eating habits—"the food Americanization of an entire population."[40] Social workers would write of their clients, "Not yet Americanized, still eating Italian food."[41] Campaigns extolled the value of canned and ready-made food, and the substitution of white bread for black or for the different varieties of Italian bread.[42] Mary Simkhovitch, among others, was critical of these campaigns from a nutritional point of view, feeling that both the

Italian and Jewish diets were varied and wholesome: "The Italian soup, black bread, vegetables, fruit, and cheese make a good combination. The Jews eat meat, fish, bread, pickles, and fruit."[43] She saw the food problems of immigrants as one of quantity, not quality.

Between 1913 and 1920, inflation caused by war production and profiteering started eating into the sparse family economy. In a study that used figures compiled by the National Industries Conference Board, *Survey* estimated that between 1914 and 1920 there was a 104.5 percent increase in the cost of living for wage-earning families: food rose by 199 percent, shelter by 58 percent, clothing by 116 percent, fuel by 68 percent, and "sundries" by 85 percent.[44] This is how the situation was summed up by one woman: "My man is working steady and we ought to be getting along just fine but my money won't reach even though I look at each penny twice before I spend it. I used to go to work when my man was sick or couldn't get a job, but this is the first time I ever had to go to work to get enough money to feed the kids when he was working regular."[45]

Inflation hit the tenement districts the hardest. If the price of food was high, the price of ethnic food was higher still. From 1917 to 1920 there were food boycotts, kosher meat strikes, and food riots on the Lower East Side, as well as in tenement districts in the outlying areas of the city. In explaining the food riots, social worker Bruno Lasker argued that ethnic bias added to the effects of inflation:

> The Italians, accustomed to the flavoring of almost everything with onions, lose not only nourishment but a great deal of pleasure in their food. As for German and Jewish citizens, it would be difficult to think of any suitable substitute for sauerkraut. Not the most alluring presentations of the virtues of rice will console our Irish, German, Italian, and Jewish brethren, as one after another of their favorite staple articles of diet are going. It was easy to see that the food riots were not simply hunger riots but outbursts of exasperation as well.[46]

In 1917 the price of kosher meat went up considerably. Although this was a local industry, its prices were affected by the national price of beef, and the Jewish consumer was particularly hard hit because fresh-killed kosher meat in any case cost twice as much as nonkosher meat.[47]

Jewish women began a house-to-house campaign, asking women to pledge themselves to a boycott until the price of meat came down. The kosher meat strike spread across the nation: "There were riots, arrests, court proceedings, protest meetings in New York, Boston, Philadelphia, Baltimore, Chicago, St. Louis, and Cleveland."[48] And it worked, as the price of kosher meat came down.

Food riots broke out on the Lower East side, in the Bronx, and in Williamsburg in February and March 1917. Maria Ganz was an active participant and left a firsthand account of the riots and their cause. She described February 1917 as "the day of the food profiteer." Even though there was ample employment and people were receiving good wages, "food prices had advanced more than wages, and all of us were far worse off than when we were earning less." The concurrence of high employment and inflation was a new experience; high unemployment caused by depression was what was expected of "bad times." According to Ganz, "a pound of potatoes [that] cost two cents, now cost seven; onions had risen from three cents a pound to twenty; the price of meat had gone up fifty percent and the price of bread more than tripled."[49]

The *New York Times* conducted an investigation of the effects of inflation on tenement neighborhoods and agreed with Maria Ganz's analysis. Reporters found ample evidence of the effects of inflationary prices, and "in every household attention is now centered upon the getting of food. Such problems as heat, light and clothing are put aside for the moment."[50] One housewife told a *Times* reporter:

> I have estimated that I have $4 a week upon which to feed myself and my [four] children. It is hard work, but the greatest fear that I have is that my children will have sufficient nourishment. . . . Fish is a luxury with us and I have not had meat for so long that I have forgotten when. . . . For breakfast we have bread and coffee. For the coffee I spend 19¢ a pound. We cannot save for clothing. This dress I have worn for five years.[51]

The Reverend Mother Marianna of Jesus of the Madonna Day Nursery on Cherry Street described the situation this way:

> Any family having children and with an income of less than $10 requires some help. It must be remembered that there is not only food to be bought, but there must be wood and coal and clothing and the many other things that are absolutely necessary for life, not to say comfort. Not long ago these families could obtain meat at least once a week, usually on Sunday. Now meat is beyond their means and bread and rice are used to keep life going. Many laborers ate an onion

sandwich for lunch, but now onions are prohibitive and cheese is used sparingly.[52]

The situation was explosive; the high cost of living drove the women to action.

On February 20, 1917, Maria Ganz reported that women were standing about in the street talking and gesticulating excitedly. On Orchard Street, a main shopping street, she overheard an altercation between a woman and an onion peddler who was asking nineteen cents a pound for onions. They would have come to blows "if it had not been for the fact that striking a woman or a man with eyeglasses are the two most dastardly crimes known to the East Side." Instead, the peddler called on his wife to beat up the outraged woman. Almost as if it were a signal:

> Slam went the window; but before the peddler's wife could reach the street his cart had been overturned by a crowd of frantic women who proceeded to scatter his stock of vegetables into the gutters. This was a signal for an attack on all the peddlers on the street. It seemed only a moment before a mob of hundreds of women had gathered. Cart after cart was overturned, and the pavement was covered with trampled goods. The women used their black shopping bags as clubs, striking savagely at the men whom they regarded as their sworn enemies and oppressors. Onions, cabbages, potatoes flew through the air and in each instance the target was a ducking, wailing peddler whose stock had been ruined beyond hope of recovery. Policemen came rushing upon the scene, and they too were pelted with whatever was at hand.

As the riot spread from Orchard to Rivington Street, the women decided to hold a meeting at Rutgers Square, the traditional site of mass meetings on the Lower East Side. Thousands of tenement women gathered, organized the Mothers' Anti–High Price League, and decided to take their protest to the mayor at City Hall:

> As we marched our numbers grew rapidly as we went along, for women swarmed out of every tenement house that we passed to join us. Many in the throng carried market baskets and many had babies in their arms. Policemen came running in from every quarter, intent on driving us back, and they did succeed in hemming in huge masses of women and preventing them from following, though I think full a thousand must have remained.

When they arrived at City Hall, they were shut out by the police:

There was a mad rush for the gates, and the women battered against them furiously. "Give us bread," they cried and their cry was taken up in English and Yiddish. "Give us bread! We are starving. Our husbands are working day and night and yet we have nothing to eat." Many of the women were hysterical and were shrieking wildly. I doubt if there had been such an uproar in City Hall Park, accustomed as it is to demonstrative crowds. At any rate, it was the first time in the city's history that it had been the scene of such a demonstration by women.[53]

According to the *New York Times* account, tenement mother Ida Harris made a speech: "We do not want to make trouble. We are good Americans and we simply want the Mayor to make the prices go down. We are starving—our children are starving. But we don't want any riot. We want to soften the hearts of the millionaires who are getting richer because of the prices. . . . We are just mothers and we want food for our children."

While the police attempted to break up the crowd, several speakers (including Maria Ganz) "harangued the crowd and soon everything was in confusion." However, the sympathies of the police appeared to be with the women: "The police held themselves in control and several times were heard attempting to explain to the women that their families were also suffering from high prices."

The *Times* reported that "food riots in which about three thousand women participated occurred also in Williamsburg and Brownsville":

A woman who was apparently the ringleader of the troublemakers refused to pay the increased price and when the peddlers would not sell her goods, put her shoulder to one of the largest carts. In a moment and before the police would be summoned, at least a thousand women had joined the crowd. Several of them carried torches made of newspapers soaked with kerosene and with these they set fire to some of the carts which contained clothing and other inflammable material. Lieutenant Gellen led the reserves . . . and for forty minutes the policemen fought the excited mob.

The peddlers called a mass meeting of all the residents of the district "to put their side of the controversy before them." Over fifteen hundred people showed up. At the point of peak excitement,

a woman appeared in the meeting room followed by her five children, and forced her way to the speaker's platform. She cried out that her husband earned $8 a week as a tailor's helper and that she was unable to buy enough for her babies. Then she exhibited her children to the crowd as proof of her assertion that they did not get enough to eat. At this point the woman got so excited that Dr. Freedman was called.

At the same time, at a mass meeting at the hall of the *Jewish Daily Forward,* many of the rioters' demands were articulated. The hall seated only a thousand people, but the *Times* estimated that between 5,000 and 10,000 tried to push their way in. The crowd was so insistent that they broke down the doors.

The *Times* described this meeting as "one of the wildest the city had seen for years," claiming that "there were few men in the yelling, shrieking crowd." The hall was packed soon after seven o'clock and it was after nine before a speaker could make himself heard. The meeting was run at a fever pitch, the crowd continually interrupting the speakers with high-spirited strategic suggestions: "Louis Shaffer of the National Aid League in a much interrupted speech urged the people to organize and begged them to do no violence. Mrs. Sarah Erdman gave the same advice. . . . From time to time some speaker would yell that the people should 'throw kerosene,' meaning to ruin the stocks of the grocers whose prices were thought too high." The Socialist Party members who were in charge of the meeting advocated organization and denounced violence, but the women wanted Ida Harris as their speaker:

Mrs. Ida Harris, who had led the City Hall demonstration, tried to speak, but those who had taken charge of the meeting refused to let her be heard. She had the women of the meeting with her, and they refused to listen to anybody else. Mrs. Harris tore herself from those who tried to hold her and ran to the platform. Others, men and women, pulled her back and she fought them. Her husband came up the fire escape and tried to quiet her, but the shouts for her kept up.

Jacob Panken, "a lawyer and eloquent, got the ear of the crowd and quieted them somewhat. Panken again urged the crowed to do no violence. Uproar broke lose again as Mrs. Harris attempted to speak." In the pandemonium a plan was made for large-scale mass demonstrations, boycotts, a petition to the president, as well as a demand on the mayor. The petition to the president was read by Panken and was carried with a huge shout:

We housewives of the City of New York, mothers and wives of workmen, desire to call your attention, Mr. President, to the fact that, in the midst of plenty, we and our families are facing starvation.

The rise in the cost of living has been so great and uncalled for that even now we are compelled to deny ourselves and our children the necessities of life.

We pay for our needs out of the wages of our husbands, and the American standard of living cannot be maintained when potatoes are 7¢ a pound, bread 6¢, cabbage 20¢, and onions 18¢, and so forth.

We call to you, Mr. President, in this crisis that we are facing to recommend to Congress or other authority measures for relief.[54]

Following this, the Mothers' Anti-High Price League asked that the municipal government appropriate $1 million to pay for the distribution of food at cost to the residents of the Lower East Side.

In an attempt to discredit the food riots, word went round that they were the work of German agents. A *New York Times* editorial reprinted these rumors but decided that "nevertheless the fact remains that there is a demonstration of hunger for the poorest amid plenty for most."[55] Maria Ganz also answered the charges: "What terrible, silly lies. What do we women of the East side know of European politics? We are going hungry. The prices of food have risen beyond our means. . . . I don't care what happens to the nations silly enough to fight. What we want are the elemental things of life, food to eat, so we can live and do our work. The women are in no mood to endure such lies."[56]

Although the demonstrations and boycotts continued, the city claimed that the "law does not give us the power to purchase food and sell it." Governor Mitchell insisted that the hardships were greatly exaggerated, and that "few need suffer if discretion in purchasing and preparing food was exercised."[57]

One demonstration of about five thousand tried to reach the governor, who was staying at the stylish St. Regis Hotel. They carried banners, including one with a picture of a pitchfork with potatoes and onions on its prongs. Underneath were the words "Keep away, you slaves." Others read, "Open the warehouses, we demand food," "Uncle Sam, why feed murderers? Feed your own children," and "Greedy speculators beware."[58] Unable to find the governor, the demonstrators tied up traffic. One man who was driving by in an automobile, a hated symbol of luxury in 1917, was attacked by the crowd. Someone shouted, "You have no right to ride in an automobile while people are starving."[59] In the ensuing uproar, some women were bruised and one suffered a concussion.

The boycotts continued over the following days, and were rigorously enforced by picketing women. Maria Ganz wrote: "On Wednesday and for several days preceding, the Jewish women of the East Side and elsewhere enforced a boycott on onions and potatoes, which resulted yesterday in practically driving these products from the market. One might walk for miles between rows of pushcarts and see no onions or potatoes displayed." This action started a major discussion of inflation: "Indeed, the whole city had woken up at last to the absolute necessity of doing something, though nobody knew just what to do." Simultaneously, the tenement women had taken the problem into their own hands:

> Desperate women in several sections of the city followed the example set by their heroic sisters of Orchard Street and proceeded to upset pushcarts and attack the peddlers. There were riotous scenes in Williamsburg, in Brownsville, and in the Bronx. In the chicken market at Stanton Street and the East River women seized a crate of chickens, broke it to pieces, dismembered the chickens and marched triumphantly off waving legs and wings of fowls and crying out what they had done.[60]

The tenement women then declared a boycott on all foods except milk, bread, butter, and cereals, and "any person caught buying anything else was mobbed." The enforced boycott and riotous behavior destroyed the business of the peddlers and *Survey* reported that "after a few days of wild disturbances throughout the poor quarters, prices began to go down." The magazine continued: "As regards the fall in prices, the riots and boycotts have been remarkably successful."[61] In fact, there was little choice but to obey the strong hand of the women.

But the only official action the city took was to pass a piece of legislation aimed at eliminating the local market:

> Under a new ruling by the Commissioner of Licenses, Gilcrest, in New York City peddlers' licenses are to be issued in the future only to citizens of the United States. Two hundred older Jewish men protested but it did no good. The Commission felt there were too many peddlers and the ruling was used to reduce the number of peddlers.[62]

Although the women had made it clear that they did not want to be starved out by high prices and although the peddlers were the immediate target of their rage, rulings such as these were not what was needed. They became, in fact, "one of the actions which made the word Americanization loathed by the foreign born."[63]

In all of this activity, women were central to the organization and success of the movement. Consumer resistance flowed from the women's role in the family, their relationship to the marketplace, their ties and relationships to each other and their neighborhoods. Their collective, explosive resistance was directed not just against high prices, but against attacks on their culture as well. While they lived with social conditions that created low wages, crowded and expensive housing, dirty neighborhoods, and high prices, this did not lead to the breakdown of the family or to apathy. During these first stages of Americanization, the women created and participated in a strong and vital culture that sometimes demanded collective resistance to commercial encroachment. They acted together—for themselves, for their families, for their neighborhoods, and in defense of their world.

11
◇
New Images, Old Bonds

Come all you foreigners and jump into this magic kettle. You are colored and discolored with things that do not fit in well with affairs in America. In fact, to speak frankly, there is a certain taint about you, a stain brought from the old world. Your clothes are ugly and ill-fitting. Your language is barbaric. . . . Immediately you will become like us, your slacks will be exchanged for the latest Fifth Avenue clothes. The magic process is certain. Your money back if we fail.[1]

WITH THESE SATIRIC WORDS, TWO NEW YORK SOCIAL workers characterized the making of new Americans. The American way of life gave these Eastern and Southern European pilgrims little support for cultural assumptions that had formerly bound them together. New tensions erupted within the family, as old-world assumptions failed to find nourishment in American soil. Fathers were pitted against sons, mothers against daughters, and even parent against parent. Where paternal authority had once been a keystone of village life, here the money economy imposed a new authority on the family. In how many homes did the following scene, recorded by Leonard Covello, take place: "Work or no work, money in our house was scarce. My mother kept saying, 'What are we doing to do?' and my father would always answer, 'What can I do? If there is no work, there is no work. You'll have to do the best you can.'"[2]

Abused by the wage system and the market economy, and constantly aware that money was the key to success, first-generation immigrant fathers were often bitter about their experience in the New World. While some men openly embraced new opportunities and found it liberating to be free from the shackles of the past, others openly resented the speed and pace of their new life:

It is often what the Italian immigrant finds in America which modifies his habitual cheerfulness. For instance, in Italy all classes of people "take time to live." One of the Americanisms that greatly irritates the more intelligent and utterly bewilders the more ignorant . . . is the rate of speed which characterizes the activities of the American populace. In Italy the peasant works from sunrise to sunset but witness the proverbial singing of the *contadini* on their way home at evensfall. There was no boss to shout "hurry up." One of the first expressions an immigrant learns is hurry up.[3]

These men also resented the discipline imposed on them by the American industrial system. In the cafes, barber shops, saloons, and hiring halls, Italian men built a life that rejected the hurry-up world of American society. This was acknowledged in "the common greeting between Italians, 'Take it easy,' [which] reflects this deep-seated resistance to the speed of American industry. Such a remark in Italy would have been met with scorn and horror."[4]

For some first-generation Italian men, the search for occupations that would accommodate old-world values and dreams of returning to Italy mediated between the value sensibilities of the old-country culture and the harsh realities of the new world: "The Italian community institutions helped to keep the Italian immigrant segregated and sufficient unto himself. The Italian churches, the Italian mutual benefit societies, the Italian newspaper, the Italian theater and movie—every phase of community life which informed him was carried on in his own language."[5] While these institutions created an insular community for the older generation, new social forces were experienced by the children: "They [the first generation] lived immersed in old world customs and traditions; their children through schooling and other contacts and associations are acquiring a language and customs very unlike their own."[6]

Italian parents were often suspicious of American institutions, particularly those that involved their children. Somehow, America seemed to have the power to steal the allegiance of the young. As Julius Drachsler pointed out:

> The fear of losing the children haunts the older generation. It is not merely the natural desire of parents to retain influence over the children. . . . It is a vague uneasiness that a delicate network of precious traditions is being ruthlessly torn asunder, that a whole world of ideals is crashing into ruins; and amidst this desolation the fathers and mothers picture themselves wandering about lonely in vain search for their lost children.[7]

Some Orthodox Jewish fathers too saw American culture as a threat to the power and authority that they had had in Eastern Europe. To them, America was a godless country "with no respect for fathers."[8] American society, devoted to the more secular deities of money and work, seemed determined to eclipse traditional patriarchal values. Further, certain of the cultural symbols and practices of Eastern European Jewish life that sanctioned the rule of the fathers were challenged by the city environment. Learning and scholarship, vital to Jewish culture in Eastern Europe, provided no food for the table in America.

Eastern European Jewish life had been marked by anxiety and fear, and Rose Cohen's description of her father's life shows how that fear remained:

> [Father] had scarcely ever known what it meant to be free from anxiety. First, from early childhood it was the fear of the army where he would be compelled to violate the laws against God, "Thou shalt not kill" and the fear for his blind and helpless mother he would have to leave behind. In this fear he grew up into manhood. And then with blood money, borrowed and saved on bread and his mother's tears, he bought a false name. Then his life was in constant fear of human beings, often in fear of his own shadow. Then being found out and all seeming lost, his escape to America, then the struggle of a stranger in a strange land, which led to only a hand-to-mouth existence, without any change.[9]

In Europe he was able to counter this anxiety with religious piety, but in the American situation the symbols of that piety had to be discarded:

> As I [Rose] came into the room I saw him resting against the wall, clipping his beard. I was so surprised and shocked to see him actually do this thing that I could neither speak nor move for some minutes. And I knew he too felt embarrassed. "You had been so pious at home, father," I said, "more pious than anyone else in our whole neighborhood. And now you are cutting your beard. Grandmother would never have believed it. How she would weep." The snipping of the scissors went on. . . . At last he laid it down and said in a tone that was bitter yet quiet: "They do not like Jews on Cherry St. And one with a long beard has to take his life in his own hands."[10]

Rejecting the beard and costume of Eastern European Jewry was one price of admission into American society. As Israel Friedlander noted in *Survey*, "They have scarcely touched these shores when they throw off their ancient costume which in Eastern Europe is the mark and is hallowed by centuries of traditions."[11]

Other parts of the Americanizing experience were equally painful:

> No one except he who has an understanding of old-fashioned Jewish life in the ghetto can adequately appreciate the excruciating mental agony which the immigrant Jew must experience when, for instance, he is forced to violate the God-given command of abstaining from work on the Sabbath, or to transgress any of the Jewish regulations concerning food.[12]

Or, as Irving Howe put it in *World of Our Fathers*, there was a battle between a religious culture that demanded that economic activity be subservient to religion, and a secular culture whose primary values were concerned with money-making and business.

In *What Makes Sammy Run*, Budd Schulberg dramatically reconstructed this confrontation. At one point, Sammy brought money home on the Sabbath and explained, "'I had to make the dollar.' 'Sammy,' his father bellowed, 'Touching money on the Sabbath! God should strike you dead!' The old man snatched the money and threw it down the stairs."[13] Sammy's money-making on the Sabbath was perceived by his father as breaking a traditional Jewish taboo and the son was the material embodiment of a transgression against a sacred value.

Some children became strangers to their religious fathers. In a poignant letter to the *Forward*, a father is described who made his case against his own children. The writer of the letter had come across an old Jewish man who wore a shabby coat and an old cap and was selling cookies on the street. He found that the old man had three sons and a daughter, all quite prosperous; he asked why the old man was reduced to selling cookies. The old man explained:

> You mean, of course, why I am not living with them. I did not want to live with them. . . . I cannot live among machines. I am a live man and have a soul, despite my age. They are machines. They work all day and come home at night. What do they do? Nothing. During supper they talk about everything—friends, clothes, wages and all sorts of gossip. . . . The next day again to work and so on. . . . Books have nothing in common with them; Jewish troubles have nothing in common with them; the whole world has nothing in common with them. . . . When I first came here I used to speak and argue with them. But they did not understand. They would ask: Why this and

that? This country is not Russia. Here everybody does as he likes. Gradually I realized that they were machines. They make money and live for that purpose. When I grasped this situation a terror possessed me and I did not believe these were my children. I could not stand it to be there; I was being choked; I could not tolerate their behavior and I went away.[14]

This transformation of traditional values created particular problems for women. Caught between the desires of their children and devotion (and obedience) to their husbands, called on to reinforce the patriarchal wishes of their husbands, the women found themselves in the middle of emotionally explosive family situations. In addition, traditions of patriarchy demanded that female children be subordinate and inferior, and immigrant daughters were allowed little leeway in their desire for independence, schooling, and sexual freedom. Since these demands frequently also challenged the mother's standards of proper female behavior, she had to steer a course between the authority and discipline of her husband, the wishes of her daughters, and her own sensibilities.

Grace Grimaldi's experience was a case in point. When her family first arrived, her father wanted the children "to talk Italian and cultivate our national customs and identity." Although he was "a little strict with my brothers, he got used to the idea that things were changing here and with the times," but he was always harsher with Grace. He "wanted to keep customs too—about how to go with boys—[he was] very strict." She was "never allowed to go out, not even on Saturday with my girlfriends." She met her husband through her father—both families belonged to the Sons of Italy. She and her fiancé "kept company for a year and a half," and during that time she was never allowed to go out with him without her father or mother accompanying them. They did meet "on the sly," however. "We did play hooky. Occasionally we would take the afternoon off and go to the Hippodrome." But they did this infrequently because they feared her father. "If I catch you walking around, I'll break your neck," was his constant refrain. Her mother was more "modern" than her father: "He used to fight with her that she was too lenient. . . . My mother was discipline, but my father was very discipline. Very. One look from him and no back talk."[15]

When immigrant mothers found themselves in the position of mediators between the patriarchal demands of their husbands and the social needs of their daughters, this mediation was complicated by the economic demands of everyday life. Mike Gold, in his memoir *Jews Without Money*, recreated the polarities in his parents' marriage: "He [father] was full of temperament, and my mother had to manage him constantly. With female realism she tried to beat the foolish male dreams out of his head. But she never succeeded in converting my father into a sober family person. Alas, he was a man of quicksilver."[16] Mothers, too, feared that American institutions— the public school, the factory, and the urban street—conspired to steal their children. Feeling threatened, they tried to keep their daughters within the orbit of maternal authority, passing down the skills they thought would be useful in finding an acceptable trade.

For instance, as small children both Amalia Morandi and Adriana Valenti were taught sewing by their mothers. Amalia Morandi said that "the people from Italy were interested in learning their children a trade, because they figure when you have a trade you can get work." For her mother, Adriana's learning a trade was a must: "When I wouldn't want to sew, my mother would stick me with a needle. You had to learn. First she taught me to baste, then how to make the back stich and so on."[17] She had to learn how to sew for her livelihood—and to make her trousseau.

Bella Feiner, a Jewish garment worker, grew up in Poland near the German border. Although her parents did not "know now to write and read and they didn't even know how to tell time," her mother "paid a woman a ruble a month to teach me how to sew because she knew that the needle trade was big in America and that's the kind of job I would get." Yetta Brier succinctly expressed the general feeling of immigrant mothers when she said that "my mother had a philosophy—everyone should learn a trade. If you're rich you wouldn't practice the trade—if you're poor you would make a living by it."[18]

Most Italian and Jewish mothers were unwilling to let their daughters do domestic or clerical work, but factory work was considered a "good" occupation: "Few Italian girls were willing to do clerical work as the pay was poor. Their mothers wouldn't stand for it. Most Italian girls are operators because they can make more money."[19]

Even when the family was in dire financial need, Rose Cohen's mother refused to let her daughter do domestic work: "Is this what I came to America for, that my children should become servants?"[20]

And after her father died Maria Ganz expressed the desire to continue his peddling business but her mother would not hear of it: "Your father had a right to support his children by whatever work he thought he could the best do. . . . But no more the peddling for my family."[21] Her solution was to work finishing skirts at home while her daughter got a job in a garment shop.

Mothers often felt that their domestic training was superior to an American education, which did not teach skills but instead "made of our children persons of leisure." To many of the first generation duty to family came first; the school, they felt, trained the young to lose "the dignity of good children to think first of their parents."[22] In addition, daughters were needed at home to help with housework.

Ida Richter, for example, went to school for a year and a half but when, close to Passover, her brother broke a leg, her mother pleaded: "Have you the heart to go to school when such a tragedy happened? The house isn't Kosher, Harry broke a leg. You think you're gonna run away from everything. You better stay home." She stopped going to school and claimed not to resent it: "The women were looked on in those days as the weaker sex," she explained.[23] At fourteen she went out to work.

In some Italian families, if the children were to go to school, the mother would have to go out to work, and this was viewed with disapproval. One Italian woman complained about the effect on her family when her two children, Carlo and Jenny, went to school:

> In our old village [in Sicily] it was shameful for a wife to do outside work. When I came to America I never believed I would have to go to work outside my home. But look what happened! My husband made a meager living, so what are children for if not to help their parents. What was I to do? With Carlo in school it was bad enough. Without Jennie's help, who spent the better part of the day in school, I was compelled to go to work myself. . . . Thank God I managed to squeeze out a day here and there so that Jennie could stay home and work on pieces of embroidery. . . . I was lucky the school inspector [the truant officer] was a nice man.[24]

One father, when confronted with his daughter's truancy, had this to say, as reported to the school officer: "He stated emphatically that the only conditions under which he would send Lily to school would be if the city contributed to his family income the same amount that his wife earns so that his children (nine) could have what he considers the necessities of life and his wife could stay home and take care of them."[25]

Although the city never considered this novel idea, Lillian Wald recognized that this was a real problem and offered as many scholarships as she could to recompense families whose children were at school.[26]

Work—at home or outside—was the accepted norm for immigrant daughters. Even those families that encouraged their daughters to go to school accepted fourteen as the cutoff age. A pressing contradiction was involved in this process: free public education was one of the benefits of the New World, but economic circumstances made it difficult to take advantage of this, especially for the daughters. One Jewish woman who tried to combine work and evening school explained: "The circumstances were not there that would allow me to continue. The family promised me that I would go to high school, but I saw that I couldn't do it. I couldn't get clothed decently . . . until I earned money. This way, I could buy my clothes and pay it out weekly from the factory."[27]

And Bea Heller, a Jewish garment worker, recounted that "I had the ambition for study. I would have loved to continue. I wanted to study as a nurse, but I needed money to bring my parents over. At that time, it didn't pay in the hospitals, so I had to quit and go back to the factory." She went to work and tried to go to night school as well. In 1913 she joined the International Ladies' Garment Workers' Union: she considered "union activity another kind of school."[28]

Sometimes mothers wanted their daughters to continue in school, but the daughters thought work more important: "I graduated Eight B and I thought I was the smartest person in the world. . . . A lot of boys and girls leave in the sixth and seventh grade to support the family. My mother wanted to send me to high school, but I thought I knew it all."[29] One Italian woman who left school at the age of twelve explained: "We had hard times then. My father was a stonemason—you know how it is. He didn't have steady work and my mother used to talk all the time about how poor we were. So I had my mind on work all the time. I was thinking how I could go to work and bring home money to my mother."[30] Mary Van Kleeck, who did a study of why working-class women dropped out of night school, discovered that half of the women did so because of economic circumstances.[31]

Rachel Cohen's experience, on the other hand, demonstrated a different value system. She had had some education in Russia. Her teachers had been socialists and social democrats. When she came to the United States in 1912, she was the pride of her family. Her relatives in the United States were pushcart peddlers and they were eager for her to finish her education: "They said, 'You are not going to the factory—keep up with your studies.' But I was a socialist, don't forget. I saw it was my duty to organize the workers."[32] Her class consciousness impelled her to choose factory work even though she went against the expressed wishes of her family.

Patriarchal attitudes were another deterrent to those who desired to continue their education. Jewish daughters often went to work to support their brothers' pursuit of education. Although Italian families were less sure of the value of an American education in general, nonetheless here too "boys had always more privileges than girls and so the idea of their going to school instead of helping us [the parents] was only half bad. Boys somehow managed to make a penny or two, and in this way kept peace with my husband. But when girls at thirteen or fourteen wasted good time in school, it simply made us regret our coming to America."[33]

Patriarchal attitudes also led to the fear that education might prevent the daughter from getting married. Social worker Louise Odencrantz documented one case of an eighteen-year-old Italian girl who, when she "went to evening school to learn Engligh, her brother jeered at her until she left. 'Oh,' he explained, 'she is going to get married. She doesn't need to know English.' "[34]

Feeling that girls were "meant to take care of the home, cook and get married," fathers often actively discouraged their daughters' pursuit of education. In one Italian family, for example, the oldest daughter wanted to become a teacher:

> Everything under the sun was done to discourage her from following her desires, but to no avail. . . . The daughter couldn't ask for carfare even in the worst weather for she never got it. In fact, the father always cursed the day he came to America, because if he had stayed in Italy, no daughter of his would have the desire to become a teacher. She would have to work on the farm or in the house.[35]

Grace Grimaldi's father believed that she did not need an education beyond elementary school, and Grace acquiesced. Her sister, on the other hand, rebelled:

My sister got disgusted with shop work and told my father that she wouldn't let him prevent her from educating herself as he had with me. She told him that she would go to night school and work during the day. My father didn't like it much. He didn't want her coming home late and he thought school and work was too much of a burden. But she did it anyway. She had to work because the family needed her wages.

She went to Hunter College and became a high school teacher. Her stubbornness paid off. As Grace put it, "She put him in his place completely, and he changed his attitude."[36]

Helen Wittenberg, who had come to the United States in 1912 from Poland, also went to Hunter College—over her parents' objections:

My parents thought it's awful—to have to keep an eye on me—you're a girl and girls are very stupid. And a flirtation is the worst thing in the world—you'll smile back at a man and you're hooked—you stay where you are. You have enough education. You'll get married, you'll have children, and keep a house—what do you need it for—why do you want to be different. You're going to be looked upon like—you won't be able to make friends easily—because you'll always think you're so much above them—they are so much lower than you. I wasn't interested in boys at that time—education was everything to me—it wasn't like my father would say—you'll flirt and they'll look at you—and I didn't know men were existing—because the books were everything to me.

She tried to continue her education but quit when she met her husband: "I was impressed that he was a college graduate. I wanted a cultured person even if I was not in love with him."[37]

On the other hand, mothers sometimes battled with fathers for their daughters' right to education. In Elizabeth Stern's description, we can see the subtle interaction between education and American culture:

My father did not approve of my continuing high school. It was time for me to think of marrying a pious man. He and mother disagreed about it. . . . It was perhaps due to my going to high school, my mother said gently and dubiously, that I wanted something new. I wanted to dance, to have fun like the other girls in my class. I didn't mean to go to work at fourteen, marry at sixteen, be a mother at eighteen, an old woman at thirty. I wanted a new thing—happiness.

My mother drew her fine dark brows together. . . . "You shall learn to dance," she said, "my daughter."

Elizabeth Stern went on to college, became a social worker, and married a native-born American. The world she embraced was foreign to her mother: "Mother said goodbye to me. I went from her to a stranger whose language she did not understand, into a life she did not know. I left her as she had left her mother when she went on a far voyage to America."[38]

One Italian mother explained her dilemma:

> My daughter wanted to become a teacher. I sacrificed everything to send her to high school and college. I did not send her to a factory or shop to help along the family income, much as the family needed it. And now after all my worries and sacrifices, she can't get a job in New York. Send her away from home? . . . That's impossible. Who would look after her? A girl cannot go out alone into the world away from the family. The Americans who send their girls away don't know what they are doing. We Italians oppose that idea. A girl must sleep under her own family roof.
>
> We did send the children to high school and college and followed the American way . . . we should have followed the good customs of our native village. Send them to work soon to help the family and then arrange for them to get settled and raise a family. . . . I stay awake nights thinking of the terrible mistake my husband and I made.[39]

Exacerbating the tensions, the public schools actively encouraged the development of two different cultures within families, tenement houses, and neighborhoods. For the children, going to school was like living in two different societies at the same time—a world of Italian or Yiddish on the one hand, and a world of English, schooling, and American peer group behavior on the other. Adriana Valenti, like many others, lived in a building with sixteen other families where "all those children were learning and speaking English, but the parents continued to talk Italian."[40]

Learning English established a cultural bond between the children in a family. Often the younger children in school taught the older working children how to speak the new language. Lenore Kosloff also learned her English from children: "The children were Jews and could understand Jewish. Amongst themselves they spoke English. I followed them around and asked a lot of questions. I would speak in Yiddish and they would answer in English."[41] By the time she went to school she spoke fluent English and was able to finish seven and a half years of elementary school in three and a half.

Children would also try to teach their parents English. Anna Kuthan lived in a tenement building she described as "looking like a United Nations building, we had every nationality." She remembered that the difficulty immigrant mothers had learning English abated somewhat when they sent the children to school: "If they were smart enough they could learn English from their children . . . the children always say mother, please speak English and they translate it so nicely. . . . I hear them—mama, that's not right, you didn't say it right, say it right."[42] At the same time, however, this meant that the traditional expectations of an adult-centered culture had to be altered; the children were now teaching the parents.

Some mothers were adamant in their refusal to learn English and would not even allow their children to speak it in the house. Ida Richter recalled that the children "spoke English all the time outside the house because my mother used to say, 'This is a Yiddish house and no Gentile languages are going to be spoken here.'" Jerry Mangione's mother, as reported in his memoir *Mount Allegro*, vigorously enforced the rule that "we speak no other language at home but that of our parents. . . . Any English we spoke at home, however, was either by accident or on the sly. My sister Maria, who often talked in her sleep, conducted her monologues in English, but my mother forgave her on the grounds that ·she could not be responsible for her subconscious thoughts."[43]

But education was unavoidable—it was also in the streets. New clothes, hair styles, street life, and dating patterns all created conflicts in the family.

Clothing was a major arena of contention between mother and daughter. Immigrant mothers came from cultures where "dress served to show where one came from and who one was"—it connoted class, status, and religious affiliation. However, "in the United States dress serves to conceal one's origins and relationships. . . . Follow the Old World practice, and show who you are and where you come from and the result is that you remain alien and different and that your children will not stay with you 'outside the gates.'"[44]

When Adriana Valenti was in elementary school she helped her mother make feathers for women's hats. She remembered this because the hats "were so beautiful, a woman looked so dressed. I wanted to grow up to wear earrings and high heels and hats."[45] To do this, however, was to break an important taboo in Italian peasant culture, where "no woman of the poorer classes dared to put on a hat. She would have been the laughing stock of her community if she did. To don a hat was the privilege of the *signora* [gentry] or the whores."[46]

In one Sicilian community on the Lower East Side women who dressed American-style were considered renegades:

> If a woman is able to buy . . . they say: "In the old country she used to carry baskets of tomatoes on her head and now she carries a hat on it," or "look at the daughter of so and so. In Cinisi she worked in the field and the sun burnt her black. Here she dares to carry a parasol," . . . or "A woman bought a pair of silk stockings and the neighbors talked so much about her that her husband ordered her to take them off."[47]

In this community, the acquisition of Americanized forms of fashion was seen as jumping class and cultural boundaries, and any woman who dared to break the social codes was ostracized.

Yet hats, silk stockings, and parasols were an essential component of American fashion for *all* classes of women in the 1900s,[48] and daughters tried to teach their mothers to dress in the new styles. Anthony Mangano, in his autobiography *Sons of Italy,* documented one battle over the hat question: "What a triumph it was when [my sister] succeed in persuading [my mother] to wear a hat instead of a scarf over her head, and to put away her old shawl and wear an American coat."[49]

Rose Cohen described a similar struggle:

> Mother had been here only a short time when I noticed that she looked older and more old fashioned than father. I noticed that it was so with most of our women, especially those that wore wigs and kerchiefs on their heads. So I thought that if I could persuade her to leave off her kerchief she would look younger and more up to date. . . . I decided to go slowly and be careful not to hurt her feelings.

Rose planned carefully. One day when she and her mother were in the house alone she asked her mother to take off her kerchief and fix her hair, just to see how it would look. Her mother consented, after much pleading on Rose's part:

She had never before in her married life had her hair uncovered before anyone. . . . When I parted it in front and gathered it up in a small knot in the middle of the back of her head I was surprised how different she looked. I had never before known what a fine broad forehead my mother had, nor how soft were her blue-gray eyes. . . . She glanced at herself, admitted frankly that she looked well and began hastily to put on her kerchief. I caught hold of her hands. "Mama," I coaxed, "please don't put that kerchief on again—ever." At first she would not even listen to me. But I sat down on her lap and I began to coax and beg and reason. I drew on my year of experience and observation and pointed out that wives so often looked so much older because they were more old-fashioned, and that the husbands were often ashamed to go out with them.

Rose's mother tried to get her to stop, but she would not:

"But father trims his beard," I still argued. Her face looked sad. "Is that why . . . I too must sin?" But I finally succeeded. When father came home in the evening and caught sight of her . . . he looked at her with astonishment. "What! Already you are becoming an American lady?" Mother looked abashed for a moment. In the next moment to my surprise and delight I heard her brazen it out in her own quiet way. "As you see," she said, "I am not staying far behind."[50]

Some daughters used fashion as an antidote to the monotonous dreariness of everyday life—often to the dismay of other family members. An overemphasis on style, however, could disrupt family life, pitting sister against sister, mother against daughter. In Anzia Yezierska's *Breadgivers*, for example, Mashah, the most Americanized daughter, came home from a discouraging day of job hunting, having just purchased some new pink roses for her hat: " 'Give a look on these roses for me hat,' she said to her sister Bessie, 'like a lady from Fifth Avenue I look, and only for ten cents, from a pushcart on Hester Street.' " Hardworking Bessie attacked her for being selfish: "Here you go to look for work and you come back with pink roses for your doll face." Mashah, underscoring her new needs, talked back: "These pink roses on my hat to match my pink calico [dress] will make me look just like a picture on a magazine cover."[51] Caught between wanting to look like a princess and the family economy, Mashah had saved herself from a scene with her mother by spending part of her lunch money.

Lillian Wald was often called upon to arbitrate clothing disputes.

One incident involved a daughter who had spent $25 accumulated from several weeks' overtime work on a hat with a marvelous plume: "The hat itself became a white elephant, a source of endless embarrassment, but buying it had been an *orgy*." Since the daughter's extravagance had not used the family money but her own overtime pay, "this interpretation . . . when presented to her mother, who in her vexation had complained to us, influenced her to refrain from nagging."[52]

Having money to spend on oneself was closely connected to breaking out of the family circle. Amalia Morandi, an Italian garment worker, was a "good girl"—she always brought her pay home and stayed close to her mother. But her sister was different:

> She used to open the envelope and take a few dollars if she needed it. They [her sister and friends] would have costume balls and she would come home at 12 o'clock—that was terrible, especially for the Italian people. That was awful, when a woman, a girl at her age, which was 18 or 19, when they came home at 12 o'clock the neighbors would gossip, would say look at that girl coming home by herself. My mother would talk to her, it did no good. It went in one ear and out the other. And then one day she came home and she says to my mother, she wanted to give her board. And my mother says whatdaya mean by board—my mother knew what she meant. She says, oh I give you so much a week, and then the rest is for me. So my mother says alright, go ahead, do what you please.[53]

Mashah in *Breadgivers* was much like Amalia's older sister, and the other sisters in the family resented her:

> She took first her wages to make herself more beautiful and left the rest of us to worry about the bread and the rent. Mashah . . . on her way home from work always looked in the shop windows for what was the latest and prettiest style. Mashah was always before the mirror trying on her things . . . while Bessie would run home the quicker to help Mother with the washing and ironing or bring home another bundle of night work, and stay up hours to earn another dollar for the house.[54]

If some daughters perceived freedom in American terms, immigrant mothers measured it by a different yardstick. The most critical scene in *Breadgivers* gives us an insight into this particular conflict. One day the mother suddenly broke the routine of daily life to engage in a confrontation with her daughters:

Who'd believe me here in America, where I have to bargain by the pushcarts over a penny that I once had it so plenty. When I'd go to a fair [in the old country] everywhere I'd pass people would draw their breath, they'd stop bargaining and selling and stand back with a sudden stillness, only to give a look on my face. In my face was all the sunshine and fresh air of the open fields.

Her daughters looked at her "faded eyes, her shape like a squashed barrel of yeast and her face black with all the worries of the world," and could not believe her claim that she had once looked like her beautiful daughter Mashah, only better: "Mashah never had such color in her cheeks, such fire in her eyes—and my shape was something to look on—not the straight up and down like the beauties make themselves in America." A different standard was operative then, where a natural radiance of the face and a fuller, more "zaftig" look to the body was considered the key to beauty.

Mother and daughter also clashed about the value of homemade versus store-bought goods: "But the most beautiful thing of all was my hand-crocheted tablecloth. It was made up of knitted rings of all colors, red, blue, and purple. All the colors of the rainbow were in that tablecloth. It was like dancing sunshine lighting up the room when it was spread on the table for the Sabbath. There ain't in America such beautiful things like we had home." Her Americanized daughter broke in: "Nonsense, mamma . . . if you only had the money to go on Fifth Avenue, you'd see the grand things you could buy." The mother replied, "Yes, buy! In America rich people can only buy, and buy things made by machines. Even Rockefeller's daughter got only store-bought ready-made things for her dowry. There was a feeling in my tablecloth."

Not surprisingly, immigrant mothers were aware of this cultural barrier between themselves and American women. As Maria Zambello put it:

I don't feel as good as the American women because I am old fashioned from the other side. . . . When I am with American women, I am afraid I don't talk good enough for them. Then sometimes they serve tea or coffee in nice cups and napkins—I feel ashamed . . . and they got different manners. We put the hands on the table, they don't. That's why I don't feel so good. But the young Italian girls, my daughters, they're up to date, just as good, just as polite like the Americans. They were born here, they go to school together, they see the same movies, *they know*.[55]

In some cases an uneasy compromise between the cultures developed. Maria Frazaetti articulated this possibility:

> There are no old-country customs prevailing in our house. My children follow the American customs. I would like them to remember that the parents must be considered as an authority. I approve of allowing my children the freedom they desire; by doing so, they learn for themselves. My children misunderstand me when I advise them what style clothes they should wear. I blame styles and clothes on some of the stuff in magazines and the movies of this country. If I had my way I would like my children to follow some of the old disciplinary laws of the old country.[56]

One particularly mortifying result of the cultural chasm between parents and children was that as the children became more Americanized, a feeling of shame developed. In "The Fat of the Land," Yezierska chronicled the rise of Hanneh Breineh, a washerwoman from Delancey Street. Hanneh, using the lodge money from her husband's death, opened a grocery store, whose capital her children parlayed into the "biggest shirtwaist factory on W. 29th Street." She was moved to a fancy apartment but experienced the shame and scorn of her children; she could not change her upbringing enough to adapt to more Americanized ways of life. Her daughter constantly experienced "the shame of mother. God knows how hard I tried to civilize her. I dressed her in the most stylish Paris models, but Delancey Street sticks out from every inch of her." To the mother, however, this experience was like being imprisoned: "When I was poor I was free and could holler and do what I liked in my own house. Here I got to lie still like a broom." She constantly wondered, "What worth is an old mother to American children?"[57]

In another instance, the Henry Street Settlement invited a speaker to address a group of older girls on the obligations of children to their aging parents. Young women lingered afterward. Lillian Wald noticed that "though sensitive to the appeal, they were loath to relinquish their right of self-expression":

> One girl thought her parents demanded an impossible sacrifice by insisting on living in a street to which she was ashamed to bring her associates. The parents refused to leave the quarter where their countrymen dwelt, and although the daughter willingly gave her earnings and paid tribute to her mother's devotion and housekeeping skill . . . she felt irritated and mortified every time she returned home.[58]

An Italian-American boy expressed the same feelings, and discussed the strategy he adopted for dealing with it:

> In my early years . . . we were highly critical if not disrespectful of the many traditions that the old folks wanted us to live up to and conform to. . . . Many of my Italian friends would say, "They have lived their lives in their own way. We want to live our lives in our own way and not be tied down to fantastic customs that appear ridiculous not only to us but particularly our American friends." We never invited our "American" friends to our home. And while "American" boys took their parents to some school functions, we did not take our parents, but never even told them they were taking place. This was *our* life. . . . The deadline was the threshold of the door of our tenement. Beyond that the older folks went their way and we went ours.[59]

The immigrant mothers, outside the process of "Americanization" and abused by the society for being old-fashioned and out of date, attempted to create a cultural universe in their homes and neighborhoods that was made out of the values and principles of their own world. They experienced real pleasure in those moments when they felt freed from the conflicts embedded in the transition from one cultural universe to another. Rather than coveting material goods, as their children did, they more often treasured those moments in which generosity, love, and kindness came before the principles of money or self.

Mike Gold and Anzia Yezierska both captured this aspect of immigrant life. Mike Gold's mother "was always finding people in trouble who needed her help. She helped them for days, weeks and months with money, food, advice, and the work of her hands. She was a midwife in many hasty births, a nurse in sickness, a peacemaker in family battles." She never took money for these services: "It was simply something that had to be done for a neighbor." She exuded the major social principle of tenement life; through her activities she created a world of generous and sustaining social warmth. In fact, to the young Mike Gold his mother embodied the principles of a humane and giving socialism: "Mother! Momma! I am still bound to you by the cords of birth. I cannot forget you. I must remain faithful to the poor because I cannot be faithless to you! I believe in the poor because I have known you. The world must be made gracious for the poor! Momma, you taught me that!"

An Italian woman named Betsy lived in the next tenement.

Betsy's life had seen tragedy. Her husband had killed his brother in a quarrel over a card game. Betsy was left with three children and no friends or work. She could only speak Italian:

> My mother visited her, and through sheer sympathy, learned in the course of many visits, a kind of pigeon Italian. It was marvelous to hear my mother hold hour-long conversations with this woman in a polyglot jargon that was a mixture of Italian, Yiddish, Hungarian and English. But the two women understood each other.

His mother helped Betsy find work doing basting at home and befriended her. One night Betsy came over with a gift to repay the kindness:

> In the midst of her miseries she found time to knit a large woolen shawl as a surprise for my mother. She brought it in . . . and kissed my mother's hands. And my mother cried and kissed her, too. . . . My mother treasured this shawl more than anything she owned. She liked to show it to everyone and tell the story of how Betsy had made it. A shawl like that was worth over ten dollars, more than Betsy earned in a week. It must have taken weeks to knit, many overtime nights under the gaslight after a weary sixteen-hour day at basting clothing. Such gifts are worthy to be treasured, they are knitted with love.[60]

Anzia Yezierska, in her story, "My Own People," described a similar situation. The story begins with a description of a day in the life of an immigrant mother whose walls seem to be closing in: "There's no end of trouble! Hear them hollering for bread and the grocer stopped by to give me no credit until the bill is paid. Woe is me!" In the midst of these troubles, the old man who lived in the basement appeared at her door. A Talmudic scholar in the old country, he had been reduced to extreme poverty in the United States. He told her that he had just received a holiday present of cake and wine from a friend in Russia, and invited the woman, her children, and their boarder to a small party right then, in the middle of the day, in his apartment. Downstairs, the old man took out a large frosted cake with nuts and raisins in it and a bottle of grape juice, which he called wine. Suddenly the rhythm of daily life was transformed. The wailing woman lifted her glass and slowly drank her grape juice wine: "All of the traditions of wealth and joy that ever sparkled from the bubbles of champagne smiled at her. She sipped her grape juice leisurely, thrilled into ecstasy with each lingering drop. 'How it laughs in me yet, the life, the minute I turn my head from worries.' " The mother, resplendent in her pleasure, turned to her boarder, Sophie, and said: "Ach! What do the rich people got but dried up dollars. Pfui on them and their money." Happiness for her was not connected to dried-up dollars but to feeling the passionate surge of life through her mind and body.

Suddenly, a Jewish social worker came to the door. She was horrified by the old man's newfound wealth and threatened to cut him from the relief rolls for not reporting this income. The contrast was absolute: while the party was a communal way of overcoming the daily grind, the social worker had come to teach the poor how to live. Sophie was outraged and shouted at the representative of America:

> You call yourself Americans? You dare call yourself Jewish? You bosses of the poor. This man, Shmendrick, whose house you broke into, whom you made shame like a beggar— he is the one Jew from whom Jews can be proud. He gives all he is—all he has. But you—you are the greed and the shame of the Jews! Alrightniks in fat bellies in fur coats. What do you give from yourself? You may eat and bust eating! Nothing you give yourself till you've stuffed yourself so full that your hearts are dead![61]

The social principle behind immigrant mothering and community values lay in the practice of bread-giving, not bread-winning; yet the social basis of American culture lay in winning, taking, making it in a world where money was the reward for good behavior and hard work. Herein lay the roots of the conflict faced by immigrant women every day. To be American meant to equate independence and freedom with upward mobility, with leaving the community behind in order to become a successful individual. Although aspects of this new ideology were used by some immigrant daughters to gain more freedom in their personal life, mothers were unwilling or unable to leave their community behind, for that meant leaving their world and its generous, sharing, communal vision.

12
◇
CITY LIGHTS

I F THE OLDER GENERATION HAD DIFFICULTY ACCEPTING NEW
ways, for their daughters contact with American culture at
work, at school, or in the street created new definitions of
femininity that led to a rejection of the constriction of family bonds.
Ready-made clothes, makeup, dance halls, movie theaters, amusement parks, all were part of a cultural environment that assumed
greater individual freedom and a less formal relationship with the
opposite sex.

Immigrant mothers feared the pull of the new life. They came
from cultures where both work and recreation were organized in
family groups. As a report by Sophinisba Breckenridge put it:

> The whole family worked together and played together with other
> family groups. The mother knew what standards she was to maintain
> and had, moreover, the backing of a homogeneous group to help her.
> It was not uncommon to find singing and dancing in the evening: the
> point was that the entire family participated and the girls were well
> chaperoned.[1]

But the "old standards can scarcely be maintained in a modern
community where the girls go to work in the factories, working side
by side with men, going and coming home in the company of men."
It became difficult for the parents to supervise young women in
school or at work, and "the girl naturally thinks that if she can take
care of herself at work she is equally well able to do so at play."[2]

Jewish mothers felt it less necessary to exercise strict control over
their daughters than did Italian mothers, who demanded chap-
eronage and obedience, but both tried to keep their daughters
within the orbit of parental authority. Street life was considered
morally and physically dangerous. In the new and more anonymous
urban world, maternal concern was tied to a fear of strangers and of
unpredictable experiences. The Americanization of their daughters

was viewed with suspicion and distrust; in the city you never knew what was around the corner.

The major form of recreation for the young consisted of dance halls, visits to Coney Island and Luna Park, the movies, and hanging out in the ice cream parlors and candy stores that dotted the Lower East Side.

Dance halls were everywhere. Belle Israels, writing in *Survey* magazine, exclaimed, "The town is dance mad. . . . Down on the East Side, dancing is cheap. Twenty-five cents a couple is all it costs and ten cents for the girls."[3] To go dancing two things were needed: a nice dress and hat, and a freer attitude about meeting men. For young Jewish women who did not know how to dance American style, special dance instructors were employed.[4]

Jewish mothers were worried about the dance halls—they were concerned about their daughters' meeting strange men, suspected the dance hall's connection to prostitution, and were afraid for the daughters' sexual morality. Jewish mothers tried to forbid their daughters to attend the dance halls, or imposed curfews. Nevertheless, many single Jewish women went.[5]

Italian mothers, on the other hand, were even stricter, and forbade their daughters to attend: "Social interaction among Italian immigrants is within families. For the Italian girl to go to a dance hall is a very rare occurrence. There is much dancing but it is done within family groups."[6] Only "wild girls" transgressed family law.

While the dance hall represented a new form of recreation that asserted the freedom from family bonds as the basis of social interaction, its less familial orientation often involved estranged and anomic relations between men and women. It also embodied the seamy side of urban culture. The instructors were often pimps and procurers. Young women came in contact with strangers and were sometimes trapped by their sexual demands. The business of prostitution, a rarity in the old-world country, was far more common in the United States—and young immigrant women were particularly prey to pimps.

Mike Gold, who grew up in a neighborhood where pimps and prostitutes mingled with families and respectable neighborhood people, analyzed the relationship between young women, dance halls, and pimps:

The pimps were hunters. A pretty girl growing up on the East Side was marked by them. They watched her fill out, grow tall, take on the sex bloom. When she was fifteen, they schemed to trap her. . . . Pimps infested the dance halls. Here they picked up the romantic factory girls who came after the day's work. They were smooth story tellers. They seduced girls the way a child is helped to fall asleep, with tales of magic happiness. No wonder East Side parents wouldn't let their daughters go to dance halls. But girls need to dance.[7]

There were, however, alternative places for Jewish women who would not frequent the dance halls to meet other young people. *Landsmanshaft* societies, social organizations, union-sponsored social events, and political organizations offered young women a social life of lectures, meetings, and dances. Bella Feiner had warm memories of her social life:

The youth of that time, especially the youth from the other side, was socially minded . . . thinking what to do with our lives. Meeting young men like we ourselves. I went to the Rand School, a socialist building on 15th St. . . . lectures of great people were there. Then I went to high school lectures and museums. The lectures were about conditions, art, music, current events. The Yiddish theater was my meat.

I loved life and was anxious to go to dances. After all, "youth is youth." I didn't go to dance halls but to organizations of towns in Europe. The town organizations invited each other to affairs. That is how we melted, mixed. I went to a Rumanian affair, a Russian affair. We met different young people.[8]

Lenore Kosloff, although less politically oriented than Bella Feiner, constructed a social life for herself along similar lines:

In my spare time, I was a member of a club of young men and women composed mainly of couples. We made an organization with small dues and had dances and affairs. As we got older, the couples in the club got married.[9]

Italian mothers were more restrictive, fearing for their daughters in situations that were not family-dominated. They distrusted men as men, especially when they could not be identified by family or kinship ties, and they feared the irrationality of the sex drive when uncontrolled by family notions of proper conduct. Italian mothers repeatedly told their daughters to "keep away from men; they only want one thing and watch yourself with the men, don't let them get too fresh; they only want your honor."[10] The fear was that random contacts would lead to sex outside the marriage bond—which was in any case assumed to be the American way. While flirting and sexual banter were allowed within the family, such behavior outside the family setting was seen as potentially destructive to the family itself, as well as to its honor.

This was one of the major reasons why first-generation Italian parents were wary even of settlement houses and clubs. As Enrico Sartorio put it:

> Unintentionally, these clubs tend to train the young Italian boys and girls to stay out of the home every evening and to mix freely together. The club-trained boys and girls are easily recognized by the ease with which they get married and divorced, by their unwillingness to stay and take care of their home, and after they are married by their insane desire to be incessantly "out for a good time" and by their lack of respect for old people.[11]

He also argued that these clubs would not have been seen as threatening if they had been so organized as to include both the young people and their parents, keeping the whole family together, on the same social plane.[12] And when Marie Concistre, an Italian who wrote an excellent monograph on Italian life in East Harlem, was asked by social workers how to get young Italian girls to come to their dances, she replied: "Why not invite the parents or the mothers of these girls to your dances, and let them see for themselves that their girls are in good company or well-chaperoned, why not approximate more nearly the family group situation?"[13] Although this offered a possible compromise, neither the settlement house nor the parents adopted it.

Many more Italian daughters longed to break free of familial restraints than were able to do so. But while they approved of the occasional rebel who broke family discipline and spent money on herself, they disapproved of open sexual rebellion. Josephine Roche reported the case of Jenni Polini:

> Jenni Polini's form of rebellion—choosing a fellow for herself and seeing him on the sly—was not . . . successful. The other girls regarded her conduct with doubt and disapproval, though they shared all of Jenni's resentment against the stern discipline of her parents from which she was separated by the old abyss between the generations, widened and deepened by the disparities of the old world and the new.[14]

Adriana Valenti recalled that when she was keeping company with her fiancé she was allowed to go out with him only three times in one year—each time with a chaperone. Instead, her fiancé came to her parents' house three times a week, and the whole family would sit around the one big table. To pass the time, he taught her how to read Italian.[15]

There were, however, various ways to subvert the power of the parental hand. Fabbia Orzo's experience was a case in point. Her mother believed that children should come inside early, although she was less strict with the boys in the family, who did not have to be home until nine o'clock. As an adolescent her activities were severely curtailed: "My parents had old-fashioned ideas, you know. They were a little strict. . . . They believed that if you went out with anybody, that would be the one that you intended to marry. You brought him up to the house." So she did not date much, although her younger sisters did. Sibling solidarity protected the younger daughters from parents:

> We used to try to convince my mother that her attitudes were wrong. But my father was the most strict of the two. My youngest sister was the only one able to date more. We used to protect each other. When my little sister went out, we would say that she went with one of the two older sisters and not mention that she went out with a boy.

Even when Fabbia was twenty-four and the main economic support of her family, her father still would not let her go out: "I didn't care. I wasn't used to going out, going anywhere, outside of going to the movies. I used to enjoy going to the movies two or three times a week. I used to be home by 9 o'clock." In the end, only the youngest sister married; the two elder sisters lived together for most of their lives, taking care of their parents. The youngest sister had five daughters, and although she was less strict than her mother, she still wanted to know "every boy her daughters date. What time they're coming home. Where they go. I don't think this attitude is strict; the girls can go out with friends. They don't have to be 'steadies.' This is very different from my mother's attitudes that the boys they brought home were the boys that would marry."[16]

For Caroline Caroli female solidarity also gave her a chance to break through her father's strict attitude. Her father would not let her go out on her own, and she met her future husband in the grocery store on her block.

He spoke Italian and was bashful. He asks, "Can I meet you in the park?" "Oh," I says, "I am kept very strict. My father won't let me go from here to there." So I took a walk with my girlfriends and met him. My mother says, "Get back here before your father gets back." My mother was more generous than my father. I had a wonderful time in the park. I was 18 years old and not allowed to go out. My father was furious when he found out I was seeing a boy. He says, "You've got ten years to go." I threatened, "I'll go back to Italy." I got married at age 19.[17]

Brothers, powerful in the family hierarchy, often supervised their sisters' social lives. One Italian brother explained:

I have two sisters, one is twelve, the other sixteen. Being girls they belong to the women's department of the family and I don't stick my nose in their business. That is, as long as they are in the house. When they go out into the street or somewhere else, it is my business to see to it that they keep up the good name of my family.

They are big enough to have boyfriends and I don't object to that. If I know the fellow and he's okay by me, I know nothing can happen. But I certainly would not allow them to go out with anybody. . . . If I ever find out that my sister went out with a fellow I don't approve of, I will break her neck.[18]

Sometimes brothers covered for their sisters. Leonard Covello told the following story of an Italian son who came to him for advice:

His sister was fifteen and mature for her age. She wished to enjoy the companionship of her classmates in high school, boys as well as girls. Her parents refused to let her go out in the evening except in the company of her older brother or with an adult member of the family as chaperone. The brother, also resentful of the old world standards in the new . . . told the parents they were going out together. By previous arrangement, the two of them met the young man a few blocks from the apartment, and the brother went on to spend the evening as he chose, leaving the two to go to a movie or dance. The three met again at an appointed time, and the brother and sister came home together.[19]

Sometimes older married sisters would act as foils for younger ones. Lucia Colleti, an older sister, recounted: "I was married and lived in my own apartment four blocks away from my parents. My two younger sisters would come to my house, telling our parents that they were visiting. Then, they'd change their clothes, get dressed up and sneak out dancing. They always came back at 9:30, they'd change and I'd walk them home. Our parents never never knew."[20]

There were many kinds of recreation, however, that involved the whole family and were enjoyed by both Italian and Jewish families. The most popular were visiting other families, playing cards, and taking outings to parks and places outside the city. Judith Weissman noted that there was little difference in her family's leisure patterns here and back home: "On Saturdays they visited relatives here and talked about Europe. After a nap, they would get some fruit and sit out. Older people chatted, and being as we [the children] were never young, we used to sit and listen."[21]

Visiting was probably the most common leisure activity. Families dropped in on each other and shared a moment of hospitality. Visiting also confirmed the importance of family in a situation where many members remained in the old country. Sophie Abrams came from Minsk with her brother, but her parents remained behind. Every Saturday she and her brother visited her relatives, and they "would sing old Jewish songs and drink tea and talk about how much we missed our parents."[22]

Yet to their parents' dismay, young people's visiting patterns often adopted aspects of the new culture. One example was their enthusiastic acceptance of American music. "The reason the young people buy ragtime music is that they don't want to be different from their American friends. When they visit their friends in American homes they find that ragtime music is the music that is played. . . . Therefore, they buy the same records that their class of Americans does."[23] Ragtime was more expressive of the sounds of the city than was the folk music of their parents, and more keyed to the pace of city life. And, while the old folks looked nostalgically to the past, youth sought cultural patterns that were more in tune with the present.

Visits to parks and to the country were also important ways of spending leisure time. Adriana Valenti's mother took the children to Central Park, a big treat for the family:

Before we would go she would make us all sit on the chair and we all had high shoes at the time—and she would see that they were all buttoned, and if we looked presentable. And then she would lecture us. "Now you are doing to the park." Me, I loved flowers, and

"Don't pick any flowers, the flowers are for beauty." And they had signs—keep off the grass. We would take a rope and a ball . . . oh, my God, what a treat it was to go to Central Park.[24]

Yetta Adelman contrasted visits to Central Park with her past life in Poland: "Who had leisure time? You work till five o'clock Saturday, from dark to dark. The people from the old country would meet in Central Park on Sunday. Central Park was different from the old country—there you could do nothing. Five people were too many in Poland. After that, you think this is heaven."[25] And Evelyn Vogelman, a Lithuanian immigrant who arrived in 1905, noted that it was possible to take advantage of city life because "at that time everything was so cheap. We went to theaters, we took subway rides, double-decker trolley rides, boat rides. There were so many things."[26]

Mike Gold recalled that after the elevated train was built, his mother would take the entire family to a park in the Bronx that looked like the Hungarian forest of her youth. He called the train a "super tenement on wheels, with excited, screaming mothers and children, and fathers sagging under enormous lunch baskets." Here his mother became a different person, telling her children forest lore, searching for mushrooms, reporting that "birds talked to each other," and madly hugging her children. The historical space between generations was expressed in her statement, "Ach Gott! I'm so happy in the forest. You American children don't know what it means. I am happy."[27]

Some, such as Caroline Caroli, had to wait until they were married to explore leisure possibilities. She and her husband bought an apartment house with three other couples, and they all took turns being the super. The three women friends joined an all-woman poker game and used it as an excuse to get out and explore: "We told our husbands we were going to play cards. But we really went out with the girls. We would take off our wedding rings and flirt with boys on the Hudson River, at Roseland Dance Hall and at the movies. We gave false names and addresses to the boys who tried to pick us up." In this way, she made up for the social life her father never allowed her. On the other hand, Carmella Caruso's husband went out far more nights a week than she did. "You know how men are. He played cards. I stayed home."[28]

Families also took advantage of immigrant versions of high

culture: the Yiddish theater and the Italian opera were thriving institutions on the Lower East Side. Gaining access to American institutions of high culture was more difficult, however. Wealthy Anglo-Saxon New Yorkers were loath to open the doors of culture to the tenement population, and only mass petitioning forced the barriers to break down: "New Yorkers need to be reminded that the Metropolitan Museum of Art was effectively closed to a large proportion of its citizens until May 31, 1891, when it opened its doors on Sunday. It is interesting to recall that of 80,000 signatures that signed the petition for this privilege, 50,000 were residents of the Lower East Side." Still, Lillian Wald, who wrote this report on the incident, observed that "the Sunday opening had offended some of the Museum's best friends and supporters" and "had resulted in the loss of a bequest of $50,000."[29]

The most popular activity of all was the movies, the newest—and cheapest—form of entertainment on the Lower East Side. Most historians of the cinema agree that the industry found its first audience in the poor tenement districts of America's larger cities.[30] By 1909 New York City alone had over 340 movie houses, called nickelodeons, with 250,000 people attending every week day and 500,000 on Sundays. It was a nickel per person, twenty-five cents for the entire family. Survey magazine wrote that "in the tenement districts, the moving picture has well-nigh driven other forms of entertainment from the field" and that it was "the first cheap amusement to occupy the economic plane that the saloon has so exclusively controlled."[31]

Thousands of immigrants went to the movies, where they could be enveloped in a new world of perception, a magical universe of motion and madness. The silents created a visual universe that did not demand an extensive knowledge of English. Families went together, local merchants advertised on the screen, people sang along and read the captions out loud, and socializing was common. Lewis Palmer, writing in Survey, was taken by the spirit of the nickelodeon:

> Visit a moving picture show on Saturday night below 14th St., when the house is full, and you will soon . . . be convinced of the real hold this new amusement has on the audience. Certain houses have become social centers where neighborhood groups may be found . . . where the regulars stroll up and down the aisles between acts and visit friends.[32]

And in 1908 the *Jewish Daily Forward* commented on the grow-ing popularity of the new medium: "Hundreds of people wait on line. . . . A movie show lasts half an hour. If it's not too busy you can see it several times. They open at one in the afternoon and customers, mainly women and children, gossip, eat fruit and nuts, and have a good time." The movies also sponsored special nights: "The movies have candy nights, grocery nights and chicken nights. At intermission, the audience draws lots and the lucky ones win a present. You can pay a nickel or a dime and go home with a whole chicken."[33]

The movie advertisements were pitched to working-class au-diences. One ad said:

If you're tired of life, go to the movies,
If you're sick of troubles rife, go to the picture show,
You'll forget your unpaid bills, rheumatism and other ills,
If you'll stow your pills and go to the picture show.[34]

One woman vividly remembered her experiences at the movies:

A nickel, the movies. For 2¢ you'd buy a bag of peanuts. You was walking around in the movies, and like you'd walk between papers and peanut shells, so much peanut shells. People was sitting around and enjoying. A picture didn't talk, a silent picture and you could read what it says. After they were making the movies, they made it that you could win when you had a card. And if you had the right card and they called it out with your number you could win $5. I won once. My God, I was afraid to go up, $5! I was so happy. I didn't know what to do, what to buy with it. But I didn't buy. I paid the rent.[35]

The industry proved fertile ground for the careers of young Jewish men. They started out as the owners of small nickelodeons and, on the basis of the nickel-and-dime trade, became the "movie moguls" of the next decade.[36] William Fox and Adolph Zukor, both Hungarian Jews, were the first of these titans of the movie industry and they were followed by Samuel Goldwyn, who in 1923 made a movie of Anzia Yezierska's novel of immigrant life, *Hungry Hearts*. Both Jews and Italians found work as actors and two of America's first celluloid "stars"—Theda Bara and Rudolf Valentino, the sex god and goddess of the silent screen—were immigrants. Both had short-lived and tragic careers: Theda Bara's lasted for four years, from 1913 to 1919, and Valentino's from 1918 to 1926. Both upset the American middle class and provided important new sexual images during the revolution of modern American sexual attitudes and behavior of the early twentieth century. As outsiders and immigrants, playing to largely ethnic audiences, these two stars provided images of new possibilities.

Theda Bara, whose original name was Theodosia Goodman, was the daughter of a Jewish tailor from Cincinnati. William Fox, then head of the Fox Film Company, catapulted her to fame through the use of a sensational publicity campaign, changing her name and her background in order to present her to the public. Theda Bara was an anagram of Arab Death, and she was said to be "the child of a French artist by his Arabian mistess, born on the desert sands in the shadow of the Sphinx"[37]—all this in preparation for the portrayal of Cleopatra.

Theda Bara's role in *A Fool There Was* (1915), based on the Rudyard Kipling poem "The Vampire," created the word "vamp" as both noun and verb and indicated the emergence of a new image of the female on the screen—sexy and sultry. Her appearance was closer to older European standards of beauty—heavy-set and full-bodied—than the slim, diminutive look of such clean-cut Anglo-Saxon film stars as Mary Pickford and Lillian Gish. In the American lexicon of sexual values, the European was identified with passion and sexual eroticism, sometimes allowing within that stereotype the reversal of sex roles and the triumph of the female over the male. Bara played the role of a brazen hussy many times over and was thought of as exotic, sultry, and dangerously wicked. Yet ironically this allowed her to play roles in which the woman had the upper hand. As film writer Edward Wagenknect observed, "Most of the time she was *The Vixen, The Serpent,* or the *She-Devil* . . . in which she had no function save to lure some helpless and completely 'dumb' male to his ruin."[38]

Rudolph Valentino played a similar role within the pantheon of male stars.[39] Born Rodolfo Pietro Filiberto Gugiliemi in Castellaneta (Taranto), he failed his course at the Venice Military Academy and instead trained in agriculture. He migrated to the United States in 1913, and worked as a gardener, waiter, and dancer. He began his film career in 1918 playing the part of the "dago villain," and finally in 1921 he broke into romantic drama with *The Four Horsemen of the Apocalypse,* followed by *The Sheik.*[40]

Valentino's cinematic presence was a contrast to the traditional notions of American masculinity. Robert Sklar, in *Movie-Made*

America, compared the appeal of Valentino to that of the American hero Douglas Fairbanks: "The telling difference between the two men was that Valentino always projected himself in a way that Fairbanks, the smiling, clean-cut genteel American hero rarely did, if ever—as a sexual being."[41] Enormously attractive and compelling to women because of his sexual presence, grace, and ease, he also created a web of "tangled resentment and emulation . . . in American men," who denounced him as effeminate.[42]

The other major figure in mass entertainment was Harry Houdini, who was also from a poor Jewish background. Houdini worked with his father, a tailor, until he was about thirteen and then broke away from this life to become a master magician and escape artist. Yet his family remained important. When his earnings

> first reached the amazing figure of $1000 a week, Houdini impulsively asked to be paid in gold. As soon as this unusual request was granted, he ran off with the heavy bag of gold and dashing into his mother's room, bade her hold out her apron, while he poured the gold into her lap. It was this event, he would later assert, that gave him the *greatest* thrill of his life.[43]

The early movies, dependent on a working-class audience, existed outside the moral universe of correct and mannered middle-class life and the middle class in turn perceived these movies as the lurid embodiment of proletarian culture. While the comedies, especially those of the Keystone Cops and Charlie Chaplin variety, took the artifacts of the new consumer culture—automobiles, vacuum cleaners, and so forth—and stood them on their heads, making a mockery of uptight Protestant attitudes, the melodramas were concerned with romance and sexual behavior. The new industry combined the trappings of modern American culture, based on a critique of Victorian morality, and an emerging working-class culture whose basic life-style was also anti-Victorian.[44]

To immigrant audiences, the early movies often appeared as ironic and fantastic expressions of their own experiences in the New World. They showed a society in which the relationship between people and objects was reversed. Vachel Lindsay perceptively analyzed this development: "It is a quality, not a defect, of all photoplays that human beings tend to become dolls and mechanism, and dolls and mechanism tend to become human."[45]

To the nomadic tenement dwellers of the Lower East Side, the movies confirmed, in comedy form, their own experience. Take, for example, this description of an early movie called *Moving Day:*

> The representatives of a moving firm are sent for. They appear in the middle of the room with an astonishing jump. They are told that the household desires to have its goods . . . transplanted two streets east. The agents salute. They disappear. . . . The books and newspapers climb out of the window. They go soberly down the street. In their wake are the dishes from the table, then follow the . . . kitchen dishes, then the chairs, then the clothing, then the carpets from the floor. The most joyous and curious spectacle is to behold the shoes walking down the boulevard, from the father's large boots to those of the youngest child. The new apartment is shown. Everything enters in procession. Then the human family comes in, delighted to find everything in order.[46]

This presentation of a common experience in ironic form touched a deep vein of humor about the tribulations of everyday life.

Sometimes silent movies took on immigrant themes directly. A movie made by Thomas Ince and G. Gardner Sullivan called *The Italian* expressed a common immigrant experience, although in somewhat romanticized form. The bold contrasts and visual content provided a prism through which the audience could look at and recognize itself:

> The first part, taken, ostensibly in Venice, delineates the festival spirit of the people. It gives out the atmosphere of town crows' happiness. Then comes the vineyard, the crows' sentiment of a merry grape harvest, then the massed emotion of many people embarking on an Atlantic liner . . . then the drama of their arrival in New York. Then we behold the seething human cauldron of the East Side, then a wedding dance, then the life of the East Side. . . . It is hot weather. The mobs of children follow the ice wagon for chips of ice. . . . Passing through the crowds are the Italian and his sweetheart. They owe the force of their acting to the fact that they express each mass of humanity in turn. Their child is born. It does not flourish. . . . The gondolier [in Venice] becomes a bootblack. The grape-gathering peasant girl becomes the suffering slum mother.[47]

If melodramas sometimes took up immigrant themes, spectaculars used Old Testament biblical themes. Occasionally they touched on episodes in the history of Judaism that related particularly to women. In 1919, for instance, D. W. Griffith made one of the first spectaculars and based it on the biblical story of Judith, an important Jewish heroine of the Old Testament. Judith of Bethulia was a dynamic and apocryphal cinematic version of a beloved and familiar story:

> The particular history of Judith begins with the picture of her as the devout widow. She is austerely garbed, at prayer for her city, in her own quiet house. Then later she is shown decked out for the eyes of man in the camp of Holofernes, where all is Assyrian glory. Judith struggles between her unexpected love for the dynamic general and the resolve to destroy him that brought her there. . . . Alternated with these scenes is the terrible rush of the Assyrian army. . . . At length the Assyrians are along the hills and valleys and below the wall of [Jewish] defense. . . . In a lull of the siege, by the connivance of the elders, Judith is let out of a door. . . . She is shown in the quiet shelter of the tent of Holofernes. Sinuous in grace, passionately in love, she has forgotten her peculiar task. . . . When her love for her city and God finally becomes paramount, she shakes off the divine honor [of love] . . . and by the very transfiguration of her figure, we know that the deliverance of Israel is at hand. She beheads the Assyrian. The people arise in a final whirlwind of courage.[48]

Judith is presented as a figure of dignity, forced to make a dramatic choice between individual passion and collective responsibility—a theme that was clearly present in the lives of the Jewish daughters and mothers of immigrant New York.

As the audience developed a facility for the English language, so too did the movies themselves. This took about two decades and the first sound movie was released in 1928. Even then, however, first-generation parents found the transition difficult, and to some the movies remained mysterious. This led to the curious situation where the older generation felt secure in having enough money in the pocket to go to the movies, but did not actually go: "A case worker reported the situation of an older Italian woman who felt a sense of prestige and secure in having money to go to a theater within easy reach. She could then pass by and say to herself, 'I no go today.' She could then continue on her way without the devastating sense of frustration so common in modern life."[49] For younger people the situation was different: they would rush to the movies "before the money finishes out."[50] The popularity of movies, their cheapness and their being in the neighborhood, all encouraged the parents to allow their children to attend.

By 1920 the movie industry had become a major corporate enterprise, committed to a national audience. The content of the movies changed, revealing a new definition of Americanization, of the consumer society as an ideal way of life. The new "formula" was revealed most notably in the films of Cecil B. DeMille. Realizing that "a new generation of moviegoers, not in sympathy with its elders,"[51] was growing up, DeMille redefined the subject matter of films, which now "withdrew the curtains that had veiled the rich and fashionable and exhibited them in all the lavish and intimate details of their private lives."[52] The DeMille movies *Old Wives for New* (1918), *Male and Female* (1919), *Why Change Your Wife?* (1920), and *Forbidden Fruit* (1920) created a fantasy world where sex, romance, marriage, and money were intertwined to show that metamorphosis was possible through consumption—the vamp becomes respectable.

In DeMille movies, the key to a successful modern marriage lay in the ability of the wife to maintain a sexually attractive appearance. In *Old Wives for New*, for instance, a slovenly, lazy wife is in danger of losing her dapper husband. She changes her appearance and keeps him. In *Why Change Your Wife?* a dowdy, modest woman interested in high culture is embarrassed by her husband's gift of a risqué negligee. The marriage begins to break until the wife experiences a metamorphosis: she realizes that sexual appeal is crucial and buys sexy new clothes that change her life.

In *Male and Female* and *Forbidden Fruit*, DeMille explores class relations through the lens of sexuality and consumption. *Male and Female*, a satire of aristocratic manners, contrasts the exquisitely coiffured and well-mannered mistress (Gloria Swanson) with the sloppy and ill-mannered servant girl, Tweeney. One scene shows contrasts in the way in which each of them eats breakfast, and Edward Wagenknecht, a DeMille defender, argues that this may have taught table manners to the working-class moviegoer: "It is just possible that some of the comfortable gum chewers in our 'movie palaces' may have learned that it is not good form to leave your spoon standing in your cup or to cover a whole slice of bread with jelly and then bite into it."[53]

In *Forbidden Fruit*, DeMille gave the Cinderella myth a modern twist. The heroine, Mary Maddock, is the wife of a lazy working-class husband who lives off her earnings. Mary is asked by the oil magnate for whom she works to help him and his wife vamp another oil magnate in order to close a business deal. She accepts an offer of

$20. The film then details her transformation: the wealthy wife phones for "jewels from Tiffany, gowns from Poiret, and perfumes from Coty." The servants dress her and a hairdresser does her hair; she becomes an object subject to the manipulation of experts. The only obstacle to her success is her manners, and in a key scene Mary triumphs by choosing the correct fork. The rest of the film revolves around the conflict between Mary's duty to her husband and her newly found life and "love" in the upper classes. Ultimately, "Cinderella" wins over her love choice and escapes her husband and her class.[54]

The DeMille films openly attacked the customary assumptions, behavior, and style of their audience and pointed the way to the appropriation of a new definition of self. In this sense they became an agency of Americanization. After the success of *Why Change Your Wife?* and *Forbidden Fruit,* many producers "turned their studios into fashion shops and the screen was flooded with imitations. . . . Wise wives, foolish wives, clever and stupid wives were portrayed in every variety of domestic situation that gave an opportunity for displays of wealth, money getting, money making, smart clothes and romance."[55] Movies with titles like *The Amateur Wife, The Misfit Wife, Poor Men's Wives,* and *Behold My Wife* "all lectured to the frump who learns that it is important to remain stylish and good looking after marriage."[56] All emphasized that the metamorphosis of the female self was the new condition for securing the means to survival in modern society—getting and keeping a husband.

For second-generation immigrant women, one step away from arranged marriages and family obligations, these new movies provided a glimpse into the ways of a new culture. DeMille's movies were a visual textbook of American culture, a blend of romantic ideology and practical tips for the presentation of self in the new marriage market of urban life. Here was guidance that mothers could not offer.

With the change in content came a dramatic change in the movie theater itself. Movie houses were designed to win over the "steady patronage of a new class" and were built to hold their audiences in the dark somnambulism of celluloid fantasy. The form itself was a demonstration of new content. If the old noisy neighborhood nickelodeons were an experience of community, the new palaces were a reprieve from community, a vision of wealth, a touch of royalty. If there was sexuality and romance inside the frame, the dark interiors, away from the watchful eyes of parents and neighbors, encouraged sexuality outside the frame, creating a new definition of a participatory audience. One critic observed:

> In the dim auditorium which seems to float on the world of dreams . . . an American woman may spend her afternoon alone . . . she can let her fantasies slip through the darkened atmosphere to the screen where they drift in rhapsodic amours with handsome stars. In the isolation of this twilight palace . . . the blue dusk of the deluxe house has dissolved the Puritan strictures she had absorbed as a child.[57]

Indeed, moving pictures were the most universal form of cheap and satisfying entertainment in urban immigrant communities. As escape, education, or pleasure, they constituted a major source of new ideas; they presented a beguiling view of American dress, manners, and sexual freedom. And they pointed to a mode of existence predicated on a commitment to individual survival in a consuming world.

13
◇
THE TIES THAT BIND

WHILE OUTINGS AND MOVIES BECAME AN INTEGRAL PART OF immigrant life in the early decades of this century, family celebrations remained the main form of recreation for the women. Weddings, holidays, Sabbath suppers, fiestas, christenings, bar mitzvahs, and even funerals were social and familial events that demanded celebration and festivity. The daily experience of suffering and isolation was temporarily forgotten; passionate joy or passionate mourning were the order of the day. And for poor communities with scant resources, these celebrations also provided a way of sharing food, wine, and social life, a mode of redistributing what little wealth there was throughout the community. While Americans watched with disapproval or envy, the new immigrants found ways to maintain culture and create community.

Here, too, however, there was a conflict between the old ways and the new, between the parental wish to preserve the customs of the old country and the younger generation's desire to be free of these restrictions and adopt a more "modern" outlook. Old-world conventions concerning love and marriage were challenged by the young, who were exposed to different ideas and new passions. In the Old World both Jewish and Italian marriages had been arranged; here these practices had to be modified. The large number of Jewish women who came to the United States because "there were no Jewish men for the girls to marry" back home altered the customary patterns of arranged marriage.[1] In the Old Country, many arranged marriages had worked out well: love followed marriage instead of preceding it. This was the case with Mike Gold's parents: "[My mother] and my father had married in the old Jewish style; that is, they were brought together by a professional matrimonial broker. He charged them a commission for the service. It is as good a method as any. My parents came to love each other with an emotion deeper than romance."[2] But other marriages ended in disaster and were gossiped about by the younger women, who were both fearful of marrying a man they did not know and determined to break out of the intricate web of parental control.

Anzia Yezierska's *Breadgivers* was a fictional account of the struggle between a patriarchal father and his daughters over the issue of marriage. The father, dependent on the labor of his daughters for income, bitterly resented losing them even though according to Jewish custom it was the duty of the parents to find marriageable men for their daughters. Bessie, his oldest daughter and hardest worker, wanted to marry a man she had met at work and invited him home to meet her father. The young man explained that he wanted to marry Bessie so badly that he would marry her even without a dowry. The father exploded: "Why don't you ask me first what I want? Don't forget when she gets married, who'll carry for me the burden from this house. She earns the biggest wages. . . . With Bessie I can be independent. I don't have to grab the first man that wants her." The father then demanded payment: "You must pay me . . . you got to pay all the expenses for the wedding and buy her new clothes. I need an outfit for myself. And all I ask more is enough money to start myself up in business so I can get along without Bessie's wages." But the democratization of the New World allowed the fiancé to take on this patriarchal attitude: "I'm marrying your daughter—not the whole family. Ain't it enough that your daughter kept you in laziness all these years? In America they got no use for Torah learning. In America, everybody got to earn his living first."

Bessie, however, felt responsible to her father and could not make the break. The father then undertook what he understood to be the proper form of marriage for his daughters: he went to a matchmaker. Matchmaking in the Old World had depended on the dowry and on the matchmaker's knowledge of the background and social status of the parties involved, but since the first-generation Eastern European Jewish population in America was poor, dowry was replaced by an assertion of the economic usefulness of the daughter: "She'd cook for you and wash for you, and carry the whole burden of the house for you . . . and you will have a wife like in the good old days and not one of these smart young women that boss their husbands." Although Bessie's father arranged the marriages of three of his four daughters and even enjoyed a brief matchmaking career himself, the mother heaped invective on the old patriarch: "Woe to us women, who got to live in a Torah-made world that's only for men." The mother felt the pain of her daughters' lives—all had married men they did not love. The youngest daughter, seeing the fate of her three sisters, refused to follow the same path. She made the break with the power of a new culture behind her. Asserting that "in America women don't need men to boss them," she moved out and into a small basement room. Although she did not even have the money to feed herself, she carried with her a fervent dream to become a teacher.[3]

Although in this case the father managed to intervene in the lives of at least some of his daughters, in general the institution of matchmaking was losing ground to more social forms of courtship, organized more along the lines of individual choice. In addition, the definition of the "good man" was transformed: high status no longer came from being a pious scholar but from being wealthy or "on the make." Maria Ganz wrote of the time she was sent to a matchmaker at the request of her mother, who was anxious that Maria make a good match even though the family's fortunes had been reduced to practically nothing. The potential husband, a clothing manufacturer, was fat and ugly. He took Maria to the Yiddish theater, bought her peanuts and candy, and talked of the things he would buy her. She was revolted and fled the theater. Her mother was disappointed but understood her daughter's feelings.[4]

New ideals of romantic love were taking precedence over customary values. "In this country," as Ruth Katz succinctly put it, "my generation got married for love."[5] One matchmaker, interviewed by the *New York Tribune* in 1898, talked of his dilemma:

Once I lived off the fat of the land, and most marriageable men and women in the quarter depended on me to make them happy. Now they believe in love and all that rot. They are making their own marriages. . . . They learned how to start their own love affairs from the Americans, and it is one of the worst things they have picked up. How can a Jewish couple expect to be happy in a marriage of their own making when it has been the custom of their fathers and mothers for ages not to see each other until after marriage?[6]

Helen Reif, a Jewish woman who migrated to the United States with her parents in 1910, married a man of her own choosing: "It was the most fortunate thing I ever did. My family wanted me to marry the son of someone who owned shoe stores. I almost had a nervous breakdown. If I had remained with my family, it would have destroyed me completely."[7]

Establishing one's independence was often equated with getting married. As Yetta Bursky explained: "I got married for one reason (can't say I didn't like my husband), to get out of the house and become independent."[8] Although she saw marriage itself as a "sacrifice," she also felt it was a way of becoming free from her parents.

But there were difficulties with the new situation as well. In America, according to Anna Kuthan, "love is blind and marriage was an eyeopener. In a big city like New York you go to work and you never know, you could meet your future husband in the subway, because it's crowded, in the bus, in the place where you work, you see, you never know."[9] Sometimes this led to false promises and exploitation. A letter written to the *Forward* from an unmarried Galician woman provided an example of this. After describing herself as a single factory girl who had saved up several hundred dollars and telling of her initial courtship by poor young countryman whom she had helped out financially during a strike, she told how they planned to get married and were on their way to the bank to draw out her money for the wedding when they met some musician friends of his:

> One musician's boy gazed at me and remarked: "Are there not enough people from the old country to ask for their opinion?" I understood the hint and asked him for an address. . . . I rushed over to his countryman and inquired about him. They were surprised at my question and told me he had a wife and three children.
>
> I found out the existence of a gang of wild beasts, robbers who prey on our lives and money. I then advertised in a Jewish newspaper warning my sisters . . . the East Side has become full of such "grooms," matchmakers, "sisters" and "brothers." Inquire of their countrymen. There are plenty of their kind.[10]

In the urban world there was always the threat that a man could claim to be other than what he was. One way of avoiding this was to know the family and village background of potential boyfriends. Fanny Rosen, who migrated from Russia in 1907, met her future husband in a restaurant: "My father had a very good name in the old country. He was very religious. It turned out that my future husband knew my family from the old country and my family had a very good name. I inquired of my family, who said he was a good boy. So we married."[11]

Others were not so lucky. The fairly high desertion rates in the Jewish community, estimated at 10 percent, compounded the problem. Desertion was so common that the *Forward* had a special column called "The Gallery of Missing Husbands," which printed photographs and worked with a Jewish agency called the National Desertion Bureau.[12] The fear of being taken, being deserted, or marrying a "bum" contributed to the women's fear of marriage.

If the desire to marry for love motivated the women, the men had a different agenda. Anna Kuthan, for instance, felt that the experience of boarding increased the men's desire to marry:

> Everybody wants to get married, they want to get their own homes, because they don't want to stay on boarding, they have to walk the street because the people where they live they have children, and he can't stay there during the day so he has to walk the streets, so it makes him so sick and homesick so everyone wants to get married. So we married again poor men because everyone was poor, so we have no better choice and myself I got married that way too. Because my husband he wants to get his own home, that's how I get into that marriage.[13]

This was the old male logic in a new guise: men felt they needed a home and a wife, and marriage for them remained practical and unromantic. For women it was a little different. As Anna Kuthan put it:

> It was always the men who wanted to get married more than the girls. They didn't like boarding, missed their mother's cooking. They can't look on good looks . . . they have to look for a girl so she could help him when they got married and also when the children comes that she would be a good mother and a good homemaker, that was more important.[14]

For women, marriage usually meant an end to much of their contact with the outside world. Both middle-class American culture in general and immigrant men in particular considered it demeaning for women to work outside the home after marriage. It was assumed that husbands who allowed this were incapable of supporting their families on their own. Most women had therefore stopped working outside the home by the age of twenty-two to "choose" the only adult option left—marriage—despite their mixed feelings about marriage itself.

Becky Brier stopped working when she got married even though she was making more money than her fiancé. Her father told her that "only widows went to work." She thoroughly resented giving up her job, but "in those days, you respected your parents or you got a crack in the face."[15] Shirley Levy, a Russian Jew who came to the United States at the age of sixteen and was active in union organizing in her factory, resented the fact that marriage meant leaving this work: "In those days a Jewish girl gets married and she doesn't work anymore. It was a terrible thing."[16]

Katy Bluestone, another Russian Jewish woman, noted that women wanted to work not "just for the money, it's to get out of the house and see people." When her first marriage ended in divorce and she remarried, she insisted on working in her husband's tailoring business even though "he didn't like it. He was ashamed and didn't want to teach me anything."[17] And Lenore Kosloff reported a double standard concerning the work of married women: "They said that only widows went out to work and it demeaned a man for his wife to go out to work, although if he had his own business his wife could work extremely long hours."[18]

For these women who had worked before marriage, the transition to a more isolated life was difficult. The new czars of the household commanded their activity. As Judith Weissman put it, "If a wife worked, the husband couldn't dominate as much as he could with a girl who depended on him for all the income. When a man came home from work . . . they were kings in the house . . . he would sit and order you around. Cooking, cleaning and catering to our husbands" became the definition of marriage.[19]

For some, however, marriage was a way to get out of working to support the family, and for others it allowed escape from the demands of exploitative work situations. One woman, the oldest of six children, worked in a box factory for three years:

> I earned a lot of money, maybe twelve dollars a week, but I had to sit in one place all the time and suffered from bleeding hemorrhoids. It was hard work . . . the machines were noisy and the smell of glue gave me headaches. I couldn't say to my father and brothers "I'm tired." I had to work. And I finally left because my future husband said "enough."[20]

When she decided to get married and quit her job, she told her father that she was going to keep her last month's wages for herself.

Since her earnings had been used to put her brothers through school, there was little he could say.

Many of the same struggles—over matchmaking, arranged marriages, and work—took place in the Italian community. There too the institution of overt matchmaking was beginning to be challenged in the new country. As one study reported:

> It was still the custom in the Italian community to arrange weddings by conference between the parents, though some of the girls had been independent enough to adopt the American method of making their own choice and had even gone so far as to turn down their fathers' "suggestions." The service of "ambassadors" were occasionally made use of to suggest marriage to young men. The suggestion would be followed by a call on the girl by the man, after which the business negotiations had been taken up by the parents. But whether the new or the old method of matchmaking was followed, it was considered essential for every girl to be married before she was twenty-one.[21]

Even if a woman met a man on her own, she had to obtain her parents' permission to marry him and the courtship was carefully scrutinized. Some parents even went so far as to use the power of the state to block an alliance. For example, Rosina Giuliani entered this country in 1906 with her two small children, having been deserted by her husband in Italy. She was a good seamstress and earned her living as a forewoman in a hat factory. When she met a man considerably younger than herself and decided to marry him, his family intervened by denouncing her as a bigamist to the deportation officials at Ellis Island. She countered by hiring a Legal Aid lawyer, who argued before the judge that she had a right to stay in this country and marry her fiancé because she was self-supporting and a skilled worker. She won the case, but was ostracized by her husband's family.[22]

In Italy, the wish to date was considered evidence of the desire to get married and the same was true in America; dating without a chaperone was rare, and to want to date many men was out of the question. Fabbia Orzo told how parental control was so strict that her friends had only two ways to meet their future husbands, either "outside on the corners" or being "matched."[23]

Lily Cortina was never allowed to date and was never taught "the facts of life," a fact noted by both Italian and Jewish women. One

Italian woman revealed how she had learned the secrets of sexual behavior:

> As a young girl, I knew nothing about the sexual side of marriage. I thought that the husband and wife slept in the same bed and that's how babies were born. When I was seventeen and working for my mother, I had a friend who had just been married. One day she came to see me very upset. I said, "What's the matter, you just got married." She said, "Oh, you don't know what marriage is really like." I said, "What do you mean? You just sleep together in the same bed." Then she shocked me. She said, "No, the man has a penis and it gets very big!" "Very big," I shouted, "very big, but where does it go? Where can it go into?" She told me where it went and I thought that was the worst thing I had ever heard.[24]

Since Italian culture, like Jewish culture, was largely family centered, young women often met their husbands at family celebrations; this had the added benefit of making it possible for the parents to judge the young man's background. Agnes Santucci met her husband at a birthday party for her sister's baby: "My brother-in-law asked his friend to be the godfather. Because of this, I knew he was a good man. He didn't like to go out. He liked to stay home."[25]

Although some women rebelled against these parental restrictions, others thought they offered protection. Letitia Serpe arrived in New York when she was seventeen, fresh from an Italian convent school, and worked in her mother's hat store. One day a friend of her mother's came into the store, saw her, and decided that she was the right woman to marry her son:

> The two mothers got together and agreed that I should be married to the woman's son. So, the next Saturday he showed up at the house with flowers for my mother but he asked me for my hand. I told him, don't ask me, ask Mama. She will tell you. Mama agreed to a three-year engagement. During the whole time I never went anywhere with him alone. I never wanted to. My aunt would go with us or he would come over and play cards with my family. I always thought it was right to never be alone with him.[26]

For Italian women even more than for Jewish women, work outside the home was seen as a prelude to the real work of life: housework and raising a family. Agnes Santucci was happy to quit work when she got married: "My husband says you no makka too much money, you stay home and cook. I wanted to stay home. I didn't like to go to work. I worked hard in the house to raise my family."[27]

Sometimes, however, economic circumstances meant that the women continued working. Caroline Caroli was one of these. She and her husband and three other couples had bought an apartment building and at one point the bank took over the house. "All the girls went out to work to buy back the house. Thank God, we were healthy, we've got the house. We *had* to work. Thank God—all the brothers and wives—none of them were lazy."[28] But work after marriage was regarded with disapproval. Fabbia Orzo argued that those who went back to work after they married did so because "they couldn't manage on their husband's salary. They wanted a little more for themselves and their children." She also reported that "once they started to work, and especially when the man couldn't get any jobs and they had to work, they got so used to it that even if they were able to stay home they didn't want to . . . even back then."[29] Grace Grimaldi tried to continue working after marriage while her mother took care of her children, but eventually found it too difficult. Adriana Valenti worked until the force of social custom stopped her:

My mother said, "Don't work. Now that you're so used to earning money you don't want to leave. But your daughter is growing and your husband is working now so stay home and take care of your daughter." You know, the Italian people—you gotta starve but your honor is first. They drilled that into you that that's it. And my daughter was thirteen at the time.[30]

Carmella Caruso met her husband "on the block" when she was seventeen. She described him as "the most jealous thing in the world. . . . He wanted me cooped up in the house. What could I say?" While she disliked married life, she saw change coming in her daughters' lives:

I didn't like my husband ordering me around. I like to do something but not compulsory. My daughters used to see how I hated the way I was treated, and now they are the boss, not the men—especially my little one. Her husband's a piece of bread. Sometimes she tosses so many words at him—this and that—and I tell her, "Mary, if your father was alive and I say words like that—bing! my teeth would be on the floor." But Mary says, "Hey, Ma, it's how you train 'em. You train 'em this way, they go straight this way. If you don't put your foot down in the beginning, it's too bad for you."[31]

And after they married these Italian daughters found themselves caught between their strict parents and their children, who could not accept the old ways. Grace Grimaldi lived with her parents, her sister, her husband, and her three children. Her mother helped her with the children, but not without problems:

I must mention there was eternal conflict. I had three generations in one. I tell you it's the worst thing to have. My father expected that I would bring up my children the way he did me. I wouldn't do that. My children used to tell me not to listen to my parents. My father pointed to any wrongdoing as evidence that his ways were better. My mother resented my different ways of running the household. My husband didn't get involved in these conflicts. He left everything to me. I used to get it from both sides. I generally sided with my children because I thought I was doing the right thing. Many, many times I argued with my parents. Now I want to live alone.[32]

In spite of new ways and generational conflict, the wedding was the high point of family and community life. If the daughters of Irish or American parents spent their money on clothes and recreation and often eloped to save the cost of the wedding, Italian and Jewish daughters and their mothers denied themselves such pleasures in order to save for the wedding and trousseau. And with few recreational activities outside the immediate family, weddings were an important part of social life. As Josephine Roche put it:

To the daughter of fourteen a wedding party is the summit of bliss. She lives from wedding to wedding, treasuring memories of the last one or preparing for the next until her own turn comes to be the central figure. She cannot fancy her stealing away in a secret marriage as so many of the [more Americanized] daughters are inclined to do. That would be the most glorious day of her life. The fine net gown and veil, the white slippers and gloves, must have meant months of savings and stern denials of necessity.[33]

Weddings were large, festive affairs in which the ties between the couple, the two families, and the larger community were sanctified. Social workers often contrasted immigrant and American weddings:

In weddings the entire community participated; no one was left out. Grandmothers were led out for a gay turn by grandsons who cavaliered their little sisters in the next dance. Fathers and mothers, mothers and sons, made lighthearted couples. It was a sight never to be seen at an American gathering, but common enough whenever Italians are assembled for any celebration or enjoyment. In pleasure as in work, the family rules.[34]

Letitia Serpe confirmed this observation when she vividly recalled her own wedding:

> I got married in Mama's store. Mama went all out for my wedding. Even though we didn't have a lot of money, she gave me such a beautiful wedding. Everyone was there, the whole family, all the friends, practically the whole neighborhood. Mama gave me a beautiful trousseau . . . all kinds of beautiful linen that she embroidered herself. I still have some of it. Everybody ate, drank, and danced so much. It was so beautiful. If I close my eyes I can still see it in my mind. Mama gave me a beautiful day.[35]

No tenement mother would voluntarily give up the pleasure of marrying her daughter or son, even if it meant going into debt or scrimping on food or rent. Irving Howe quoted a Yiddish memoirist who explained that "the aristocrats and the radicals preferred 'private' weddings without a big fuss, but ordinary people were not satisfied with this. They would not forgo the opportunity of dancing at their own children's wedding."[36] Weddings were celebrations for the parents, not just the children. Maria Ganz remembered the wedding of her neighbor, Zalmon Eckstoff, as a great event on her block: "No matter how many hours of work we might lose, mother and I simply couldn't stay away from the long anticipated celebration. Everyone in our house went. Who could miss the wedding of such a near neighbor?"[37]

Weddings, however, were far more expensive in the United States than they had been in the Old Country. "The ceremony in the old country was an occasion for great celebration with feasting and dancing for several days, but was perhaps not expensive when the necessary articles were produced at home or received in exchange for home products."[38] In the United States similar results cost money. Halls were usually too expensive and the family would search for an apartment or a shop big enough for the wedding party. Special food and wine were an additional expense. Among Italians, the fathers of the bride and bridegroom shared the expenses, with the bridegroom's family paying for the music and the hall and the bride's family furnishing the food.[39] Nevertheless, weddings were bountiful. In contrast to the daily routine where every morsel was measured out, the wedding turned everyday practice on its head. One man caught Maria Ganz's eye during a wedding feast: "It seemed as if he couldn't get enough of that roast chicken. The contents of fully half of one of those platters he deposited before himself and Yankel [his son], and I discovered that he was providing for the future as well as for the present for I saw him wrap up a wing and a leg in paper napkins and stuff them into his son's pockets."[40]

Custom decreed that wedding gifts should take the form of money or useful articles for the home, and gift money would sometimes be used to help pay for the wedding itself, although this left very little for the couple to start off their new life. Wedding clothes were important symbols, but were also expensive—a wedding dress in 1918 cost over $200. In addition, the bridegroom had to provide "not only the household furniture and his clothing, but the wedding ring, earrings, a gift for the bride."[41]

Flowers, clothing for the maid of honor and bridesmaids, rented automobiles, and photographs added to the cost. The tradition of photographing the wedding party was especially important: "It is the custom of most foreign-born groups to have large photographs, not only of the bride and groom but of the whole wedding party. These photographs cost $30 a dozen."[42] The wedding picture captured the moment of adulthood and the possibility of a future. They were hung up in the parlor and "sent to friends' and relatives, especially in the old country."[43] The wedding photograph thus also provided a sense of the continuation of culture in the new country, a connection between estranged family groups.

To the first generation, the wedding was worth the sacrifice. But to the younger generation, economy was becoming more important and second-generation children sometimes exchanged an elaborate wedding for a stake in a furnished home. This new practice caused enormous conflict: "Even second generation Italians do not really feel properly married without the offices of the Church. On the other hand, the expense of the ceremonial has prompted more and more young couples to be married by the justice of the peace."[44]

The attitude toward weddings was similar to attitudes toward other major events in the life cycle. Christenings and bar mitzvahs were also days of celebration, and gifts were a required part of the ceremony: "Christening celebrations are often held in halls, but more often in the home. The gifts in this case are given to the baby. The godmother, as a rule, buys the whole baptismal outfit for the child and ever after the two families involved address each other as *compare* and *comparee*, meaning godmother and godfather."[45] The role of godparent was an important continuation of an Italian cultural practice. It helped create a bond between immediate family and others in the community. Godmothers were expected to give their godchildren special attention; they were in turn given special respect and honor by the children.

Funerals were also important social events. Even for families with insurance, funerals were costly: unscrupulous undertakers often got possession of the insurance policy and charged an amount equal to the whole of it.[46] During the 1917 influenza epidemic, Sophinisba Breckenridge interviewed an Italian woman who was the president of one mutual-benefit society and a member of four others, and who told her about going to buy a casket when a friend died from influenza: "The cheap wooden casket cost $150. The next day when we went back with another friend to the same undertaker, the casket which had been $150 was $175."[47] Social customs attached to funerals added to their cost: a proper casket, the service of a priest, charges for bell-tolling, and so forth:

> Italian funerals and weddings are elaborate. In the home, no matter how strained the circumstances, there must be nothing lacking in the funeral setup. The poorer families often go into debt in order to have everything as beautiful and elaborate as possible. Underlying the funeral customs is the sentiment that it is the last thing that can be done for those who pass on and it must measure up to the memory of the dead.[48]

Women bore the responsibility for mourning. Italian and Jewish women mourned the dead in similar fashion. Richard Gambino described how Italian women mourned: "The women mourn dramatically. . . . They mourn for the whole family . . . these women weep, wail, and rage against death, berating its shamefulness at taking a member of the family. Their behavior seems excessive and, second, the more extreme it is the greater catharsis for other family members. The women scream their screams of loss, frustration, and rage."[49] Mike Gold recorded the activity of Jewish women at funerals: "They [the women] made an awful hullabaloo. It pierced one's marrow. The East Side women have a strange keening wail, almost

Gaelic. They chant the virtues of the dead sweatshop slave. . . .
They fling themselves about in an orgy of grief."[50]

While Jewish and Italian women were part of different cultures, with different religious and social traditions, both experienced the joy and social solidarity that came with family celebrations. Both experienced the pleasure of children's weddings, shared the responsibility for mourning the dead, and were responsible for planning how the family's income would cover these special events. While Americans watched with either Victorian disapproval or simple envy of the festive community spirit, these immigrant women found their own ways to maintain culture and community.

14
◇
SWEATSHOPS AND PICKET LINES

Hail the waist makers of 1909
Making their stand on the picket line

Breaking the power of those who reign
Pointing the way and smashing the chain

In the black winter of 1909
When we froze and bled on the picket line
We showed the world that women could fight
And we rose and we won with women's might. [1]

THE FACTORY, THAT OUTER WORLD THROUGH WHICH NEW immigrants were introduced to American industry, separated the experience of daughters from the homebound history of their mothers. While the home had encompassed the mothers' labor, concerns, and vision of womanhood for generations, the experience of being "factory girls" provided a different, wider, world view for their daughters. Social theorists and social workers often interpreted this as a sign of a developing modern consciousness. In *The New Basis of Civilization*, a book based on a series of lectures given at the New York School of Social Work in 1905 and reprinted eight times, Simon Patten argued that modern industry aroused and cultivated the economic instincts of working-class family life, and noted two different responses on the part of women: resistance and adaptation. He identified resistance with the mother:

The woman in the shelter is slow to leave the base on which a multiplicity of home industries long since established her. She often lags behind the man in a slough of confusion and dejection for the old idealism of which she is the center [and which] had not yet been penetrated and broken by the imperative necessities that readjusted men to modern production. Women feel that their times are out of joint because they are not yet coordinated with the industrial civilization which is penetrating their home and sifting through their activities.[2]

The weapon in industry's arsenal against the mother was factory work. Patten argued that the decisive break with the past would come as women entered production:

> The woman who in her girlhood learned to be punctual at her factory bench, impressed her acquired quality upon her family and is proud to be named by her tenement neighbors as the most particular woman in the house. Thrilling with pride in the appearance of people for whom she is responsible, and in objects she now possesses, she has a delight—new to her class—in precision, simplicity of form and in order. Her desire is to add to the number of her things, and because of the rapid cheapening of commodities this primary aesthetic longing is among the first to be gratified.[3]

Factory work, in this analysis, was a primary means for internalizing habits and practices necessary for bringing women into the industrial world, and the factory girl was in the vanguard of this movement: by absorbing industrial discipline at work, she would transform her home life with the public display of newly acquired habits and consumer values.

If this was the social worker's image of the factory girl, the reality of work and the understanding of that work were quite different. Factory managers may have attempted to impose discipline on the workers, but the women did not immediately accept the new order. If going to work separated mothers and daughters, the reason for going in the first place was intimately connected to the home, and if work was an educational experience, it was an education in exploitation.

The Lower East Side was the most industrialized neighborhood in the city. It housed many small garment shops and factories, as well as a host of other kinds of light industry. Women found jobs through kinship and community networks. A study of Italian women in industry reported: "Of 874 who told of how they had secured their first position in New York City, 685, or over three-fourths, had found their first job through some friend or relative."[4] Factory work required little training, and a recommendation from a friend or relative was enough for most employers.

During this period, the manufacturers were replacing artisan labor with factory workers and there was a growing division of labor; one worker rarely put togther a whole garment from start to finish. One manufacturer explained the system: "Coats go through forty-odd processes in the making. There is no such thing as a tailor in the ready-made business now."[5] If this created jobs for unskilled workers, it also meant that the "prime requisite for success is not any special skill, but speed, and this comes with practice after the worker has been shown how to do the work."[6] The need for training was greatly reduced: " 'The forelady showed me once,' usually summarized how a girl learned the work and practiced did the rest. Speed, with accuracy, was the only qualification necessary for the slight advancement possible."[7]

Some Italian women had been trained as artisan clothesmakers, and came from a tradition of craft and pride of work. These women were often critical of the organization of the clothing industry in New York:

"Your work is all right provided it is done quickly enough" was the criticism frequently made. "They only do cheap work in this country. Everything must be done in a hurry. In Italy it would take six months to do a pillow and here it was done in three or four hours. Cheap work!" A finisher on dresses complained that she had to learn the trade all over again when she came here because in Italy there was more handsewing, and no subdivision of processes. If one worked fast there, people would say that the work was badly done and everyone was taught to do as beautiful sewing as possible.[8]

Adriana Valenti, still imbued with a craft sense, took a job making men's cuffs but "got tired of doing cuffs all day. I says no, I don't want this. I'll never learn how to do things." Her next job, making skirts, she liked better "because I made it complete, at least I learned to sew for myself."[9]

Rosina Giuliani was known in her town in Italy for her expert millinery skills. When she came to the United States, she landed a job as the forelady of a hat factory, where she made $25 a week. Her daughter talked about the use that was made of her skill:

Mama always knew how to make beautiful hats. When she first came here, they used to tease her in the factory. Rosina, Rosina, you're the fastest in the shop, they used to say. Mama became a forelady because she showed the boss how to make her beautiful hats. He used her skill and made her a forelady. Mama taught Papa how to make hats. They tried to go into business themselves, but failed because they never had enough money to get started. That's why they ended up in the factory for most of their lives.[10]

In Eastern Europe, the industrial process was farther advanced than in Italy, but there was still a mixture of artisanal craft, apprenticeship systems, and machine work. Judith Weissman, for example, got her training in the garment industry from her father, who designed and cut garments that young girls would baste and male apprentices would finish on a sewing machine. He had five people working in his shop, which was also his home. People came to his house, ordered their clothes, and he gave each garment special attention. Wealthy Gentiles sent a wagon for him, and he would load the sewing machine on the wagon and make their clothing in their homes. His apprentices, according to custom, received board but no pay.

Yetta Bursky learned to be a dressmaker in Galicia. As an apprentice, she made patterns. She then became the "supporter of the family" with her dressmaking. By the time she was sixteen, she had started her own shop:

> When I was sixteen I made a bunch of dresses for a woman and I delivered them. I expected about $15 but she gave me $1.50. She was an aristocrat, but money she didn't believe in paying. I burst into tears, went home and told my mother, "I'm going to America." I had to make money to help the family. I did that, but I ended up in the factory making waists by machines.[11]

Bella Feiner trained as a dressmaker in Poland, beginning as an apprentice when she was twelve years old. In the United States, however, she was an operator. She summed up the feelings of other artisan dressmakers when she said, "When I came here, I knew more than I know now. I knew how to make a whole dress."[12]

The seasonal nature of certain light industries and the consequent yearly periods of slack time meant that women shifted from one job to another, often working in several different kinds of industry over one year:

> During the course of two years, sixteen-year-old Maria Viviana had tried her hand in eight such different industries as the making of aprons, straw hats, dresses, shirtwaists, gloves, underwear, dresses and silk embroidery. "I have worked in every trade in New York City," exclaimed Emilia, a girl of twenty, as she told of her working on women's neckwear, hats, pins, suits, children's cloaks. . . . Another

girl had run the gamut of the trades, from packing candy to spooling thread. "I have worked in lots of places. You see, I have been working for ten years."[13]

The conditions of work provided an education in the excesses of discipline. A twelve- to fourteen-hour day was common. Workers were often cheated out of their full wages—clocks were slowed down during working hours or sped up at lunchtime. Workers were charged for needles, thread, mistakes, and even electrical power (if there was any). They were fined for being late, talking, singing, and taking too much time in the bathroom. The sanitary conditions were deplorable, the working conditions unsafe; floors collapsed in small lofts incapable of carrying the weight of machines and people, the doors were locked when work began, and shop fires were common. The speed of the work was intense. Maria Ganz's first work experience was instructive. She got a job putting small pearl buttons on cards at a wage of $2.50 a week:

> If a girl came in even a few minutes late, the lost time was charged against her pay. We were not permitted to talk to each other. Sometimes, some girl, unable to endure the silence any longer, would begin humming a tune which would be taken up by others near her. Marks, the foreman, would question us until he had learned who began the singing. Then he would deduct three hours from her pay. If any girl objected to this treatment she was told to look for work elsewhere. It was my first real job and I was afraid of losing it, so I tried to keep silent. But for a lively girl like me to keep her mouth shut for eleven hours is torture; it almost drove me wild.[14]

Agnes Santucci, in describing her first job, gave a similar account:

> The machine used to go, keep agoing, keep agoing. I was so unhappy to stay there all day, no go out like it was a prison. I couldn't speak English. I used to stay at the machine all day without seeing anybody. The forelady used to be back and forth, back and forth, look this way, look the other way. Do your work, do your work. An Italian girl fell asleep at the machine and she was fired.[15]

Grace Grimaldi described her work life in a blouse-making factory as a kind of slavery:

> Between the years 1914 and 1918, it was a slavery really. You couldn't open your mouth. God forbid you came five minutes late or they'd actually throw you out of the place. You couldn't talk. . . . You couldn't even go to the bathroom. We were treated like slaves. I

worked for Scher Brothers—a place people of my generation never forgot. He was a real slavedriver. He used to pick people from the boat and use them for slavery. But people had to earn. So when you want to earn your own, you take anything.[16]

Ida Shapiro's first job was equally typical: "You didn't have a little water to drink, you didn't have nothing. Everything was dirty. The bosses could fire girls for any reason they liked. The boss fired women who fought back, women who were smart. Getting on those American clothes every morning always made me five to ten minutes late. You had to punch a clock you know. I got fired."[17]

Bessie Gitlin's first real disappointment in life came from her first job in New York: "I came here, my god was I disappointed. It was the first time in my life in a shop where you couldn't just leave, but I got over it. After all, I was responsible for bringing over my sister. But I was very unhappy."[18]

Deductions were made for time lost opening bundles or learning new styles:

> The bosses would count the stitches. I would try to make my bosses understand, it's not only the stitches to make the garment, but the labor. When you open a bundle, time goes by. We were supposed to make so much an hour. And it takes about five minutes—you have to write out your ticket . . . and every time you open a bundle you lose five minutes which equals two hours by the end of the week. You have to turn it, you have to study the garment. We always have new styles. We have to have new styles, makes people buy, this gives us work . . . but the bosses would feel by giving the workers less they had more in their pocket.[19]

Shirley Levy explained how this system worked in her shop: "In my shop, we worked on the same style, because you could produce more. You don't have to look at the sample. First week on a style you might make $9. Second week $10. But even when we produced more than that, the boss gave us the same amount. No matter how much we produced on the same sample we never got ourselves higher than $9."[20]

One of the evils of the needle trades was the subcontracting system, whereby a factory owner would give out jobs to several men who would then hire young women to work for them—all in the owners' factory. Shirley Levy went to work in a ladies' waist factory that used the subcontracting system:

My friend got me a job in a waist factory. The factory was very large, about two hundred workers. The factory was owned by five brothers, they had a very good income. The rates the workers got were indescribable. Most of us were under twenty and came from small towns and we didn't know a trade or anything. They gave the men four or five machines, and he'd take on four or five immigrant girls and anybody with a little intelligence could learn how to run the machines in an hour or so. The men that hired the girls would pay a small wage—$2 or $3 a week. The boss would give the man the work, he would give it to the girls, he made his money by the piece.[21]

Sonia Farkas worked with three women who had come over on the boat with her. She wanted to go to school, but her family could not afford it, and at fourteen she went to work. She got a job as a finisher because she knew how to sew:

It was a big shop, it has three floors and five hundred people. All the three of us got jobs as finishers. In those years the operator would take a finisher and one finisher would work for two or three operators. They would pay me. They would get the money from the boss and we would get it from them. The boss exploited us that way. That's how it used to be.[22]

There were two ways of being paid: by the piece or by the hour. Most women seemed to have preferred piece work. Bessie Polski worked in a shirtwaist factory that employed Jewish and Italian women. She identified being paid at the end of the week—"week work"—with slavery: "We were week workers. We were like slaves. You couldn't pick your head up. You couldn't talk. We used to go to the bathroom. The forelady used to go after us, we shouldn't stay too long. We hardly had a chance to wash our hands."[23]

Andriana Valenti also preferred piece work: "When I was a piece worker, I would sing. I would fool around, say jokes, laugh, talk to the girls. With time work, I would put my head down and I would work . . . and it seemed to me the day would never pass."[24]

With piece work there was more room for socializing, and the work itself seemed more human. Yetta Bursky put it this way: "I admired the operators on piece work. They were sitting and talking and were jolly, having fun. I became a piece work operator as soon as I could." And Katy Bluestone explained how socializing and work could go hand in hand: "We were six or eight girls and we talked and enjoyed ourselves. It was piece work so it was our own time. We used to sing and talk. The boss never minded if the work was good and fast."[25]

But piece work also had its problems. Fania Horvitz reported: "In piece work you can socialize because it's your own time. But I preferred week work to piece work. In piece work you rush yourself to death." Another woman explained the advantages of week work: "You don't have to rush. You don't have to be jealous—this one gets a bigger bundle—you get a smaller one and believe me there were plenty of arguments like that—'oh, Sarah got a bundle twice as large as mine'—like that."[26]

The work was debilitating mentally and physically; a combination of monotonous work, constant supervision, and long hours led to feelings of isolation, frustration, and depression. Industrial accidents were frequent, as were such health problems as tuberculosis, pneumonia, backaches, and general physical deterioration. In addition, the women suffered sexual abuse by the bosses and male workers in the shop. One woman recalled how she was afraid of her boss: "He tried to hug me and I was so ashamed because I didn't know what to say or do. No man had ever kissed me except my father before. Finally, I told my father and he wouldn't let me go back."[27] The bosses often expected sexual favors from the women and would hold back wages if they were refused. Cutters—always men—who taught the women how to work the machines often made "fresh remarks" and were sexually insulting. Some bosses would even require that their female workers wear makeup in an effort to hide their pale faces and make them more alluring.

It was also difficult for Jewish women who did not work in all-Jewish shops to keep up dietary and religious practices. Garment worker Lillie Tamarakin worked in one such shop:

> It was filled with machine operators, mostly single Italian women, they thought I was German. When it came to the Jewish holidays, I took off and they were surprised. During Passover, I couldn't eat *hometz* [food not prepared for Passover], so I ran all the way home for lunch and then came back. God knows how I did it.[28]

Saturday was the Sabbath for Jews, and working the usual half-day was often a problem for many Jewish women. Bella Feiner was fired several times because her mother would not allow her to break the Sabbath taboo on work: "I lost many jobs. My mother didn't let me go to work. I had to work a half day on Saturday and my mother objected because it was the Sabbath—so they used to fire me for that."[29] Doria Shatsky described herself as a "Sabbath observer" and said she never "worked a half day Saturday. If I was fired, I found another job."[30]

Despite the exploitative conditions, there was camaraderie among the women that helped to relieve the situation. Women helped each other with their work in times of accident or distress, told jokes, laughed, sang, and tried to slow down the pace of the work itself. They talked about men, marriage, the social conditions of the job, the neighborhood, and their families. One woman recalled how one day she hummed an old Russian love song, only to see the young woman working the next machine break into tears. Hearing the song brought back the memory of her love, who had died in a pogrom. Then, at her request, all of the women began to sing the song to ease the pain of her memory.[31]

During slack times, when there was not enough work to go around, the women also helped each other out. Yetta Adelman described how she shared: "When I worked on samples and the other girls didn't have work, I divided my money with them because we had to make the same thing. Because if they didn't call me in, I would have to be out too. So we shared."[32]

Shop forewomen had reputations like supers, good or bad depending on the degree of solidarity they showed with the workers. To Bella Cohen the "forewomen were like everybody else. We were all workers."[33] Lenore Kosloff, herself a forewoman, demonstrated her solidarity by socializing with the other women and repairing their mistakes: "I socialized with the other girls in the shop. They were in the same station as I was. I stayed at work and repaired mistakes the operators had made. I spent my lunch hours fixing up mistakes. I didn't want them to lose money. In my position I could act as a mediator."[34]

Lillie Tamarakin noted that there was a clear distinction between the bosses, the male workers, and the women workers. The bosses kept their distance, the male cutters made sexual comments, but the women got along well together. When she left the shop to get married, the women workers "showered" her with gifts.[35] Getting married was a big event in the factory and the women would pool what little surplus cash they had to give each other presents. Maria Ganz ran into the wife of one wedding couple, the Eckstoffs, who had to return to factory work because they had used up their wedding money and pawned their furniture. The wife had only kept a few pieces, along with a set of four framed pictures—"The pictures were a wedding present from the employees of the shop where the bride was employed at the time of the marriage."[36]

Ida Shapiro was working in a ladies' waist shop that employed fifty Jewish and Italian women when she got married: "They gave me a surprise party in the shop when I got married. The machines even were decorated. The girls gave me a crystal candlestick and flowers. I had a big wedding and everyone in the shop came. The Italian girls came too."[37] Bella Cohen also worked with Italian and Jewish women, and had a similar experience: "Whenever a girl got married the workers made a collection. Everyone chipped in. I didn't tell them but they found out and came to my apartment and gave me a beautiful roll of Irish linen. I was overwhelmed."[38]

Industrial accidents were frequent and fellow workers took care of each other, even when the boss took that time out of their pay. For example, Lillie Tamarakin had an accident at work: "I once got my finger caught and badly mangled in the machine and I had to be taken to the hospital. One of the machine operators, a young girl, took me. But she was an hourly worker so they didn't pay her for the time she spent taking me. I felt terrible."[39]

While they worked, the women stole time for themselves by daydreaming and singing. Dreams of marriage, of freedom from work, and songs of love allowed the young women to create visions of another life for themselves as they sat locked up in the factory. Adriana Valenti described her daydreams:

> I'd make up stories in my mind while I'm working. I'd say, "What kind of a person's going to wear this dress. Is she in good health, is she a good person? Where is she going to go? . . . Will she just throw this dress aside [laughs] . . . because on each ticket you put your name or number so you know who made it. Like you're creating something and someone is going to enjoy it. And then I'd think—what kind of a person? Is she going to be careful? Is she going to keep it well? It's not mine. I only made it and got paid for it.[40]

In her daydream, Adriana Valenti was able to establish a more direct relationship between the creator/producer and the consumer/enjoyer than was possible in reality. Her reverie pierced the exploitative nature of the work to grasp the real meaning of work as creation and of consumption as pleasure.

Bella Feiner's daydreams were more romantic:

All of us young people were sitting and dreaming in the shops. Well it's only for a season or two. I'll be doing this, I'll be doing that. I'll get married. An aunt will be able to take care of me. We used to even sing songs—Yiddish naturally . . . singing the dream songs, the love songs and this is how we dreamed away our youth and go out gay and happy and what not. We enjoyed it, our young life with all its problems.[41]

Another woman explained why she used to sing to herself all day:

You know what I used to do. I used to sing the whole day when I worked with the machine. So the boss used to say, "Oh Irene's really working." You know, I sing that I want to forget that I'm working the whole day by the machine. There were about twenty-five girls there. They all said, "Irene, oh look how happy she is all the time!" I used to sing Hungarian all the time. I told them I used to sing the whole day there with the machine to forget that I had to work there. I used to sing love songs.[42]

But the women never forgot the exploitation, and, infused with old-world radical traditions and new-world ideas of freedom, they took part in creating a militant, organized labor movement on the Lower East Side, electrifying a stagnant American labor movement.[43] For the first time, new immigrants took center stage in the history of organized labor in the United States.

The Lower East Side had long had a thriving radical culture that stimulated the organization of labor unions and the more general fight against industrial exploitation. Given new fuel by the influx of Russian Jews following the abortive Russian revolution of 1905, the movement to transform social conditions on the Lower East Side grew rapidly. Women garment workers formed the vanguard of this movement.

Adriana Valenti had learned about the power of collective action from her father. When she was a child, he had told her of the fear that would come from isolation and of how the people of his village would stick together in the face of the landowners' demands. As she put it, "So that's what I always remembered, that's why I love the union, because unity, strength, power, you're together, you're not alone." When she went to work she found that it was hard for the European people to stand up to the boss because they were so grateful to be earning a little money, but "I was the youngest there. And I would tell them, let's ask for more money, let's stick together." Since she had the support of her mother and no family of her own, she wasn't afraid to be fired: "I was a fighter. I always fought. I didn't worry because if I didn't work, I didn't have to pay board—whatever I earned I took it to my mother."[44]

Many of the Jewish women who came to the United States had been politically active at home. Rachel Cohen argued that the "girls who were the organizers were the ones who had been socialists in the old country and who had never worked in the shops before." Although her family was opposed to her organizing in the shops, her father's greatest moment in life had been the Russian Revolution, when he knelt down in prayer, saying "Thank God, I lived to see the Czar overthrown."[45]

Sonia Farkas had been active in the revolutionary movement in Kiev when she was young. She had gone to meetings, done undercover work, and participated in the general strikes:

> We had a general strike once where everything stopped. The cars and everything. It was like you make a revolution. It was 1905. A lot of people were beaten up and arrested but we had it for one day. But we had quite a nice revolution that day. It didn't last long because the police weren't with us. I couldn't understand when I came to the U.S. why we couldn't make a revolution in the U.S.[46]

On the Lower East Side she became a union organizer:

> I went to look for a union because I worked in a non-union shop. They threw down sixty pressers. The pressers wanted a union so the boss threw them out. I saw that and started to cry. I went to look for a union. Where can I get a union so they could come and organize a strike. I knew what movement meant and I knew what a union was. I found one on East Broadway. In 1906 the union was very small. So when I came to the union, I said that I want to organize the shop. He says, "Where you working?" I told him. He said, "It's five hundred people in that shop and we don't have five hundred members. How can you take on a shop like that?" So he laughed at me. I started to bang on the table and crying, "I want a union." They had to take me from that job and put me in a union shop. A small shop. They had a couple, but very few.[47]

Yetta Bursky's father had been arrested during a strike in a factory in Poland and her mother had not known if she would ever see him again. Yetta grew up in the midst of pogroms and the mass slaughter of Jews, at a time when it was dangerous for more than a few people to gather together in the same house. Her parents and their friends used to take out marriage permits and then hold political meetings instead. She came to the United States when she was twelve, got work in the garment industry, and became "a fighter":

> I got a job in a waist factory. It was the rottenest boss I ever worked for. I refused to work on a particular garment and I convinced the others not to also and I got into trouble. But we made a stoppage. Oh, I loved it. If the boss didn't do the right thing, a stoppage. See, in the beginning the boss could do anything he wanted. The boss used women and paid them less than men. He hated me. He used to say, "If she wouldn't be a woman, I'd cut her into pieces." But we could make a stoppage.

She also hated the forewoman, but felt that the union could deal with her demands: "She was a little runt. You have to take this from her. With the union, you make a stoppage. She has to stop it. Before the union she liked us but we don't have to stand for this. As long as we have the union, the hell with them." Sometimes the women in the shop were more courageous than the union's business agents: "The boss once maltreated a male worker. The union business agent encouraged us to go back to work before the incident was settled, but we refused to until the man was given an apology. I forced the boss to apologize." Yetta took part in many strikes and walked many picket lines. Following Polish custom, she used to follow the scabs home from work and harass them. She always carried her lunch when picketing in order to convince the police that she was a good worker—she thought this gave her a kind of tactical protection. She was once arrested for pinching a scab but she was not afraid. Eventually she became a union organizer. She would get a job for a few weeks and organize until she was fired. As she herself summed up her own history, "Kids like me made the union."[48]

Adriana Valenti got a job in a shop where thirty-five operators worked for practically nothing, and became angry thinking of what this meant for the women's families. Although she knew it was wrong she shut the power off in the shop. The wife of the owner came after her with an umbrella, poked her in the stomach, and ordered her to get out, but, as she ironically put it, "We got out, but we took the girls with us."[49]

When Judith Weissman was working in an underwear factory, she met an older woman who had been educated in radical politics in Europe and was the chairperson of the union; although she came from a religious family, all of her children were socialists. Judith admired the woman and "followed her around." She carried an umbrella to protect herself from the goons who attacked her during the many strikes the union called. The police would arrest her, but she would show the judge a book of U.S. history and be freed. On one occasion, all of the pickets were locked up, including Judith, who did not get home until one o'clock in the morning. Although her mother was crying, thinking her daughter dead, Judith "loved it."[50]

Bessie Polski went to work in a big factory that had 120 machines. The operators, Jewish and Italian women, told their union local that they wanted a piece-work system and better working conditions. When their demands were rejected, they went on strike. The bosses brought in scabs and called in the police, but "the police didn't club the scabs, they clubbed the strikers. You know how police are. The bosses used to look through the windows and they had the pleasure of it." Bessie Polski and an Italian woman were arrested for using a "female weapon" against a scab—a hat pin. The Italian woman decided to act hysterical, and cried and carried on until she was released the next day. Bessie was taken to night court, where "no nice girls go." The judge told her that he "sympathized very much with the girls, they were fighting for their rights. But you have to have respect for an officer and not spit in his face." She said she had not spit in the officer's face, "it was not in my nature I should spit on somebody," but she got locked up for three days anyway. The union finally won the strike, and Bessie argued that "we made the union, all those European boys and girls, we made the union. Otherwise, there still wouldn't be a union."[51]

Shirley Levy worked in a factory run by five brothers. A union representative came to organize the shop:

> The five brothers nearly broke his head and threw him down the stairs. So it was like a fortress—couldn't organize the place. My friend and I decided that we would try to go out and find a job in a union factory. So we did. And it was all the difference in the world. The first week I earned $16. I helped maintain the shop. The boss was very annoyed at me because I fought for good prices and pulled all kinds of tricks.[52]

Grace Grimaldi became involved in union activities because she worked for a slave driver. Joining the union was an important step for her:

> I was praying for someone to come and help us change the working conditions. I was always for the union. It really helped change the slavery conditions of the workers. It was really for the workers. My father was afraid to let me go to the picket line. I used to do behind-the-scenes work in the office. But the women who went out to the picket line—you've got to be a fighter. It's in you. Some people are more fighters than others so they take the front. For twenty years, things were very bad. Only those who were here before 1930 can understand the difference between 1910 and 1930.

Her husband was also active in the union—they were a union family. She described her husband as a "fighting idealist" who "sold his mind and body to the ideals of the cause."[53] Even when raising a family inhibited her full-time participation, Grace Grimaldi always supported the union's work.

The strike was the key weapon in the union's battle, and two mass strikes—the shirtwaist strike of 1909 and the cloakmakers' strike of 1910—revolutionized the labor movement, both in New York City and across the nation. The shirtwaist strike of 1909, which became known as the "uprising of the 30,000," was not only the first large-scale protest in a new and rapidly growing industry but was the largest strike of women workers in the United States up to that point.

Responding to the growth of the national market—production in 1909 was worth about $50 million retail—the shirtwaist industry was in the process of changing from domestic manufacture to factory production. Most of the shops were medium sized, but some were large, employing over one hundred workers in one shop.

In 1909 a series of local strikes culminated in a strike in the two biggest shirtwaist factories, the Leierson and Triangle Shirtwaist shops. Striking pickets were met by the combined force of scabs, police, and thugs hired by management. The women began to feel that a general strike was the only effective weapon against the police power of the employers. The middle-class members of the recently organized Women's Trade Union League came to picket in solidarity with the striking women and were also arrested by the police. This brought the strike new publicity, as well as support from progressive elements across the city.

A leaflet calling for a general meeting of all workers in the shirtwaist trade printed in Italian, Yiddish, and English was distributed across the Lower East Side. The meeting was held at Cooper Union and illustrated dramatically the potentially explosive alliance between new forms of rank-and-file militancy and old-world traditions of community and solidarity. The speakers were moderate and uninspired until Clara Lemlish, a striker from the Leierson shop, spoke up—in Yiddish: "I am a working girl. One of those who are on strike against intolerable conditions. I am tired of listening to speakers who talk in general terms. What we are here for is to decide whether we shall or shall not strike. I offer a resolution that a general strike be declared—now." The speech electrified the audience and cries of support and enthusiasm swept the hall. A second was called for, people jumped to their feet, and the chairman called for the taking of the old Jewish oath: "Two thousand hands were raised in the air with the prayer: 'If I turn traitor to the cause I now pledge, may this hand wither from the arm I now raise.' "[54] Thus a general strike, the newest weapon against industry, was cemented by an oath of solidarity emanating from a communal past.

As the general strike began there were over fifteen thousand shirtwaist makers on the picket lines. The strike itself was held together by the women. As Louis Levine wrote:

> In fact, though the principal union officials were men and the direction of the strike was in the hands of men, the women played a preponderant role in carrying it through. It was mainly women who did the picketing, who were arrested and fined, who ran the risk of assault and who suffered ill treatment from the police and the courts.[55]

One sympathetic social worker, writing in *Survey* magazine shortly afterward, described the spirit of the strike:

> Into the forefront of this great motion picture comes the figure of one girl after another as her services are needed. With extraordinary simplicity and eloquence she will tell before any kind of audience, without false shame and without self-glorification, the conditions of her work, her wages and the pinching poverty of her home and the homes of her comrades. Then she withdraws into the background to undertake quietly the danger and humiliation of picket duty or to

become a nameless sandwich girl selling papers on the street, no longer the center of attention but the butt of the most unspeakable abuse.[56]

One judge expressed the outrage of official society at the idea of women on strike. While sentencing one woman striker, Judge Olmstead told her pointblank: "You are on strike against God and Nature, whose firm law is that man shall earn his bread by the sweat of his brow. You are on strike against God."[57] The activities of the women strikers were perceived as a blow against a civilization that demanded submission and docility on the part of its women.

The Progressive coalition that formed around the strike demanded a different definition of civilization and Americanization. Made up of the families of the strikers, socialist organizations on the Lower East Side, Progressive social workers, and the middle-class Women's Trade Union League, the coalition represented the interests of trade unions, suffragettes, and socialists, all of whom wanted a different kind of country. Unionists demanded higher wages and better working conditions because they believed that true Americanization occurred when workers stood up for their rights and demanded the reappropriation of the profits of their labor. Suffragists demanded the vote because they believed that the rights of women extended beyond the home to include an active participation in the affairs of civil society. Socialists (and varieties of anarchists) demanded the redistribution of the wealth created by industrial capitalism to the workers who had produced it in the first place. This vision of Americanism was voiced by Elizabeth Gurley Flynn during a strike at the textile mills in Lawrence, Massachusetts, in 1912:

> We talked of "Solidarity," a beautiful word in all languages. Stick together!—Workers unite! One for all and all for one! An injury to one is injury to all! The workers are all one family! It was internationalism. It was also real Americanism—the first they had heard. "One nation indivisible with liberty and justice for all." They hadn't found it here, but they were willingly fighting to create it.[58]

The coalition was unified in a series of public meetings. At one, where the stage was set up like a rally for woman suffrage, "flags of blue on both side walls carried the words in white 'Votes for Women,' the *New York Times* reported that 'socialism, unionism, women's suffrage and what seemed to be something like anarchism was poured into the ears of fully 8,000 people who gathered.' "[59]

Nevertheless, ethnic barriers did not fall all at once, and there were some uncomfortable moments during the shirtwaist strike. Since the strike was organized primarily by the Jewish labor movement, its leaders were not always sympathetic to the Italian women, who found it more difficult to join the strike than did their Jewish sisters. Some Italian families were unwilling to allow their daughters to go on picket duty or to be involved in strike activities that took them out of the house. A common divisive tactic on the part of the bosses was to deliberately seat Jewish workers next to Italian workers. Language barriers and ethnic contempt made the situation worse. Yet this was the first time that Jewish and Italian women had worked together in an organized fashion, and in time the problems were somewhat overcome. Through the work of the Italian organizers of the Italian branch of the Socialist Party, anarchist societies, women's mutual-benefit societies, and individual contacts, increasing numbers of Italian women joined the strike and became active in the union.[60]

After three grueling months the strike ended, with some gains and some losses. The employers agreed to shorter hours and the abolition of charges for needles but refused to recognize the union or to employ only union help. But even this partial success inspired the workers in the men's clothing industry to strike in 1912, when about 115,000 people went out on strike, including 10,000 Italian women finishers. The bosses attempted to buy the women off with promises of higher pay, but failed. One woman had been out six weeks when she was interviewed by Louise Odencrantz. She stayed on strike because, she said, "I will not betray my *patria*."[61]

In both strikes there was a tension between male trade union officials and women workers. The male officials often made policy decisions that were to the women's detriment. During the shirtwaist strike, for example, the male negotiators won on wage and hour demands but compromised on health and safety issues—issues on which the owners refused to budge. A year later the Triangle Waist Company went up in flames. On the day of the fire there were about eight hundred workers in the plant, and all the doors were locked—company policy in order to keep track of the women. One hundred and forty-six people died and hundreds more were injured.

One reporter who covered the scene wrote: "I looked upon the dead bodies and I remembered these girls were the shirtwaist makers. I remembered their great strike of last year in which the same girls had demanded more sanitary conditions and more safety precautions in the shops. Their dead bodies were the answer."[62]

In the 1912 strike, the male union leadership agreed to a settlement that set different standards of pay for male and female workers. In the famous "Protocols of the Dress and Waist Trade of 1913," the first labor agreement to use outside arbitrators, the lowest paid male earned more than the highest paid female, and the highest paid jobs were reserved for men only. These conditions made it difficult for women to remain in the industry, and showed the extent to which the industry and the union were intent on maintaining the sexual division of labor. The male-dominated trade union movement, by accepting a pay scale based on the sexual division of labor, in effect agreed that the principles of the family economy should be replaced by the more "Americanized" idea of a wage-earning father who was the sole support of the family.

In a larger sense, however, the shirtwaist strike was a real victory for the women. It lifted the work of immigrant women out of obscurity and into public consciousness, and helped demonstrate the power of organized resistance. It was a living example of the American radical tradition—of spontaneous activism, solidarity, and the promise inherent in American ideals of democratic action.

In addition, the activity of the women and their emergence as a public force created new alliances in the community. The previously middle-class suffrage movement was bolstered by the power of women workers who were challenging the prevailing ideology of a woman's place, and in 1917 the referendum on women's suffrage was carried by 100,000 votes in New York City alone.[63] Mary Simkhovitch thought that it passed because of

> the plain fact that though indeed the women's place is in the home, in our neighborhood it is also largely in the factory, workshop, the store and office, [and] that fathers and brothers and sons have long been convinced of the inevitability of this great political change. In the case of the Italians in our district, the fact that their women are beginning to work so largely in factories was the dominant reason for the change in attitude about suffrage. "My daughter she works, she must vote like me." It is indeed obvious.[64]

The collective activity of immigrant women also demonstrated that the atomization inherent in American society could be confronted with the dignity and collectivity of labor. The union was often described as a family—a collective family that could provide for the needs and the well-being of the community itself.

Rebecca Markowitz expressed her understanding of the intimate connection between home and workplace: "If industry is sick—nobody makes any money. It's like housekeeping. If you don't have the money, you can't be a good housekeeper. In order to make good meals and take care of your family, you need the what with. That's why we needed the union."[65] Bella Feiner articulated the same thought in a more political way: "Poor people didn't have anything. We had to seek ways of bettering our lives. The union was the way of meeting our economic and political needs. We had to deal with the present and the future.[66]

Most women felt that the union had made a big difference in the shops. Fabbia Orzo reported that conditions improved after the union came in: "Quite a lot of improvement came after the union came in. Before the union came in, the hours were 48 a week at most of the shops. There were no breaks except for lunch. After, the hours were down to forty, then down to thirty-six. We got better pay."[67] Bella Feiner expressed the same sentiment: "When the union came, it was wonderful. Before we had to work so long that I used to faint many times when I came home from work. I enjoyed working but we didn't get nothing before the union. After, it was a pleasure."[68]

The union did, however, create class cleavages within the community. Garment manufacturers who prided themselves on their radical past in Eastern Europe were threatened by union activists in the United States. Fanny Rosen recalled: "My boss was a so-called liberal. He called himself a liberal and became a millionaire. He had been a student radical who fled Russia in the Revolution of 1905. He believed that strikes were legitimate but when it came to bargaining, he bargained like all the rest and kept informers in his shop."[69]

Becky Brier summed up the feeling about bosses when she said, "You never liked a boss. He always lived better than the rest. He had a nicer home, even automobiles and vacations. He got that by paying us starvation wages. So, you never liked a boss."[70]

The response of the clothing manufacturers to union organizing was twofold: some compromised their need for profit to meet the demands of the workers, while others began to move their factories and shops out of the city. By 1921 union organizers were facing the realities of the "runaway shop." As one official survey of the region noted: "The clothing manufacturer who announced to an investigator his intention to move his plant from New York to some town where he could tell 'those damned Bolsheviks to go to hell' undoubtedly voiced the sentiments of many exasperated fellow employers."[71]

Ultimately trade union activity created an alternative to Americanization for immigrant women—and particularly for their daughters. If the Americanization movement assumed that it could change the immigrant working class, the trade unions offered a way for them to change America.

CONCLUSION

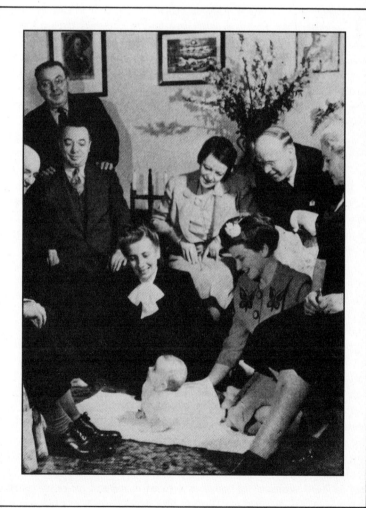

THROUGHOUT AMERICAN HISTORY THE IDEA OF PROGRESS HAS persisted as a national destiny and a personal dream. The story of American life often resembles a Hollywood narrative, a miraculous metamorphosis in which people of humble origins, using simple implements, ascend to a "city on a hill." Through the elixers of *virgin land, streets of gold, industry, enterprise,* and *opportunity,* common folk become comfortable residents in paradise. The past is left behind. A new world is born.

The tale of the *immigrant* is a particularly ubiquitous variation on this myth. Despised refugees from misery and want reach the borders of the promised land. After an apprenticeship of hard work, discipline, and denial, they reap the rewards of their journey: a bank account; a new suit of clothes; a house in the suburbs; a college degree; an Oldsmobile Cutlass; a partnership in a thriving retail business; a son as class valedictorian, despite the fact that their parents were illiterate.

But the lives of the two generations of women examined in this book reveal a more textured and ambivalent history. It is true that if one were to scrutinize particular family biographies over generations, many would show a significant transformation in material conditions. A considerable number of Americans whose families migrated at the turn of the century today enjoy the benefits of better housing, access to jobs or professions that were inaccessible to their grandparents, and the ability to purchase a growing number of mass-produced consumer goods and services. The children of immigrants have also found a degree of acceptance that has generally been greater than what their parents experienced in their native lands. The opportunities for women also changed. In twentieth-century America, many women found a kind of independent identity that would have seemed unimaginable in the Old World. If the cliche of the "modern woman" of today is defined more and more by work and career in a public sphere, the cliches that surrounded immigrant women at the turn of the century were home-bound and family-centered.

Yet analyzing these developments simply as milestones of "progress" conceals important historical questions. What were the human costs of these changes? Is the new-found independence of women solely emancipatory? Can the evolution of a consumer/industrial society be understood as the unequivocal advancement of material conditions? At the heart of these questions lies an analysis of the way in which American society has tended to characterize the "rising standard of living." In common parlance "standard of living" is usually measured by the extent to which a given society has made available the particular goods and services associated with a middle-class lifestyle. Thus the move from self-sufficiency to daily involvement in the confusions of a money economy becomes a mark of progress. Similarly, the growing link between personal identity and external appearances is also seen as part of the "rise."

What we confront in the standard-of-living argument is a very strange mix. On the one hand it claims that there is an objective standard for measuring the quality of life; yet it uses a highly politicized and one-dimensional vision of modernity which fails to consider the social, familial, individual, and spiritual implications of modern industrial culture. Among the "life quality" issues that are surely part of any "standard" and yet are ignored by this perspective are family solidarity, networks of care among women, instincts of sharing and generosity, bonds of mutual interest. Instead we confront a self-selected frame of reference which reinforces the consumerized value system and the definition of success based on valuing aggressive individualism, accumulation, mobility, and assimilation. But twentieth-century American society is not merely about more things for more people; it is also about the elaboration of a fundamentally new fabric of existence.

The lives of first- and second-generation immigrant women at the turn of the century were deeply affected by this process. Pulled from the isolated hill towns of the *mezzogiorno* or the shtetls and ghettos of Eastern Europe, they were deposited in a world that was undergoing the turbulent eruptions of mass production, consumption, and the teeming metropolis. They stepped off the boat into a world where the most basic elements of daily life, from cooking to child-rearing, from courtship to community life, were part of a rapidly changing, unfamiliar, and market-dominated mode of existence. They could take nothing for granted. New industries called for their labor. New goods and images claimed their wages and their imaginations. A new culture demanded their attention.

Some of the know-how and traditions that they brought from the old country helped them meet the challenge. A sense of family and community provided a system of mutual protection against the dangers and deprivations that were an intrinsic part of tenement life. The old culture provided a cement which held people together. Yet aspects of the New World intruded, eroding the mortar. New voices were heard within the home. Social workers, missionaries from a Protestant American elite incessantly preached the *correct, American* way of doing things. Within the family circle, young children became emissaries from a new culture which vied for their loyalty: school, the streets, sweatshops, movies, the allure of city lights. The history of these women, then, as mothers and as daughters, reveals a crazy-quilt of custom and assimilation, of resistance and complicity, of understanding and confusion.

In the period this book covers, therefore, the lives of immigrant women were torn between traditional affections and the promise of modernity. Daily life became a theater of cultural conflict. Work, family, shopping, personal appearance, and amusement were all in dispute. Social workers and other agents of assimilation aimed much of their assault at those aspects of life which were the customary provinces of women. The household, and particularly the mother, was seen as the linchpin holding an anachronistic way of life together. How to wash dishes, how to bathe the baby, how to decorate the home, what to eat—all these and other arenas became contests between custom and progress, barbarism and civilization.

The emerging consumer culture celebrated itself as the embodiment of forward motion. Against this claim, European culture was depicted as a backward and disposable remnant of the past. The message carried to the immigrants was that their cultural traditions must be given up if they were to enter the present. In a mass-production world, the making of people was as important as the making of goods. Home production gave way to factory production, and the rootedness of family was consumed by mobile individualism.

This crusade for modernization, which marks the particular period this book addresses, was also an earmark of twentieth-century American culture in its relationship to the rest of the world. From the time of the Spanish-American War, the United States enunciated a global mission—in the name of "international responsibility"—to remake the world in its own image. This included the new immigrants, but pointed outward as well. An aggressive approach to "cultural modernization," at home and abroad, was marketed as progress. In all cases, the asking-price of "development" was the obliteration of the traditional fabric of daily life.

Yet the campaign of the modernizers could not be accomplished overnight. Social and economic circumstances curtailed the ability of the consumer culture to make good on its promises. The hard economic realities of urban working-class life demanded that immigrant families and communities retain their bonds of obligation and care. While the cultural dispatches from the consumer society lured the immigrants with promises of bounty and independence, the hardships of everyday life taught another lesson—and mothers were its primary teachers. Drawing upon all the weapons at their disposal, and resisting the endless demands for change, immigrant mothers used their power in family and community to protect family life and to preserve those features of tradition that were essential to survival. If the new culture preached independence, mobility, and modernity, the economic context conspired with strong Old World custom to forge an urban ethnic working-class culture that sustained family, community, and organization over time.

By the mid-1920s the influx of "new" immigrants had been halted by law and what had appeared to be an endless infusion of people came to an end. For these new Americans, the 1920s and 1930s were a period of see-sawing between old patterns of working-class cohesion and new forces of dispersal. In New York City a period of post-World War I economic prosperity gave rise to a construction boom in the outer boroughs, and an intricate web of subways, ferries, and bridges. A new migration began, out of the close quarters of the Lower East Side and into Brooklyn, the Bronx, and later, Queens. Among those immigrants who had become successful in businesses of their own, many were drawn to the newly developed Upper West Side of Manhattan.

Economic growth also fueled the further development of the consumer culture. Along with new neighborhoods, automobiles, household appliances, and radios became fixtures of immigrant working-class life. As these altered the customary terms of existence, sociologists, journalists, and others spoke increasingly of a national "generation gap." Clothing, cosmetics, automobiles, and the movies all became arenas of contestation between mothers schooled by the old culture and daughters of the New World.

The depression of the 1930s put a temporary cramp in these strides, and economic necessity rekindled the importance of family and community connections. The labor movement, which had been largely suppressed during the 1920s, reawakened. This revitalized political and cultural radicalism posed alternatives to the individualism of the consumer culture.

By the end of World War II, however, the consumer culture was back on track. A plethora of consumer goods was pouring out of America's born-again industries. These products, along with the related development of the suburbs and of an individualistic automotive culture, constituted a new ideal of citizenship. The children and grandchildren of the immigrants joined the ranks of the American middle class. Patriotism, freedom, and consumption became interchangeable ideas, continually reinforced through the magic of television. And as the immigrants of the turn of the century left their history behind, new populations replaced them at society's bottom: blacks from the rural south, peasants from Puerto Rico. For these people the cycle of urban poverty began again.

Meanwhile, second-generation Americans, many by now living in the suburbs, were becoming part of a milieu of economic and political conformity. Successful adoption of the suburban consumer ideal meant hiding all traces of one's roots. All telltale signs of the old way were smothered. Nuclear ideals of family life—working father, housewife mother, and dependent children—became signs of belonging. Those left over from the old culture, the parents, were seen as hopeless anachronisms.

Ironically, the conditions of women became more, not less, stultified and stultifying. While the early promise of the consumer culture had been to liberate women from the insularity of the home—to make them "new, independent women"—by the 1950s this promise had been dramatically broken. If women at the turn of the century found themselves actively engaged in a public world of life and labor, women of the 1950s were expected to return home. There they sat, in quiet desperation, not even expected to carry out the intricate homecrafts of their foremothers.

Compared with the home activities of early immigrant mothers, the life of the suburban woman lacked a clear sense of purpose. Women were trapped again, trapped by marriage, by new middle-class lifestyles, drifting amid the burdens of assimilation. The Italian and Jewish housewives of the 1950s had considerably less power in the home than did their mothers or grandmothers whose world they had escaped. Economically dependent, secluded in suburban tracts, servants to their husbands, infantalized by the demands of a child-centered world, they became what Mary Simkhovitch had disparagingly termed "middle-class wives." As it turned out, it was *their* daughters—beginning in the 1960s—who rediscovered the dream of women's liberation.

The fact that women rediscovered struggle in the 1960s and 1970s provides an ironic link to a past that had ostensibly been laid to rest. Many years before, it had been their mothers or grandmothers who fought to move beyond the legacy of the home. With strikes and trade union activity, boycotts and food riots, rent protests and demonstrations, these women had begun to lay out a vision of society in which the freedom of women and the commitment to social responsibility were joined. They saw intimate connections between the world of work and the world of the home, and launched their struggle in both workplace and community. In so doing they began to lay out an alternative view of what it might mean to be an American. For them, freedom *from* the past was not enough. The freedom to take control of one's life, at home or in the marketplace, was at issue. This is their legacy. This is our task.

NOTES

PREFACE

1. For the standard interpretation, see Marcus Lee Hansen, *The Immigrant in America* (New York, 1948); Lloyd Warner and Leo Srole, *The Social System of American Ethnic Groups: Yankee City* (New York, 1946); Oscar Handlin, *The Uprooted* (Boston, 1971); Humbert S. Nelli, *Italians in Chicago, 1880–1930: A Study in Ethnic Mobility* (New York, 1970). For the new approach, see Virginia Yans McLoughlin, *Family and Community: Italian Immigrants to Buffalo, 1880–1930* (Ithaca, 1978); Josef Barton, *Peasants and Strangers: Italians, Rumanians and Slovaks in an American City, 1890–1950* (Cambridge, 1975); John Briggs, *An Italian Passage: Immigrants to Three American Cities, 1890–1930* (New Haven, 1977–78); Thomas Kessner, *The Golden Door: Italian and Jewish Immigrant Mobility in New York City* (New York, 1977). For an excellent critique of the literature, see Laura Schwartz, "Immigrant Voices, From Work, Family and Community," Ph.D. diss., SUNY/Stony Brook, 1983.
2. See Yans-McLoughlin, *Family and Community;* Carolyn Golab, *Immigrant Destinations* (Philadelphia, 1977); Tamara Hareven, *Amoskeag: Life and Work in an American Factory City* (New York, 1980). For a more feminist approach see the pathbreaking study of European women, Louise A. Tilley and Joan W. Scott, *Women, Work, and Family* (New York, 1978); Miriam Cohen, "From Workshop to Office: Italian Women and Family Strategies in New York City, 1900–1950," Ph.D. diss., University of Michigan, 1978; Judith Smith, "Remaking Their Lives: Italian and Jewish Immigrant Family, Work and Community in Providence, Rhode Island, 1900–1940," Ph.D. diss., Brown University, 1981; Schwartz, "Immigrant Voices." Although Irving Howe's *World of Our Fathers* (New York, 1976) has been correctly criticized for its obvious male bias, it still contains a great deal of material on daily life that is missing from other studies of immigration. See also Charlotte Baum, Paula Hyman, and Sonya Michel, *The Jewish Woman in America* (New York, 1976); Betty Boyd Caroli, Robert Harney, Lydia Tomasi, eds., *The Italian Immigrant Woman in North America* (Toronto, 1978).
3. Mary Kingsbury Simkhovitch, *Neighborhood* (New York, 1938), p. 138.

1. A TALE OF TWO CITIES

1. Maria Ganz, *Rebels: Into Anarchy and Out Again* (New York, 1920), pp. 20–25.
2. Thomas Kessner, *The Golden Door: Italian and Jewish Immigrant Mobility in New York City* (New York, 1977), p. 17; Phillip Taylor, *The Distant Magnet* (New York, 1971), pp. 192–96.

3. Lillian Wald, *The House on Henry Street* (1915; reprint ed., New York, 1971), pp. 2–3.
4. Sheila Rothman, *Women's Proper Place: A History of Changing Ideas and Practices, 1970 to the Present* (New York, 1978), pp. 16–21; Susan Strasser, *Never Done: A History of American Housework* (New York, 1982), pp. 6–10. *Never Done* is a comprehensive study of these changes. See also Siegfriend Giedion, *Mechanization Takes Command* (New York, 1948), Part VI.
5. Susan Porter Benson, "Palaces of Consumption and Machines for Selling: The American Department Store, 1880–1940," *Radical History Review*, Fall 1979, pp. 199–221; Lewis Erenberg, *Stepping Out: New York Nightlife and the Transformation of American Culture, 1890–1930* (Westport, Conn., 1981), pp. 31–59; Stuart and Elizabeth Ewen, *Channels of Desire: Mass Images and the Shaping of American Consciousness* (New York, 1982), pp. 68–71.
6. Ellen Richardson, *The Woman Who Spends* (Boston, 1913), pp. 34–35. See also Joseph Lee, "The Integrity of Family Life," *Survey* 19 (1909): 306; Talcot Williams, "The Full Stature of the Public Schools," *Charities and the Commons* 12 (1904): 573. *Charities and the Commons* was the precursor of *Survey*, the main journal of social work. For a discussion of the change from *Charities and the Commons* to *Survey*, see Clark Chambers, *Paul U. Kellogg and the Survey* (Minneapolis, 1971), pp. 35–46.
7. In oral interviews, Italians continually referred to the United States as the land of "sweet money," a common vernacular for America in Italy.
8. See Erenberg, *Stepping Out*, parts 2 and 3. See also John Kouwenhoven, *The Columbia Historical Portrait of New York* (New York, 1953), and Grace Meyer, *Once Upon a City* (New York, 1958), for a photographic rendering of these themes.
9. Robert Haig and Roswell Morea, *Regional Survey of New York and Its Environs*, vol. 1 (New York, 1927), p. 36. For an excellent critique of the regional survey see Robert Fitch, "Planning New York," in *The Fiscal Crisis of American Cities*, ed. Roger Alcoy and David Mermelstein (New York, 1977), pp. 246–84.
10. Louise Odencrantz, *Italian Women in Industry* (New York, 1919), p. 38. See also Alice Kessler Harris, "Organizing the Unorganizable: Three Jewish Women and Their Union," *Labor History* 17 (1976): 6; Melvin Dubovsky, *When Workers Organize: New York City in the Progressive Era* (Amherst, 1968), pp. 73ff.
11. Quoted in Joel Seidman, *The Needle Trades* (New York, 1942), p. 37.
12. Isaac Hourwich, *Immigration and Labor* (New York, 1912), p. 235.
13. "Keeping in Style," *New York Tribune*, 3 July 1898; reprinted in Allon Schoener, ed., *Portal to America: The Lower East Side 1870–1925* (New York, 1967), p. 120.
14. Ibid., p. 121.
15. Kessner, *The Golden Door*, p. 134.
16. This situation was the basis of the Save New York Movement, an organization of wealthy retail merchants, financiers, and Wall Street brokers who wanted to rid the downtown area of the "blight of manufacturing." See Albert Ashforth, "Fighting to Save New York City's Retail Center from the Blight of the Manufacturers," *New York Times*, 4 February 1917. This long article, one of many, contained a "doctored" picture of lower Manhattan being overrun with hordes of workers, crowding out business. The picture, practically a full page, bore a remarkable resemblance to the opening scene of Charlie Chaplin's *Modern Times*, but the point of view is obviously different.
17. Viola Paradise, "The Jewish Girl in Chicago," *Survey* 30 (1913): 701.

2. IN THE OLD WORLD

1. It is obviously beyond the scope of this book to detail main differences of culture, work, and life that existed in southern Italy between the peasant hill towns, the fishing villages, and those peasant communities that existed near large cities; or to account for regional and cultural differences over such a vast area as the Jewish sections of Eastern Europe. Recent work in social history such as Josef Barton's *Peasants and Strangers: Italians, Rumanians, and Slovaks in An American City, 1890–1950* (Cambridge, Mass., 1975) makes clear the need to understand local chain migration patterns, but such detailed investigation, especially for women, is an area yet to be fully explored.

   On migration, see J. S. MacDonald, "Agricultural Organization, Migration and Labor Militancy to Rural Italy," *Economic History Review,* August 1963, pp. 68–70; Barton, *Peasants and Strangers,* pp. 30–35; Gino Speranza, "The Effects of Emigration in Italy," *Charities and the Commons* 12 (1904): 470.

2. Barton, *Peasants and Strangers,* p. 38; Leonard Covello, *The Social Background of the Italo-American School Child* (Totowa, N.J., 1972), p. 56; Phyllis Williams, *South Italian Folkways in Europe and America* (New Haven, Conn., 1938), pp. 4, 20.

3. Robert Foerster, *The Italian Emigration of Our Times* (Cambridge, Mass., 1924), p. 85; Virginia Yans-McLaughlin, *Family and Community: Italian Immigrants in Buffalo* (Ithaca, N.Y., 1977), pp. 182–83; Emiliana P. Noether, "The Silent Half: *Le Contadino del Sud* Before the First World War," in *The Italian Immigrant Woman in North America,* ed. Betty Boyd Caroli, Robert Harney, and Lydia Tomasi (Toronto, 1978), p. 7.

4. Williams, *South Italian Folkways,* p. 4.

5. Covello, *Social Background,* p. 263.

6. Ibid., p. 264.

7. Noether, "The Silent Half," p. 5; interview with Carmella Caruso (tapes 22, 23). Most of the oral interviews used in this book were done by the Oral History Project of the City University of New York, directed by Herbert Gutman and Virginia Yans. In accord with the release signed by those interviewed, real names have been deleted and fictitious ones substituted. The tapes are on file at the Tamiment Library at New York University, and are numbered. I have therefore used fictitious names and real tape numbers. I have used those interviews done between 1973 and 1976 with immigrant women who lived in the International Ladies' Garment Workers' Nursing Home and other retirement homes or private residences, or who were members of the Brooklyn chapter of the Italian organization Ciao. The age of those interviewed was between seventy and ninety; the ethnicity, primarily Italian and Jewish.

8. Williams, *South Italian Folkways,* pp. 16, 26.

9. Ibid., p. 73.

10. Covello, *Social Background,* 149. For a similar viewpoint on peasant families, see William I. Thomas and Florian Znaniecki, *The Polish Peasant in Europe and America,* vol. 1 (Boston, 1919), pp. 89–90. For a more detailed description of family relations, see Franc Sturino, "Family and Kin Cohesion Among South Italian Immigrants in Toronto," in *The Italian Immigrant Woman,* pp. 292–94.

11. Covello, *Social Background,* p. 235.

12. Ibid., p. 213. See also Noether, "The Silent Half," pp. 8–9.

13. Richard Gambino, *Blood of My Blood* (New York, 1974), p. 7; Williams, *South Italian Folkways,* pp. 76–77; Covello, *Social Background,* pp. 213–14.

14. Williams, *South Italian Folkways,* p. 60.

15. Gambino, *Blood of My Blood*, pp. 198–99; Covello, *Social Background*, p. 203.
16. Covello, *Social Background*, p. 179.
17. Thomas and Znanieki, *The Polish Peasant*, p. 181.
18. Covello, *Social Background*, p. 121.
19. Ibid., p. 127.
20. Moses Rischin, *The Promised City* (Cambridge, Mass., 1942), p. 26.
21. Diane K. Roskies and David G. Roskies, *The Shtetl Book* (New York, 1975), p. 25.
22. Jack Kugelmass and Jonathan Boyarin, *From a Ruined Garden* (New York, 1983), p. 30. Both Roskies and Roskies, *The Shtetl Book*, and Kugelmass and Boyarin, *From a Ruined Garden*, are collections of translated documents, referred to here by page number. The reader is encouraged to read these books in their entirety; they show the rich texture of Eastern European Jewish life.
23. Irving Howe, *World of Our Fathers* (New York, 1976), pp. 13–14.
24. Barbara Myerhoff, *Number Our Days* (New York, 1978), p. 245.
25. Roskies and Roskies, *The Shtetl Book*, p. 121.
26. Ibid., p. 105.
27. Ibid., pp. 123–24.
28. Roskies and Roskies, *The Shtetl Book*, p. 73.
29. Kugelmass and Boyarin, *From a Ruined Garden*, p. 79.
30. Sydelle Kramer and Jenny Masur, *Jewish Grandmothers* (Boston, 1976), p. 21.
31. Anuta Shurrow in ibid., p. 77; "Skutsim" from ibid., p. 32.
32. Quoted in Myerhoff, *Number Our Days*, p. 235.
33. Ibid., pp. 234–35.
34. Kramer and Masur, *Jewish Grandmothers*, pp. 5–6.
35. Myerhoff, *Number Our Days*, p. 256.
36. Roskies and Roskies, *The Shtetl Book*, pp. 308–9.
37. Gitl in ibid., p. 309; Sarah Rothman in Kramer and Masur, *Jewish Grandmothers*, p. 20.
38. Kramer and Masur, *Jewish Grandmothers*, p. 77.
39. Ibid., pp. 4–7.
40. Ibid., pp. 80–81.
41. Roskies and Roskies, *The Shtetl Book*, pp. 298–99.
42. Mark Zborowski and Elizabeth Herzog, *Life Is with People* (New York, 1952), p. 270.
43. Kugelmass and Boyarin, *From a Ruined Garden*, pp. 123–24.
44. Kramer and Masur, *Jewish Grandmothers*, p. 108.
45. Myerhoff, *Number Our Days*, p. 232.
46. Roskies and Roskies, *The Shtetl Book*, p. 237.
47. Kramer and Masur, *Jewish Grandmothers*, p. 6.
48. Zborowski and Herzog, *Life Is with People*, p. 262.
49. Ibid., p. 265.

3. STEERAGE TO GOTHAM

1. Silvano M. Tomasi, "The Ethnic Church and the Integration of Italian Immigrants in the United States," in *The Italian Experience in the United States*, ed. Silvano Tomasi and Madeline Engel (New York, 1970), p. 164. Tomasi is paraphrasing a 1911 Italian government report on conditions among the southern peasantry.

2. Quoted in Gino Speranza, "The Effects of Emigration on Italy," *Charities and the Commons* 12 (1904): 470.
3. Grazie Dore, "Some Social and Historical Aspects of Italian Emigration to America," in *The Italians: Social Backgrounds of an American Group,* ed. Francesco Cordasco and Eugene Buccioni (Clifton, N.J., 1974), p. 31.
4. Quoted in Tomasi, "The Ethnic Church," p. 164.
5. Quoted in Speranza, "The Effects of Emigration," p. 468.
6. Thomas Kessner, *The Golden Door: Italian and Jewish Immigration Mobility in New York City* (New York, 1977), pp. 28–30.
7. Interview with Agnes Santucci.
8. Interview with Rosina Giuliani's daughters Letitia Feltrinelli and Francesca Campanile (author's file).
9. Virginia Yans McLaughlin, *Family and Community: Italian Immigrants in Buffalo* (Ithaca, N.Y., 1977), p. 91. For an excellent discussion of this point, see also pp. 96–100, as well as G. E. Di Palma Castiglione, "Italian Immigration into the United States," *American Journal of Sociology* 2 (1905): 185.
10. Irving Howe, *World of Our Fathers* (New York, 1976); Samuel Joseph, *Jewish Immigration to the United States, 1881–1910)* (1914; reprint ed., New York, 1969), pp. 41–44.
11. Interview with Bessie Polski (tape 139); Carlotte Baum, Paula Hyman, and Sonia Michel, *The Jewish Woman in America* (New York, 1978), pp. 76–89; Sydelle Kramer and Jenny Masur, *Jewish Grandmothers* (Boston, 1976), p. 127.
12. Anzia Yezierska, *Hungry Hearts* (New York, 1920), pp. 115–19, 121, 122–24.
13. Kramer and Masur, *Jewish Grandmothers,* p. 7.
14. Howe, *World of Our Fathers,* p. 27.
15. Ibid.
16. Ibid.
17. Diane K. Roskies and David G. Roskies, *The Shtetl Book* (New York, 1975), p. 282.
18. Howe, *World of Our Fathers,* p. 26.
19. Yezierska, *Hungry Hearts,* pp. 254–55, 259.
20. Elizabeth Gurley Flynn, *Rebel Girl* (New York, 1955), p. 134.
21. Dore, "Social and Historical Aspects of Italian Emigration," p. 19.
22. Ibid., p. 19.
23. Quoted in Isaac Hourwich, *Immigration and Labor* (New York, 1912), p. 94.
24. Francesco Carase, "Nostalgia or Disenchantment: Considerations on Return Migration," in Tomasi and Engel, *The Italian Experience in the United States,* p. 233; Hourwich, *Immigration and Labor,* p. 96.

4. First Encounters

1. Maria Ganz, *Rebels: Into Anarchy and Out Again* (New York, 1920), p. 4.
2. Leonard Covello, *The Heart Is the Teacher* (New York, 1958), p. 19.
3. Anzia Yezierska, *Hungry Hearts* (New York, 1920), p. 264.
4. Ibid., p. 263.
5. Covello, *The Heart Is the Teacher,* p. 21.
6. Leonard Covello, *Social Background of the Italo-American School Child* (Totowa, N.J., 1972), p. 94.
7. Quoted in Elizabeth C. Watson, "Home Work in the Tenements," *Survey* 25 (1910): 772.

8. Interview with Anna Kuthan (tape on file but unnumbered).
9. Yezierska, *Hungry Hearts*, p. 264.
10. Covello, *Social Background*, p. 13.
11. John Berger, "Homegrown," *Village Voice*, 3 July 1984.
12. Jane Addams, *Twenty Years at Hull House* (1910; reprint ed., New York, 1961), pp. 110–11.
13. Rose Cohen, *Out of the Shadow* (New York, 1918), p. 246.
14. Simon Patten, *The New Basis of Civilization* (1907; reprint ed., Cambridge, 1968). For an intellectual biography of Simon Patten and his effect on the evolution of modern social work, especially those social workers allied to *Survey* magazine, see Daniel Fox, *Simon Patten: The Discovery of Abundance and the Transformation of Social Theory* (Boston, 1967).
15. Ganz, *Rebels*, p. 10.
16. Covello, *The Heart Is the Teacher*, p. 22.
17. Interview with Anna Kuthan.
18. Josephine Roche, "The Italian Girl," in Ruth S. True, *The Neglected Girl: West Side Studies*, vol. 2 (New York, 1914), p. 116.
19. Gino Speranza, "The Italians in Congested Districts," *Charities and the Commons* 20 (1908): 56.
20. David Blaustein, "Oppression and Freedom," *Charities and the Commons* 10 (1903): 339.
21. Louise Odencrantz, *Italian Women in Industry* (New York, 1919), p. 233.
22. Interview with Sophie Abrams (tape on file, unnumbered).
23. Viola Paradise, "The Jewish Girl in Chicago," *Survey* 30 (1913): 704.
24. Sophinisba Breckenridge, *New Homes for Old* (New York, 1921), p. 173.
25. Andria Taylor Hourwich and Gladys Palmer, eds., *I Am a Woman Worker* (1936; reprint ed., New York, 1974), pp. 22–23.
26. Ellen Richardson, *The Woman Who Spends* (Boston, 1913), pp. 77–78.
27. Jane Addams, *Democracy and Social Ethics* (1902; reprint ed., Boston, 1964), pp. 34–35.
28. Lillian Wald, *The House on Henry Street* (1915; reprint ed., New York, 1971), pp. 193–94.
29. "Keeping in Style," *New York Tribune*, 26 August 1900, reprinted in Allan Schoener, *Portal to America* (New York, 1967), p. 122.
30. Odencrantz, *Italian Women in Industry*, p. 233.
31. Covello, *The Heart Is the Teacher*, p. 22.
32. Interview with Anna Kuthan.
33. Paradise, "The Jewish Girl," p. 701.
34. Covello, *The Heart Is the Teacher*, p. 23.
35. Quoted in Robert Park and Herbert Miller, *Old World Traits Transplanted* (New York, 1921), pp. 63–64.
36. Covello, *The Heart Is the Teacher*, p. 25.
37. Lawrence Veiller, "New Ideas in Social Work: Posters and Tuberculosis," *Charities and the Commons* 20 (1908): 563–64.
38. Mary McDowell, "The Struggle in Family Life," *Charities and the Commons* 16 (1904): 196.
39. Israel Friedlander, "The Americanization of the Jewish Immigrant," *Survey* 38 (1917): 105.
40. Interview with Anna Kuthan.

5. AGENTS OF ASSIMILATION

1. Alan F. Davis, *Spearheads for Reform: The Social Settlements and the Progressive Movement, 1890–1914* (New York, 1967), pp. 26–37.
2. Margaret Byington, "The Normal Family," *The Annals of the American Academy of Political and Social Science* 88 (1918): 17; Jane Addams, *Democracy and Social Ethics* (1902; reprint ed., Boston, 1964), p. 18.
3. Addams, *Democracy and Social Ethics*, p. 74; see also pp. 84–85. For harrowing descriptions of late-nineteenth-century middle-class women trapped inside the home, see Charlotte Perkins Gilman, *The Yellow Wallpaper* (1892; reprint ed., Old Westbury, N.Y., 1973); and Kate Chopin, *The Awakening* (1904; reprint ed., New York, 1984).
4. Paul Boyers, *Urban Masses and Moral Order in America, 1820–1920* (Cambridge, 1978), pp. 150–51; Anzia Yezierska, *Hungry Hearts* (New York, 1920), p. 24.
5. Davis, *Spearheads for Reform*, p. 31.
6. Addams, *Democracy and Social Ethics*, p. 18.
7. Ibid., p. 38.
8. Lillian Wald, *The House on Henry Street* (1915; reprint ed., New York, 1971), pp. 7–8.
9. Mary Kingsbury Simkhovitch, *Neighborhood* (New York, 1938), pp. 60–61, 80–83, 86–87.
10. Wald, *The House on Henry Street*, p. 8.
11. Simkhovitch, *Neighborhood*, p. 92.
12. R. L. Duffus, *Lillian Wald: Neighbor and Crusader* (New York, 1938), pp. 71–73.
13. Quoted in *Survey* 28 (1912): 183.
14. Quoted in Duffus, *Lillian Wald*, p. 75.
15. Ibid.
16. Simkhovitch, *Neighborhood*, p. 151.
17. Wald, *The House on Henry Street*, p. 13.
18. Simkhovitch, *Neighborhood*, p. 93.
19. Ibid., p. 96.
20. Walter Weyl, cited in Robert Bremmer, *From the Depths: The Discovery of Poverty in the United States* (New York, 1955), p. 129.
21. Cecilia Razovski, "The Eternal Masculine," *Survey* 39 (1917): 117.
22. Byington, "The Normal Family," p. 18.
23. Edward Devine, "The Family," *Survey* 43 (1919): 396.
24. Eva White, "The Immigrant Family," *The Annals of the American Academy of Political and Social Science* 88 (1918): 728.
25. Addams, *Democracy and Social Ethics*, p. 20.
26. Wald, *The House on Henry Street*, pp. 17, 21.
27. Quoted in Sydelle Kramer and Jenny Masur, *Jewish Grandmothers* (Boston, 1976), p. 99.
28. S. Adolphus Knoph, "The Smaller Family," *Survey* 37 (1916): 161.
29. Simkhovitch, *Neighborhood*, p. 136; see also Addams, *Democracy and Social Ethics*, pp. 40–41.
30. Charles Bernheimer, "The Social Settlement and New York's Lower East Side," *Charities and the Commons* 20 (1908): 728.
31. David Blaustein, "Oppression and Freedom," *Charities and the Commons* 10 (1903): 339.
32. Walter Weyl, "The Deserter," *Survey* 27 (1911): 396.
33. Covello, *The Heart Is the Teacher* (New York, 1958), p. 33.

34. Cited in Richard N. Juliani, "The Settlement House and the Italian Family," in *The Italian Immigrant Woman in North America*, ed. Betty Boyd Caroli, Robert Harvey, and Lydia Tomasi (Toronto, 1978), p. 119.
35. Quoted in Duffus, *Lillian Wald*, p. 75.
36. Simkhovitch, *Neighborhood*, p. 136.
37. Razovski, "The Eternal Masculine," p. 117.
38. Wald, *The House on Henry Street*, p. 201.
39. Ibid., pp. 202–3.
40. Simkhovitch, *Neighborhood*, p. 63.
41. Wald, *The House on Henry Street*, p. 189.

6. Our Daily Bread

1. Interview with Grace Grimaldi (tapes 25, 26).
2. "Americanization and the Italian Colony," *Survey* 45 (1920): 277.
3. "Language and Home Links," *Survey* 45 (1920): 20.
4. Lillian Brandt, "In Behalf of the Overcrowded and the Apathy That Arises from It," *Charities and the Commons* 12 (1904): 503.
5. Mary Kingsbury Simkhovitch, *The City Worker's World* (New York, 1917), pp. 73–74.
6. Ibid., pp. 79–80.
7. Jane Addams, *Democracy and Social Ethics* (1902; reprint ed., Boston, 1964).
8. Katharine Anthony, "Mothers Who Must Earn," *West Side Studies*, vol. 1 (New York, 1914), p. 45.
9. Ibid.
10. Ibid.
11. Edna LoZebnik, *Such a Life* (New York, 1978), p. 13; Leonard Covello, *Social Background of the Italo-American School Child* (Totowa, N.J., 1972), p. 304; Sydelle Kramer and Jenny Masur, *Jewish Grandmothers* (Boston, 1976), p. 155.
12. Josephine Roche, "The Italian Girl," in Ruth S. True, "The Neglected Girl," *West Side Studies*, vol. 2 (New York, 1914), pp. 105–6, 114.
13. Interview with Yetta Adelman (tapes 3, 4); interview with Grace Grimaldi.
14. Interview with Judith Weissman (tapes 135–137).
15. Roche, "The Italian Girl," p. 109.
16. Interview with Lenore Kosloff (tapes 116, 117).
17. Elizabeth Dutcher, "Budgets of the Triangle Fire Victims," *Life and Labor*, September 1912, p. 267.
18. Interview with Fabbia Orzo.
19. Interview with Jennie Matyras, in *Women in the American Economy: A Documentary History, 1675 to 1929*, ed. Elliot Brownlee and Mary Brownlee (New Haven, 1976), pp. 229–30.
20. Sophinisba Breckenridge, *New Homes for Old* (New York, 1921), p. 50.
21. Thomas Kessner, *The Golden Door: Italian and Jewish Immigrant Mobility in New York City* (New York, 1977), pp. 75–77. Kessner, from his census study, found that in 1905, only 6 percent of Italian married women and 1 percent of Jewish married women worked at paid labor outside the home. Oral history and contemporary sources confirm this observation, although economic circumstances compelled some women to seek outside employment.
22. Mario Puzo, *The Fortunate Pilgrim* (New York, 1964), p. 83.
23. Louise Bolard More, *Wage Earners' Budgets: A Study of Standards and Costs of Living in New York City* (New York, 1907), p. 28.

24. Robert Chapin, *The Standard of Living Among Workingmen's Families in New York City* (New York, 1901), p. 22.
25. Simkhovitch, *The City Worker's World*, p. 102.
26. More, *Wage Earners' Budgets*, p. 28.
27. Louise Odencrantz, *Italian Women in Industry* (New York, 1919), p. 176; Anthony, "Mothers Who Must Earn," p. 6.
28. Interview with Anna Kuthan.
29. Anthony, "Mothers Who Must Earn," p. 36.
30. Ibid.
31. Interview with Fabbia Orzo (tapes 10, 11).
32. More, *Wage Earners' Budgets*, p. 12.
33. Ibid., p. 87.
34. Interview with Amalia Morandi (tape 38); Mollie Linker quoted in Kramer and Masur, *Jewish Grandmothers*, p. 96.
35. Interview with Yetta Adelman.
36. Interview with Agnes Santucci (tapes 39, 40).
37. Addams, *Democracy and Social Ethics*, p. 46.
38. Roche, "The Italian Girl," p. 109.
39. Charlotte Baum, Paula Hyman, and Sonia Michel, *The Jewish Woman in America* (New York, 1978), p. 127; Irving Howe, *World of Our Fathers* (New York, 1976), pp. 256–71. Compare Howe's account of the play of young boys, pp. 256–64, with the play of young girls, pp. 265–71. Howe sums up the difference: "Jewish boys faced the problem of how to define their lives with relation to Jewish origins and the American environment, but Jewish girls faced the problem of whether they were going to be allowed to define their lives at all" (p. 267).
40. Odencrantz, *Italian Women in Industry*, p. 176.
41. Roche, "The Italian Girl," p. 111.
42. Abraham Bisno, *Union Pioneer* (Madison, 1967), p. 212; emphasis added.
43. Breckenridge, *New Homes for Old*, p. 170.
44. Anthony, "Mothers Who Must Earn," p. 45.
45. Phyllis Williams, *South Italian Folkways in Europe and America* (New Haven, Conn., 1938), p. 36.
46. Roche, "The Italian Girl," p. 112.
47. Interview with Sophie Abrams.
48. Interview with Becky Brier (tape 108).
49. Interview with Judith Weissman.
50. Interview with Fania Horvitz (tapes 110, 111).
51. Quoted in Kramer and Masur, *Jewish Grandmothers*, p. 98.

7. How Many Tears This America Costs

1. Louise Boland More, *Wage Earners' Budgets: A Study of Standards and Costs of Living in New York City* (New York, 1907), p. 6. See also pp. 16–21 for an income breakdown of 200 New York City working-class families. Although income varies from a low of $200 a year to a high of $1,000, the average yearly income falls between $500 and $700. See also Robert Chapin, *The Standard of Living Among Workingmen's Families in New York City* (New York, 1970), pp. 61–63; his figures concur with those of More.
2. Isaac Hourwich, *Immigration and Labor* (New York, 1916), p. 268.
3. Cited in ibid., p. 271.

4. Frank M. White, "How the United States Fosters the Black Hand," *Outlook* (1909); reprinted in *A Documentary History of the Italian Americans*, ed. Wayne Moquin, Charles Van Doren, and Frances Ianni (New York, 1974).
5. Mark Zborowski and Elizabeth Herzog, *Life Is with People* (New York, 1962), p. 261.
6. Antonio Mangano, *Sons of Italy* (New York, 1917), p. 23. See also Antonio Stella, "Tuberculosis and the Italians in the United States," *Charities and the Commons* 12 (1904): 486–89.
7. Grazie Dore, "Some Social and Historical Aspects of Italian Emigration to America," in *The Italians: Social Backgrounds of an American Group*, ed. Francesca Cordasco and Eugene Buccioni (Clifton, N.J., 1974), p. 31.
8. Hourwich, *Immigration and Labor*, p. 272. For the official view on sending back money and the mercantilist prejudice, see W. Jett Lauck and J. Jenks, *The Immigrant Problem: A Study of American Immigrant Conditions and Needs* (New York, 1911), p. 16. Jeremiah Jenks was the chief researcher for the influential government-sponsored study of the new immigration called the Dillingham Commission, *Report on Immigration* (1911), whose forty-five volumes provided a racial interpretation of the new immigration, replete with statistical "proof." Lauck and Jenks's book was an attempt to distill the findings of the commission report and serve as the official viewpoint on the new immigration. Isaac Hourwich's *Immigration and Labor*, on the other hand, was intended as a historical refutation of the arguments presented in the report. See also Oscar Handlin, *Race and Nationality in American Life* (New York, 1950), pp. 57–135, for an analysis of the racism implicit in the commission report.
9. More, *Wage Earners' Budgets*, p. 104.
10. Moses Rischin, *The Promised City* (Cambridge, 1942), p. 105; Irving Howe, *World of Our Fathers* (New York, 1976), pp. 183–84. See also Arthur Gorin, *New York Jews and the Quest for Community—The Kehillah Experiment, 1908–1922* (New York, 1970).
11. Chapin, *The Standard of Living*, p. 193.
12. More, *Wage Earners' Budgets*, pp. 42–43; Paul Starr, *The Social Transformation of American Medicine* (New York, 1982), p. 207.
13. Hutchins Hapgood, *The Spirit of the Ghetto* (New York, 1902), p. 13.
14. Rose Cohen, *Out of the Shadow* (New York, 1918), p. 196.
15. More, *Wage Earners' Budgets*, p. 42.
16. Ibid., p. 43.
17. Ibid.
18. Josephine Roche, "The Italian Girl," in Ruth S. True, *The Neglected Girl: West Side Studies*, vol. 2 (New York, 1914), p. 107. For an analysis of Italian communal forms that, although particularly in reference to Chicago, suggests that Italians made greater use of local institutions than the literature indicates, see Rudolph Vecoli, "Contadini in Chicago: A Critique of the Uprooted," *Journal of American History* 54 (December 1964): 404–17; see also idem, "Italian American Workers, 1880–1920: Padrone Slaves or Primitive Rebels," in *Perspectives in Italian Immigration and Ethnicity*, ed. S. M. Tomasi (New York, 1977), pp. 25–50.
19. Louise Odencrantz, *Italian Women in Industry* (New York, 1919), p. 208.
20. Elizabeth Gurley Flynn, *Rebel Girl* (New York, 1955), p. 133.
21. Cohen, *Out of the Shadow*, p. 73.
22. Robert Park and Herbert Miller, *Old World Traits Transplanted* (New York, 1919), p. 11.
23. Phyllis Williams, *South Italian Folkways in Europe and America* (New Haven, Conn., 1938), p. 49.

24. More, *Wage Earners' Budgets*, p. 33.
25. Ibid.
26. Anzia Yezierska, *Breadgivers* (1925; reprint ed., New York, 1977). See Alice Kessler-Harris's introduction to the reprint of *Breadgivers* for an excellent essay on Anzia Yezierska's life and the problems she faced both as an immigrant writer and as a woman. Compare Kessler-Harris's analysis of Yezierska with the less sympathetic treatment given her in Howe, *World of Our Fathers*, pp. 268–70.
27. Ibid., p. 27.
28. Anzia Yezierska, *Hungry Hearts* (New York, 1920), pp. 67, 68, 73, 82, 84, 93.
29. Maria Ganz, *Rebels: Into Anarchy and Out Again* (New York, 1970), pp. 77–78.
30. Ibid.
31. Mike Gold, *Jews Without Money* (New York, 1930), p. 94.
32. Hourwich, *Immigration and Labor*, p. 251; Tamara Haraven and John Modell, "Urbanization and the Malleable Household: An Examination of Boarding and Lodging in American Families," in Tamara Haraven, *Family and Kin in Urban Communities, 1700–1930* (New York, 1977), p. 166. Reformers in the housing movement, especially Lawrence Veiller, saw immigrant boarding practices as spurring the breakdown of the family and encouraging sexual immorality (Lawrence Veiller, "Room Overcrowding and the Lodger Evil," in *Housing in America: Proceedings of the Second Annual National Conference on Housing* [Philadelphia, 1912], pp. 60–63).
33. E. A. Goldenweisser, "Immigrants in Cities," *Survey* 19 (1908): 1050.
34. More, *Wage Earners' Budgets*, p. 58.
35. Chapin, *The Standard of Living*, p. 83; Hourwich, *Immigration and Labor*, pp. 251–53.
36. Sophinisba Breckenridge, *New Homes for Old* (New York, 1921), p. 25.
37. Odencrantz, *Italian Women in Industry*, p. 224.
38. Interview with Evelyn Vogelman (tape 41).
39. Interview with Judith Weissman.
40. Odencrantz, *Italian Women in Industry*, pp. 224–25.
41. Ganz, *Rebels*, pp. 41, 48, 49.
42. New York State Bureau of Labor Statistics, *Annual Report* (New York, 1902), p. 46. John R. Commons authored the section on homework practices in the garment industry.
43. Elizabeth Watson, "Home Work in the Tenements," *Survey* 32 (1914): 774.
44. New York State Bureau of Labor Statistics, *Annual Report*, p. 78. Commons argued that Jewish women had been employed in homework in the 1880s and 1890s but that by 1902 homework and finishing were largely done by Italian women. This statement was verified by various social workers' field research; see Mary Van Kleeck, "Child Labor in the Tenements," *Survey* 19 (1908): 1406–13.
45. Ibid., p. 78.
46. Thomas Kessner, *The Golden Door: Italian and Jewish Immigrant Mobility in New York City* (New York, 1977), pp. 71–75; Robert Foerster, *The Italian Emigration of Our Times* (Cambridge, 1924), p. 347; Mabel Hurt Willet, *The Employment of Women in the Clothing Trade* (New York, 1902), p. 38; Mary Van Kleeck, *Artificial Flower Makers* (New York, 1913), pp. 91–97.
47. Van Kleeck, "Child Labor in the Tenements," p. 1407.
48. Ibid., p. 1408.
49. Lawrence Veiller, "To Restrict Work in the Tenements," *Charities and the Commons* 12 (1904): 529.
50. Van Kleeck, "Child Labor in the Tenements," p. 1410.
51. New York State Bureau of Labor Statistics, *Annual Report*, p. 77.
52. Van Kleeck, "Child Labor in the Tenements," p. 1410.

53. Christina Merriman, "Searchlight Turned on Child Labor and the Tailoring Trade," *Survey* 32 (1914): 304.
54. *Survey* 26 (1911): 69.
55. Annie Daniels, "The Wreck of the Home," *Charities and the Commons* 14 (1905): 1096.
56. Interview with Fabbia Orzo.
57. Odencrantz, *Italian Women in Industry,* pp. 180–83; *Survey* 19 (1908): 780.
58. Van Kleeck, "Child Labor in the Tenements," p. 1413.
59. *Survey* 27 (1911): 1775; *Survey* 25 (1910): 776.
60. Merriman, "Searchlight Turned on Child Labor," p. 303.
61. Jane Robbins, "The Bohemian Women of New York," *Charities and the Commons* 13 (1905): 194–95
62. Charles Bernheimer, "High Rent on New York's Lower East Side," *Charities and the Commons* 19 (1907): 1403–40.
63. Gold, *Jews Without Money,* pp. 179–80.
64. "The Rent Strike Grows," *Charities and the Commons* 19 (1907): 1379.
65. Ibid.
66. *New York Times,* 20 December 1907, p. 16.
67. *Survey* 42 (1919): 675. I am indebted to Daphne Kis of Yivo for showing me her unpublished manuscript "The Political Role of Women in the Community, 1900–1916."
68. Mario Puzo, *The Fortunate Pilgrim* (New York, 1964), p. 10.

8. IN SICKNESS AND IN HEALTH

1. "Large Immigrant Population Conference on Infant Mortality," *Survey* 27 (1911): 876. See also Leonard Covello, *The Social Background of the Italo-American School Child* (Totowa, N.J., 1972), p. 95. Phyllis Williams described one midwife's shop in a southern Italian village that displayed a sign, the symbol of an egg, as an occupational designation (*South Italian Folkways in Europe and America* [New Haven, Conn., 1958], pp. 87–88; Mark Zborowski and Elizabeth Herzog, *Life Is with People* (New York, 1952), pp. 313–16. It is interesting that in both Italian and Jewish culture the midwife stood in a "spiritual relationship" to the family and children she delivered.
2. Covello, *Social Background,* p. 876.
3. F. Elizabeth Croswell, "The Midwives of New York," *Charities and the Commons* 17 (1907): 667.
4. Ibid.
5. Elsa Herzfeld, "Superstitions and Customs of Tenement Women," *Charities and the Commons* 14 (1905): 984; both Williams and Zborowski and Herzog confirm that men were forbidden to attend a birth in Italian and Jewish culture.
6. Ibid.
7. Interview with Andriana Valenti (tapes 30, 31).
8. Croswell, "The Midwives of New York," p. 669.
9. Interview with Adriana Valenti.
10. Croswell, "The Midwives of New York," p. 668.
11. Interview with Adriana Valenti.
12. Interview with Letitia Serpe.
13. Croswell, "The Midwives of New York," pp. 667–68.
14. Ibid., p. 668; see also *Survey* 27 (1911): 671.
15. Emma Goldman, *Living My Life* (New York, 1913), vol. 1, p. 186.

16. Margaret Sanger, *Autobiography* (New York, 1938), pp. 80–83.
17. Interview with Adriana Valenti.
18. Thomas Kessner, *The Golden Door: Italian and Jewish Immigrant Mobility in New York City* (New York, 1972), p. 132.
19. Goldman, *Living My Life*, p. 185.
20. Ibid., p. 186.
21. Sanger, *Autobiography*, pp. 218–19.
22. Linda Gordon, *Women's Body, Women's Right: A Social History of Birth Control in America* (New York, 1976), p. 232. See the chapter entitled "Birth Control and Social Revolution," pp. 186–248, for an analysis of the birth control movement between 1900 and 1920.
23. Lillian Wald, *The House on Henry Street* (1915; reprint ed., New York, 1971), pp. 59–60.
24. Ibid.
25. Mary Boyd, "The Store of Dammerschalf," *Survey* 32 (1914): 129. See also Adrienne Rich, *Of Woman Born: Motherhood as Experience and Institution* (New York, 1976), pp. 126–85; Barbara Ehrenreich and Deirdre English, *For Her Own Good* (New York, 1977), pp. 84–88.
26. Goldman, *Living My Life*, p. 185.
27. Interview with Adriana Valenti.
28. Ignas Bernstein, *Yiddish Sayings*, trans. M. S. Zuckerman and G. Weltman (Van Nuys, Calif., 1975), p. 38.
29. Herzfeld, "Superstitions and Customs of Tenement Women," p. 985.
30. Mrs. Max West, *Infant Care*, Care of Children Series, Children's Bureau Publication No. 8 (Washington, D.C., 1914); reprinted in *Child Rearing Literature of Twentieth-Century America*, ed. David Rothman and Sheila Rothman (New York, 1972), p. 36. See also Ehrenreich and English, *For Her Own Good*, p. 182.
31. "How to Save Babies in the Tenements," *Charities and the Commons* 14 (1905): 979.
32. "The Mothers and the Baby: New York Milk Commission," *Survey* 23 (1909): 623.
33. John Spargo, "Common Sense of the Milk Question," *Charities and the Commons* (1908): 595.
34. Wald, *The House on Henry Street*, p. 57.
35. "The Mothers and the Baby," p. 623.
36. Spargo, "Common Sense of the Milk Question," p. 595.
37. "The Mothers and the Baby," p. 624.
38. West, *Infant Care*, p. 61.
39. In Anzia Yezierska, *Hungry Hearts* (New York, 1920), pp. 98–99.
40. Enrico Sartorio, *Social and Religious Life of Italians in America* (Boston, 1918), p. 58.
41. In Yezierska, *Hungry Hearts*, p. 100.
42. Wald, *The House on Henry Street*, p. 54.
43. Isaac Metzker, *A Bintel Brief* (1908; reprint ed., New York, 1971), p. 83.
44. W. A. Mannheimer, "Mikveh Baths of New York," *Survey* 32 (1914): 71. See also Zborowski and Herzog, *Life Is with People*, pp. 130, 279, on the importance of the *mikveh* as a purification of the female body after menstruation.
45. Mannheimer, "Mikveh Baths."
46. Annie O'Hagan, "Fresh Air for the Youngest Sweeney," *Charities and the Commons* 14 (1909): 980.
47. "Health Care Centers Oversee Care of the Sick at Home," *Survey* 31 (1913): 369.
48. Author's interview with Clare Kaplan.

49. Interview with Sophie Abrams.
50. Interview with Fabbia Orzo.
51. Mike Gold, *Jews Without Money* (New York, 1930), pp. 87–89.
52. Ibid.
53. "Dispensaries and Hospitals," *Survey* 31 (1913): 369–70.
54. Ibid.
55. "East Side Women Stone Schoolhouses," *New York Tribune*, 28 June 1906; cited in Allan Schoener, *Portal to America* (New York, 1967), p. 132.
56. Ibid.
57. "Dispensaries and Hospitals," p. 370.
58. "Sick and Hungry Garment Workers Fight On," *Survey* 36 (1916): 321.
59. "Pain Killers and the New Americans," *Survey* 45 (1920): 653. See also Robert Park, *The Immigrant Press and Its Control* (New York, 1922), pp. 121–34, 369–74. Park, in concluding his investigations into the sources of revenue available to the foreign-language press, states: "It is probably true that a good many of the foreign-language papers could not continue to exist if they were deprived of their medical advertisements" (pp. 373–74).
60. "Pain Killers and the New Americans," p. 636.
61. Ibid.

9. House and Home

1. Sophinisba Breckenridge, *New Homes for Old* (New York, 1921), pp. 35–44.
2. Ibid., p. 44; see also Susan Strasser, *Never Done* (New York, 1982).
3. Marie Concistre, "A Study of a Decade in the Life and Education of the Adult Immigrant Community in East Harlem," Ph.D. diss., New York University, 1943; reprinted in part in Francesco Cordasco and Eugene Bucchioni, *The Italians* (Clifton, N.J., 1974), p. 237.
4. Breckenridge, *New Homes for Old*, p. 56.
5. Phyllis Williams, *South Italian Folkways in Europe and America* (New Haven, Conn., 1938), p. 49.
6. Breckenridge, *New Homes for Old*, p. 58.
7. Ibid., p. 59.
8. Robert Chapin, *The Standard of Living Among Workingmen's Families in New York City* (New York, 1907), p. 132.
9. "The Immigrant Experience," part 1, program produced for WBAI (New York) by Gail Pellett, Nina Mende, and Beth Friend in Spring 1976.
10. Interview with Fabbia Orzo.
11. Breckenridge, *New Homes for Old*, p. 58.
12. Interview with Ruth Mishkin (tape 25).
13. Interview with Becky Brier (tape 108).
14. Interview with Yetta Adelman.
15. Interview with Fabbia Orzo.
16. Interview with Carmella Caruso.
17. Quoted in Fred Feretti, "Last of the Street Politicians," *New York Times Magazine*, 10 January 1979, p. 56.
18. Interview with Shirley Levy (tape 21).
19. Interview with Lenore Kosloff.
20. *Survey* 19 (1909): 1052; see also Chapin, *The Standard of Living*, pp. 57–64.
21. Bruno Lasker, "Fagots and Furnaces," *Survey* 40 (1917): 368.

22. Louise Boland More, *Wage Earners' Budgets: A Study of Standards and Costs of Living in New York City* (New York, 1907), p. 40.
23. Ruth S. True, "Boyhood and Lawlessness," *West Side Studies*, vol. 1 (New York, 1914), pp. 15–16. See also Breckenridge, *New Homes for Old*, p. 18; truancy, throwing stones, and playing ball were other offenses.
24. True, "Boyhood," p. 147; see also Katharine Anthony, "Mothers Who Must Earn," *West Side Studies*, vol. 1 (New York, 1914), p. 10.
25. Chapin, *The Standard of Living*, p. 115.
26. Quoted in Feretti, "Last of the Street Politicians," p. 56.
27. More, *Wage Earners' Budgets*, p. 41.
28. Isaac Hourwich, *Immigration and Labor* (New York, 1912), p. 265; Chapin, *The Standard of Living*, p. 162.
29. Chapin, *The Standard of Living*, p. 164.
30. More, *Wage Earners' Budgets*, pp. 72–73.
31. Elsa Herzfeld, *Family Monographs* (New York, 1905), p. 48; see also Thomas Kessner, *The Golden Door: Italian and Jewish Immigrant Mobility in New York City* (New York, 1977), pp. 140–44; "Moving Day," *Survey* 45 (1920): 54.
32. Mary Kingsbury Simkhovitch, *The City Worker's World* (New York, 1917), p. 39.
33. Herzfeld, *Family Monographs*, p. 47.
34. Ibid.
35. Interview with Judith Weissman.
36. Interview with Adriana Valenti.
37. Ida Hull, "Special Problems in Italian Families," *National Conference of Social Work: Addresses and Proceedings* (New York, 1924), p. 289.
38. Anzia Yezierska, *Breadgivers* (1925; reprint ed., New York, 1977), p. 6. The toothbrush was one of the most ubiquitous symbols of Americanization in the social work literature of the period. It is interesting that Booker T. Washington in his autobiography and self-help manual *Up from Slavery* (New York, 1901) uses the toothbrush as the symbol for the acquisition of civilization.
39. Yezierska, *Breadgivers*, pp. 506.
40. *Survey* 28 (1912): 183.
41. Quoted in *Survey* 25 (1910): 603. The article is quoting E. A. Goldenweisser, researcher for the immigration commission.
42. R. L. Duffus, *Lillian Wald: Neighbor and Crusader* (New York, 1938), pp. 77–78.
43. Williams, *South Italian Folkways*, p. 47.
44. Leonard Covello, *The Heart Is the Teacher* (New York, 1958), p. 29.
45. May Mabel Kittredge, "Housekeeping Centers in Settlements and Public Schools," *Survey* 30 (1913): 189.
46. Ibid.
47. Simkhovitch, *The City Worker's World*, p. 34.
48. Ibid; see also Viola Paradise, "The Jewish Girl in Chicago," *Survey* 30 (1913): 706.
49. Simon Patten, "Backsliding in Social Work," *Survey* 43 (1920): 349.
50. Simkhovitch, *The City Worker's World*, p. 32.
51. Ibid., p. 34.
52. Maria Ganz, *Rebels: Into Anarchy and Out Again* (New York, 1920), pp. 43–45.
53. Kittredge, "Housekeeping Centers," p. 190.
54. Kittredge, "Housekeeping Centers," p. 190. See Strasser, *Never Done*, pp. 210–20, on scientific housekeeping.
55. Ibid.

56. Mabel Kittredge, "Homemaking in a Model Flat," *Charities and the Commons* 15 (1905): 176. For a more general analysis of the imposition of scientific housekeeping see Barbara Ehrenreich and Deidre English, *For Her Own Good* (New York, 1977), pp. 127–81. See also Christine Frederick, "The New House-keeping," serialized in the *Ladies Home Journal* in 1912; and Bertha Richardson, *The Woman Who Spends* (New York, 1913). The scientific housekeeping development should also be seen as the forerunner of modern consumer and advertising practices. Social workers steeped in this movement, like Mable Kittredge, attempted to perform by personal witness what later became the stock in trade of modern consumer appeals to women—the external imposition of a standardized methodology of housekeeping in which direction and judgment originate outside the home and therefore are assumed to be more scientific and modern than "old-fashioned" methods.
57. Kittredge, "Homemaking in a Model Flat," p. 177.
58. Elsie Clews Parsons, "The Division of Labor in the Tenements," *Charities and the Commons* 15 (1905): 443.
59. Interview with Fabbia Orzo.
60. Interview with Judith Weissman.
61. Josephine Roche, "The Italian Girl," in Ruth S. True, "The Neglected Girl," *West Side Studies*, vol. 2 (New York, 1914), p. 191.
62. Interview with Adriana Valenti.
63. Interview with Anna Kuthan.
64. Interview with Anna Kuthan.

10. THE LAND OF DOLLARS

1. Lillian Brandt, "In Behalf of the Overcrowded and the Apathy That Arises from It," *Charities and the Commons* 12 (1904): 503.
2. Marie Concistre, "A Study of a Decade in the Life and Education of the Adult Immigrant Community in East Harlem," Ph.D. diss., New York University, 1943; reprinted in part in Francisco Cordaoco and Eugene Bucchioni, *The Italians* (Clifton, N.J., 1974), p. 228.
3. Antonio Mangano, "The Associated Life of the Italians in New York City," *Charities and the Commons* 12 (1904): 477.
4. *Survey* 25 (1910): 603.
5. Irving Howe, *World of Our Fathers* (New York, 1976), p. 164.
6. Interview with Ida Shapiro (tape 132).
7. Josephine Roche, "The Italian Girl," in Ruth S. True, "The Neglected Girl," *West Side Studies*, vol. 2 (New York, 1914), pp. 106–7.
8. Interview with Ethel Adelson.
9. Interview with Judith Weissman.
10. Maria Ganz, *Rebels: Into Anarchy and Out Again* (New York, 1920), p. 27.
11. *Report of the Mayor's Pushcart Commission* (New York, 1906), p. 39.
12. Edwin Markham, "Contractor at Center of the Sweating System," *Cosmopolitan*, January 1907; reprinted in Allan Schoener, *Portal to America* (New York, 1967). This perception is not wholly accurate, however; see Thomas Kessner, *The Golden Door: Italian and Jewish Immigrant Mobility in New York City* (New York, 1977), pp. 55–61, for an analysis of the organization of the pushcart trade.
13. *Report of the Mayor's Pushcart Commission*, p. 199.

14. Ibid., p. 200.
15. Richard Gambino, *Blood of My Blood* (New York, 1974), p. 167.
16. In Anzia Yezierska, *Hungry Hearts* (New York, 1920), pp. 311–12.
17. Ganz, *Rebels,* pp. 103–4.
18. Ibid., pp. 10–11.
19. Louise Odencrantz, *Italian Women in Industry* (New York, 1919), p. 165.
20. Mary Sherman, "The Manufacture of Foods in the Tenements," *Charities and the Commons* 15 (1906): 669.
21. Sophinisba Breckenridge, *New Homes for Old* (New York, 1921), p. 125.
22. Phyllis Williams, *South Italian Folkways in Europe and America* (New Haven, Conn., 1938), p. 64.
23. Howe, *World of Our Fathers,* p. 175.
24. Interview with Rachel Rabinowitz.
25. Odencrantz, *Italian Women in Industry,* p. 227.
26. Interview with Caroline Caroli (tape 2, second drawer).
27. True, "The Neglected Girl," *West Side Studies,* vol. 2 (New York, 1919), p. 75.
28. Breckenridge, *New Homes for Old,* p. 131.
29. Williams, *South Italian Folkways,* p. 62.
30. Ibid., p. 61.
31. True, "The Neglected Girl," p. 75.
32. Williams, *South Italian Folkways,* p. 61.
33. Simon Patten, *The Consumption of Wealth* (New York, 1892), p. 20.
34. Williams, *South Italian Folkways,* p. 122.
35. Ibid.
36. In Yezierska, *Hungry Hearts,* p. 189.
37. Ibid., p. 218.
38. Leonard Covello, *The Heart Is the Teacher* (New York, 1958), p. 36.
39. Lillian Wald, *House on Henry Street* (1915; reprint ed., New York, 1971), p. 21.
40. *Survey* 41 (1918): 166.
41. Enrico Sartorio, *Social and Religious Life of Italians in America* (Boston, 1918), p. 57.
42. *Survey* (1918): 166.
43. Mary Kingsbury Simkhovitch, *The City Worker's World* (New York, 1917), p. 58.
44. "The Cost of Living," *Survey* 45 (1920): 967.
45. Ester Packard, "My Money Won't Reach," *Survey* 39 (1918): 122.
46. Bruno Lasker, "The Food Riots," *Survey* 37 (1917): 638.
47. Robert Haig and Roswell Morea, *Regional Survey of New York and Its Environs* (New York, 1927), p. 64; *Survey* 37 (1917): 661.
48. Phil Davis, "The Kosher Meat Strike," *Survey* 38 (1917): 633.
49. Ganz, *Rebels,* pp. 246, 247, 250.
50. *New York Times,* 25 February 1917, p. 7.
51. Ibid.
52. *New York Times,* 21 February 1917, p. 8.
53. Ganz, *Rebels,* pp. 251, 255, 260.
54. *New York Times,* 21 February 1917, pp. 1, 4.
55. *New York Times,* 22 February 1917, p. 7.
56. *New York Times,* 23 February 1917, p. 4.
57. Ibid.
58. *New York Times,* 25 February 1917, p. 1.
59. Ibid., p. 4.
60. Ganz, *Rebels,* p. 260.

61. *Survey* 37 (1917): 661.
62. "Americanization by Starvation," *Survey* 44 (1920): 284.
63. Ibid.

11. New Images, Old Bonds

1. Simon Lubin and Christina Keysto, "Cracks in the Melting Pot," *Survey* 43 (1920): 258.
2. Leonard Covello, *The Heart Is the Teacher* (New York, 1958), p. 29.
3. Marie Concistre, "Study of a Decade in the Life and Education of the Adult Immigrant Community in East Harlem," Ph.D. diss., New York University, 1943; reprinted in part in Francesco Cordasco and Eugene Bucchioni, *The Italians* (Clifton, N.J., 1974), p. 228.
4. Phyllis Williams, *South Italian Folkways in Europe and America* (New Haven, Conn., 1938), pp. 32–33.
5. Concistre, "A Study of a Decade," p. 227.
6. Ibid.
7. Quoted in Leonard Covello, *The Social Background of the Italo-American School Child* (New Jersey, 1972), p. 314.
8. Anzia Yezierska, *Breadgivers* (1915; reprint ed., New York, 1977), p. 135.
9. Rose Cohen, *Out of the Shadow* (New York, 1918), p. 211.
10. Ibid., p. 106.
11. Israel Friedlander, "Americanization of the Jewish Immigrant," *Survey* 38 (1917): 107.
12. Ibid.
13. Cited in Irving Howe, *World of Our Fathers* (New York, 1976), p. 181.
14. Quoted in Robert Park and William Miller, *Old World Traits Transplanted* (New York, 1919), p. 103.
15. Interview with Grace Grimaldi.
16. Mike Gold, *Jews Without Money* (New York, 1930), p. 48.
17. Interviews with Amalia Morandi and Adriana Valenti.
18. Interviews with Bella Feiner (tape 42), Yetta Brier (tapes 6, 7).
19. Louise Odencrantz, *Italian Women in Industry* (New York, 1919), p. 35.
20. Cohen, *Out of the Shadow*, p. 156.
21. Maria Ganz, *Rebels: Into Anarchy and Out Again* (New York, 1920).
22. Covello, *Social Background*, p. 295.
23. Sydelle Kramer and Jenny Masur, *Jewish Grandmothers* (Boston, 1976), p. 130.
24. Quoted in Covello, *Social Background*, pp. 292–93.
25. Ibid., p. 301.
26. Lillian Wald, *Windows on Henry Street* (New York, 1934), pp. 142–43.
27. Interview with Rachel Cohen (tape 9).
28. Interview with Bea Heller (tape 59).
29. Interview with Amalia Morandi.
30. Quoted in Odencrantz, *Italian Women in Industry*, p. 254.
31. Mary Van Kleeck, *Working Girls in Evening School: A Statistical Study* (New York, 1913), pp. 45–57.
32. Interview with Rachel Cohen.
33. Quoted in Covello, *Social Background*, p. 292.
34. Odencrantz, *Italian Women in Industry*, p. 255; see also Covello, *Social Background*, pp. 278, 327.
35. Covello, *Social Background*, pp. 307–8.

36. Interview with Grace Grimaldi.
37. Interview with Helen Wittenberg (tape 65).
38. Elizabeth Stern, *My Mother and I* (New York, 1917), pp. 60, 160.
39. Quoted in Covello, *Social Background*, p. 317.
40. Interview with Adriana Valenti.
41. Interview with Lenore Kosloff.
42. Interview with Anna Kuthan.
43. Ida Richter, quoted in Kramer and Masur, *Jewish Grandmothers*, p. 130; Jerry Mangione, *Mount Allegro: A Memoir of Italian American Life* (New York, 1942), pp. 49–50.
44. Sophinisba Breckenridge, *New Homes for Old* (New York, 1921), p. 137.
45. Interview with Adriana Valenti.
46. Richard Gambino, *Blood of My Blood* (New York, 1974), p. 175.
47. Park and Miller, *Old World Traits Transplanted*, p. 147. On the social morality of the people from the Sicilian village of Cinisi, see Robert F. Harney, "Men Without Women: Italian Migrants in Canada, 1885–1930," in *The Italian Woman of North America*, ed. Betty Boyd Caroli, Robert Harney, and Lydia Tomasi (Toronto, 1978), p. 93.
48. David L. Cohn, *The Good Old Days: A History of American Morals and Manners as Seen Through the Sears Roebuck Catalogs* (New York, 1940), pp. 354–61.
49. Anthony Mangano, *Sons of Italy* (New York, 1921), p. 21.
50. Cohen, *Out of the Shadow*, pp. 153–54.
51. Yezierska, *Breadgivers*, pp. 4–5.
52. Wald, *The House on Henry Street*, p. 193.
53. Interview with Amalia Morandi.
54. Yezierska, *Breadgivers*, pp. 35–36.
55. Interview with Maria Zambello (WPA interview, January 1938), loaned to the author by Laura Schwartz, SUNY Stonybrook.
56. Interview with Maria Frazaetti (WPA interview, January 1938), loaned to the author by Laura Schwartz, SUNY Stonebrook.
57. Anzia Yezierska, *Hungry Hearts* (New York, 1920), pp. 201, 209.
58. Wald, *The House on Henry Street*, p. 197.
59. Covello, *Social Background*, p. 340.
60. Gold, *Jews Without Money*, pp. 96–103.

12. CITY LIGHTS

1. Sophinisba Breckenridge, *New Homes for Old* (New York, 1921), p. 63.
2. Ibid., p. 175.
3. Belle Israel, "The Way of the Girl," *Survey* 22 (1909): 494.
4. Charlotte Baum, Paula Hyman, and Sonia Michel, *The Jewish Women in America* (New York, 1978), pp. 115–17.
5. Interview with Sophie Abrams.
6. Marie Concistre, "A Study of a Decade in the Life and Education of the Adult Immigrant Community in East Harlem," Ph.D. diss., New York University, 1943; reprinted in part in Francesco Cordasco and Eugene Bucchioni, *The Italians* (Clifton, N.J., 1974), p. 227.
7. Mike Gold, *Jews Without Money* (New York, 1930), p. 92.
8. Interview with Bella Feiner.
9. Interview with Lenore Kosloff (tapes 83, 84).

10. Phyllis Williams, *South Italian Folkways in Europe and America* (New Haven, Conn., 1938), p. 96.
11. Enrico Sartorio, *Social and Religious Life of Italians in America* (Boston, 1918), pp. 72–73.
12. Ibid.
13. Concistre, "A Study of a Decade," p. 227.
14. Josephine Roche, "The Italian Girl," *West Side Studies*, vol. 2 (New York, 1913), pp. 112–13.
15. Interview with Adriana Valenti.
16. Interview with Fabbia Orzo.
17. Interview with Caroline Caroli (tape 2).
18. Quoted in Leonard Covello, *The Social Background of the Italo-American School Child* (New Jersey, 1972), pp. 358–59.
19. Ibid., pp. 352–53.
20. Interview with Lucia Colleti (author's file).
21. Interview with Judith Weissman.
22. Interview with Sophie Abrams.
23. Robert Park and William Miller, *Old World Traits Transplanted* (New York, 1919), p. 51.
24. Interview with Adriana Valenti.
25. Interview with Yetta Adelman.
26. Interview with Evelyn Vogelman (tape 41).
27. Gold, *Jews Without Money*, pp. 94–95.
28. Interview with Carmella Caruso.
29. Lillian Wald, *The House on Henry Street* (1915; reprint ed., New York, 1971), pp. 80–81.
30. See Lewis Jacobs, *The Rise of American Film* (1939; reprint ed., New York, 1969); Robert Sklar, *Movie-Made America* (New York, 1975); Larry May, *Screening Out the Past* (New York, 1980); see also Roy Rosenzweig, *Eight Hours for What We Will: Workers and Leisure in an Industrial City* (Cambridge, 1983), pp. 191–221, for an analysis of the effects of the movies on a small industrial city.
31. Lewis Palmer, "The World in Motion," *Survey* 22 (1909): 8–9, 357; Russell Nye, *The Unembarrassed Muse* (New York, 1970), pp. 362–65; Sklar, *Movie-Made America*, pp. 18–21.
32. Palmer, "The World in Motion," p. 355.
33. Cited in Howe, *World of Our Fathers*, p. 213.
34. Cited in Nye, *The Unembarrassed Muse*, p. 365.
35. "The Immigrant Experience," part 1, program produced for WBAI (New York) by Gail Pellett, Nina Mende, and Beth Friend in Spring 1976.
36. Sklar, *Movie-Made America*, p. 41.
37. Robert Stanley, *The Celluloid Empire* (New York, 1978), pp. 26–27; Edward Wagenknect, *The Movies in the Age of Innocence* (Norman, Okla., 1962), pp. 179–81.
38. Wagenknect, *The Movies in the Age of Innocence*, p. 180; Elizabeth Ewen, "City Lights: Immigrant Women and the Rise of the Movies," *Signs* 5, no. 3 (1980): 559.
39. Sklar, *Movie-Made America*, pp. 97–100.
40. David Robinson, *Hollywood in the Twenties* (New York, 1976), p. 32.
41. Sklar, *Movie-Made America*, p. 99.
42. Ibid.
43. Bernard Meyer, *Houdini: A Mind in Chains* (New York, 1968), p. 159.
44. Sklar, *Movie-Made America*, p. 99; May, *Screening Out the Past*, pp. 36–42.

45. Vachel Lindsay, *The Art of the Motion Picture* (New York, 1922), p. 53.
46. Ibid., pp. 61–62.
47. Ibid., pp. 69–70. The baby does not flourish because there is not enough mother's milk and the family cannot afford bottled milk. The child dies from "dirty milk."
48. Lindsay, *The Art of the Motion Picture*, pp. 88–92.
49. Williams, *South Italian Folkways*, p. 118.
50. Ibid.
51. Benjamin Hampton, *History of the American Film Industry* (1931; reprint ed., New York, 1970), p. 221. For an analysis of the change see pp. 197–215; see also Sklar, *Movie-Made America*, pp. 88–92; Jacobs, *The Rise of American Film*, pp. 287–301; May, *Screening Out the Past*, pp. 200–36.
52. Hampton, *History of the American Film Industry*, p. 222.
53. Wagenknect, *Movies in the Age of Innocence*, p. 207.
54. See Sumiko Higashi, *Virgins, Vamps, and Flappers* (Montreal, 1978), pp. 136–42; Hampton, *History of the American Film Industry*, pp. 220–26.
55. Hampton, *History of the American Film Industry*, p. 224.
56. Ibid., p. 401.
57. Lloyd Lewis, "The Deluxe Picture Palace," *New Republic*, March 1929; reprinted in George Nowry, *The Twenties* (Engelwood Cliffs, N.J., 1963), p. 59.

13. The Ties That Bind

1. Interview with Judith Weismann.
2. Mike Gold, *Jews Without Money* (New York, 1930), p. 98.
3. Anzia Yezierska, *Breadgivers* (1925; reprint ed., New York, 1977), pp. 96, 137–38.
4. Maria Ganz, *Rebels: Into Anarchy and Out Again* (New York, 1920), p. 140.
5. Quoted in Sydelle Kramer and Jenny Masur, *Jewish Grandmothers* (Boston, 1976), p. 147.
6. "Shadkens Find Business Bad," *New York Tribune*, 9 January 1898; reprinted in Allon Schoener, *Portal to America* (New York, 1967), p. 118.
7. Interview with Helen Reif (tape 35).
8. Interview with Yetta Bursky.
9. Interview with Anna Kuthan.
10. Robert Park and Herbert Miller, *Old World Traits Transplanted* (New York, 1919), pp. 79–80.
11. Interview with Fanny Rosen.
12. Charlotte Baum, Paula Hyman, and Sonia Michel, *The Jewish Woman in America* (New York, 1978), pp. 116–17; Irving Howe, *World of Our Fathers* (New York, 1976), p. 179.
13. Interview with Anna Kuthan.
14. Ibid.
15. Interview with Becky Brier.
16. Interview with Shirley Levy.
17. Interview with Katy Bluestone (tape 104).
18. Interview with Lenore Kosloff.
19. Interview with Judith Weissmann.
20. Author's interview with Gussie Agines.
21. Louise Odencrantz, *Italian Women in Industry* (New York, 1919), p. 204.
22. Author's interview with Francesca Campanile narrating the history of her

mother, Rosina Giuliani.

23. Interview with Fabbia Orzo.
24. Interview with Letitia Serpe.
25. Interview with Agnes Santucci.
26. Interview with Letitia Serpe.
27. Interview with Agnes Santucci.
28. Interview with Caroline Caroli.
29. Interview with Fabbia Orzo.
30. Interview with Adriana Valenti.
31. Interview with Carmella Caruso.
32. Interview with Grace Grimaldi.
33. Josephine Roche, "The Italian Girl," in Ruth S. True, "The Neglected Girl," *West Side Studies*, vol. 2 (New York, 1914), p. 116.
34. Ibid., p. 117.
35. Interview with Letitia Serpe.
36. Howe, *World of Our Fathers*, p. 221.
37. Maria Ganz, *Rebels: Into Anarchy and Out Again* (New York, 1920), p. 62.
38. Sophinisba Breckenridge, *New Homes for Old* (New York, 1921), pp. 99–100.
39. Ibid.
40. Ganz, *Rebels*, p. 64.
41. Breckenridge, *New Homes for Old*, p. 101.
42. Ibid., p. 100.
43. Ibid. See John Berger, *A Seventh Man* (New York, 1977), pp. 5–25, for the importance of photography as a means of communication and of reinforcing memory in the lives of migrant workers.
44. Phyllis Williams, *South Italian Folkways in Europe and America* (New Haven, Conn., 1938), p. 101.
45. Marie Concistre, "A Study of a Decade in the Life and Education of the Adult Immigrant Community in East Harlem," Ph.D. diss., New York University, 1943; reprinted in part in Francesco Cordasco and Eugene Bucchioni, *The Italians: Social Backgrounds of an American Group* (Clifton, N.J., 1974), p. 223.
46. Breckenridge, *New Homes for Old*, p. 98.
47. Ibid.
48. Grazie Dore, "Some Social and Historical Aspects of Italian Emigration to America," Cordasco and Bucchioni, *The Italians*, p. 26.
49. Richard Gambino, *Blood of My Blood* (New York, 1974), pp. 161–2.
50. Gold, cited in Howe, *World of Our Fathers*, p. 221.

14. SWEATSHOPS AND PICKET LINES

1. "The Uprising of the 20,000," quoted in Barbara Werthheimer, *We Were There* (New York, 1977), p. 293.
2. Simon Patten, *The New Basis of Civilization* (New York, 1907), p. 59.
3. Ibid., p. 139.
4. Louise Odencrantz, *Italian Women in Industry* (New York, 1919), p. 273.
5. Ibid., p. 266.
6. Ibid., pp. 266–67.
7. Ibid., p. 267.
8. Ibid., p. 41.
9. Interview with Adriana Valenti.

10. Author's interview with Francesca Campanile narrating the history of her mother, Rosina Giuliani.
11. Interview with Yetta Bursky.
12. Interview with Bella Feiner.
13. Odencrantz, *Italian Women in Industry*, p. 281.
14. Maria Ganz, *Rebels: Into Anarchy and Out Again* (New York, 1920), p. 73.
15. Interview with Agnes Santucci.
16. Interview with Grace Grimaldi.
17. Interview with Ida Shapiro (tape 132).
18. Interview with Bessie Gitlin (tapes 83, 84).
19. Interview with Adriana Valenti.
20. Interview with Shirley Levy.
21. Ibid.
22. Interview with Sonia Farkas (tape 81).
23. Interview with Bessie Polski.
24. Interview with Adriana Valenti.
25. Interviews with Yetta Bursky, Katy Bluestone.
26. Interviews with Fania Horvitz, Gussie Agines.
27. Author's interview with Lillie Tamarakin.
28. Ibid.
29. Interview with Bella Feiner.
30. Interview with Dora Shatsky.
31. Interview with Sophie Abrams.
32. Interview with Yetta Adelman.
33. Interview with Bella Cohen (tape 105).
34. Interview with Lenore Kosloff.
35. Interview with Lillie Tamarakin.
36. Ganz, *Rebels*, p. 80.
37. Interview with Ida Shapiro.
38. Interview with Bella Cohen.
39. Interview with Lillie Tamarakin.
40. Interview with Adriana Valenti.
41. Interview with Bella Feiner.
42. "The Immigrant Experience," part 2, program produced for WBAI (New York) by Gail Pellett, Nina Mende, and Beth Friend in Spring 1976.
43. Paul Buhle, "Italian-American Radicals and the Labor Movement," *Radical History Review*, Spring 1978, p. 130.
44. Interview with Adriana Valenti.
45. Interview with Rachel Cohen.
46. Interview with Sonia Farkas.
47. Ibid.
48. Interview with Yetta Bursky.
49. Interview with Adriana Valenti.
50. Interview with Judith Weissman.
51. Interview with Bessie Polski.
52. Interview with Shirley Levy.
53. Interview with Grace Grimaldi.
54. Louis Levine, *The Women's Garment Workers* (New York, 1924), pp. 144, 154. For other accounts of the shirtwaist strike, see Meredith Tax, *The Uprising of the 20,000* (New York, 1980); and Wertheimer, *We Were There*, pp. 291–96.
55. Levine, *The Women's Garment Workers*, p. 156.
56. Mary Sumner, "The Spirit of the Strikers," *Survey* 23 (1909): 553. See also

Constance D. Leupp, "The Shirtwaist Makers' Strike," *Survey* 23 (1909): 383–86; and Woods Hutchinson, "The Hygienic Aspects of the Shirtwaist Strike," *Survey* 23 (1909): 541–50.

57. Leupp, "The Shirtwaist Makers' Strike," p. 385. When George Bernard Shaw heard about this incident, he commented, "Delightful medieval America always in the intimate personal confidence of the Almighty" (quoted in Levine, *The Women's Garment Workers*, p. 159).

58. Elizabeth Gurley Flynn, *Rebel Girl* (New York, 1955), p. 135.

59. *New York Times*, 6 December 1909, p. 3. See also Levine, *The Women's Garment Workers*, p. 160.

60. Levine, *The Women's Garment Workers*, p. 156; Alice Kessler-Harris, "Organizing the Unorganizable: Three Jewish Women and Their Union," *Labor History* 17 (1976): 12; Charlotte Baum, Paula Hyman, and Sonia Michel, *The Jewish Woman in America* (New York, 1978), pp. 137–40. One of the most important organizers of Italian women during the 1909 and 1910 strikes was writer and socialist Arturo Carot. In 1909 he allied himself with the Women's Trade Union League to organize Italian women in the garment industry. He had to overcome problems of organizing that were compounded by male patriarchal attitudes. He did this by first organizing a primarily social organization, the Italian Women's Mutual Benefit Society, and then using it as a forum for the discussion of trade unionism. For information on his work see Adriana Spadoni, "The Italian Working Women of New York," *Colliers* (1912); reprinted in Wayne Moquin, Charles Van Doren, and Frances Ianni, *A Documentary History of the Italian Americans* (New York, 1974), pp. 126–31. For additional information, see Tax, *The Uprising of the 20,000*, pp. 66–72.

61. Odencrantz, *Italian Women in Industry*, p. 105.

62. Cited in Baum, Hyman, and Michel, *The Jewish Woman in America*, p. 151.

63. Eleanor Flexner, *Century of Struggle* (New York, 1970), p. 290.

64. Mary Kingsbury Simkhovitch, "Some Casual Reflections on the Elections," *Survey* 39 (1917): 160.

65. Interview with Rebecca Markowitz.

66. Interview with Bella Feiner.

67. Interview with Fabbia Orzo.

68. Interview with Bella Feiner.

69. Interview with Fanny Rosen.

70. Interview with Becky Brier.

71. Robert Haig Roswell, *Regional Survey* 1 (New York, 1927), p. 25.

Index

Abortion, midwifery and, 133
Addams, Jane, 76, 77, 78, 79, 86, 97–98
Adolescence, and conflict in immigrant families, 99–100, 106–9
Advertising: by quack doctors, 145; to recruit immigrants, 55–56
America, first impressions of, 60–74. *See also* American dream; Americanization
American dream: immigrant women and, 264; migration of Eastern European Jews and, 53–57
American household culture. *See* Household culture
Americanization: of children, 72–73, 88–89; and clothing, 25–26, 66–71, 197–201; consumerism and, 64–67, 71–73; and conflict between parents and children, 201–3; demise of midwifery and, 135; and factory work, 242–62; and food, 172–76; impact on immigrant families, 186–90; movies and, 222–24; myth of, 14, 15; name changes and, 72–73
Anti-Semitism, and Eastern European Jewish migration, 37–38
Arranged marriages, 226–29, 232–33
Association of Neighborhood

Workers, Public Health Committee of, 131

Bara, Theda, 217–18
Birth control, 133–34
Black Americans, and melting pot myth, 13
Boarders, 119–21
Breast feeding, cultural conflict over, 135–39
Bureau of Charities, 159

Cardplaying, 214, 215
Celebrations, 226–39; in Italian peasant culture, 36; meeting future husbands at, 233. *See also* Bar mitzvahs; Christenings; Weddings
Central Park, 214–15
Ceremonies. *See* Celebrations
Charities magazine, 67–68
Charity, in Eastern European Jewish culture, 42–43, 47
Charity Organization Society, 78
Charity workers. *See* Charity; Settlement workers
Child care, by older children, 125
Childbirth, in Italian peasant families, 33. *See also* Midwivery
Children, in Eastern European Jewish culture, 46–47. *See also* Family life; Immigrant children;

Fairbanks, Douglas, 219
Family economy: and clothing costs, 153–54; and control of family income, 98–106; during depression of 1907–1908, 126–27; and frequent moving, 154; and heating costs, 152–53; and home-workers, 121–26; and indebtedness, 112; and inflation between 1913 and 1920, 176–78; insurance and, 113–15; living expenses and, 116–21; midwifery and, 132–33; and money sent to Old World, 112–13; and rent payments, 116–21; and small shopkeeping, 167–68. *See also* Family life; Immigrant families
Family life, 63; and children's sense of responsibility, 98–101, 104–6; and attitudes toward speaking English, 196–97; and attitudes toward wages of sons and daughters, 105–8, 200; disruption in New World, 72–73; and economic problems, *see* Family economy; and family size, 133; and generational conflict, 106–9, 201–3; influence of public schools on children and, 88–89; in Italian peasant culture, 33–36; role of mother in, 97; settlement workers and, 85–90. *See also* Household culture; Immigrant families; Immigrant mothers; Social life
Fashion: and immigrant women, 25–26, 66–71; movies and, 223
Flower makers, 123
Flynn, Elizabeth Gurley, 258
Folk medicine, 141–42
Food: availability of meat, 172–73; changes in, 172–76; and conflict between immigrants and American society, 174–76; and emotional communication, 174
Food boycotts, 176–83
Food riots, 176–83
Friendly Aid Society, 80–81

Funerals, 226, 238–39; cost of, 113–15. *See also* Ceremonies
Furniture. *See* Home decoration

Gambling, immigrant men and, 103–4
Garment industry: and division of labor, 244–45; and home-workers, 121–26; and immigrant women, 24–26; liberal bosses in, 261; and spread of tuberculosis, 139–40; subcontracting system, 247–48; union organizing in, 254–62; work conditions in, 246–49
Generational conflict: and family life, 106–9; after marriage, 235
Gish, Lillian, 218
Gold, Mike, 118–19, 141–42, 203, 209–10, 215, 226, 238–39
Goldman, Emma, 89, 135
Goldwyn, Samuel, 217
Goodman, Theodosia. *See* Bara, Theda
Greenwich House, 80, 81, 83, 84, 131
Griffith, D. W., 220–21
Gugiliemi, Rodolfo Pietro Filiberto. *See* Valentino, Rudolf

Hairdresser, role in Italian peasant culture, 33
Haskala movement, 39
Health care: costs of 114–15; distrust of hospitals and, 142–43; and factory work, 249; folk medicine and, 141–42; and home treatment of disease, 141; and lack of parks, 140–41; and midwifery, 130–35; *mikveh* baths and, 140; in Old Country, 130; and quack doctors and patent medicine men, 144–46; and scarlet fever, 139; social workers and, 143–44; and tuberculosis, 139–40; vaccination and, 142. *See also* Breast feeding; Food

Henry Street Settlement House, 80, 84, 202
Hines, Lewis, 123
Home decoration, 156–59
Homeworkers, 121–26; child labor and, 125–26; ethnic backgrounds of, 122
Hospitals, lack of use of, 142–43
Houdini, Harry, 219
Household culture: boarders and, 120; and cleanliness, 154–57; and clothing, 153–54; and community cooperation, 161–63; of Eastern European Jewish women, 40–41; and heating problems, 152–53; and home decoration, 156–59; in Old and New Worlds compared, 148–50; and "scientific housekeeping," 159–61; transformation of, 148. *See also* Cooking; Laundry
Household production: and early garment industry, 25; and Italian peasant families, 33. *See also* Homework
Housekeeper, of tenement, 154–55
Housework. *See* Household culture
Housing: description of, 150–53; of Italian peasant women, 32; lack of heating in, 152–53; model tenements, 156; in Old and New Worlds compared, 148–49
Housing reform movement, division of labor by gender in, 83

Il Proletario, 51
Immigrant children: Americanization of, 88–89; of homeworkers, 123; and hunting for fuel, 153; impact of Americanization on, 187–89; and rejection of European culture, 72–73; relationships between brothers and sisters, 213–14; relationships with mothers, 96–98, 100–1, 104–5; and "right to personality," 106–8; wages of, 98, 100–1, 104–6; of

working mothers, 94–95. *See also* Immigrant daughters
Immigrant daughters: conflict with mothers over clothing, 197–201; conflict with parents over traditional values, 190–214; education of, 191–96; and factory work, *see* Factory work; as "middle-class wives," 267–68; relationships with mothers during pregnancy, 132; social life of, 208–24 *See also* Immigrant children; Immigrant families
Immigrant families: adolescence in, 99–100; attitudes toward landlords, 116–18; conflict between parents and children in, 187–214; goals for children, 145–46; and health care, *see* Health care; impact of American way of life on, 186–90; impact of factory work on, 242–62; Italian peasants of *mezzogiorno*, 30–37; and marriage of daughters, 226–38; as shopkeepers and peddlers, 167–71; stereotypes of, 113; trade unionism and, 90–91. *See also* Family economy; Immigrant children; Immigrant mothers; Immigrant fathers; Immigrant women
Immigrant men: attitudes toward education of daughters, 193–96; attitudes toward marriage, 230–32; reaction to speed up of work, 186–87; social life of, 103–4. *See also* Patriarchal traditions
Immigrant mothers: attitudes toward American women, 201; attitudes toward Americanization of daughters, 208–9; attitudes toward childhood and adolescence, 98–100; attitudes toward education of daughters, 191–96; and breast feeding, 135–39; conflict with daughters, 16, 190–214; conflict with social workers over childrearing prac-

tices, 138–39; and control of children's wages, 94–109; economic role of, 101–4; importance of community to, 203–5; isolation from American culture, 96–97, 109; and preservation of tradition, 267; relationships between, 161–63; relationships with children, 96–98; and role of mother in Italian peasant families, 34–35; working, 94–95. *See also* Immigrant women

Immigrant Protective League, 27

Immigrant sons. *See* Immigrant children

Immigrant women: and abortion, 133; American culture and, 71–73; American dream and, 264; attitudes toward charity workers, 78; attitudes toward settlement workers, 83–84; and birth control, 133–34; contrasted with middle class, 20–24; cultural background of Italians, 30–37; cultural background of Jews, 37–47; cultural similarities of Jews and Italians, 30–31; and fashion, 25–26, 66–71; first impressions of U.S., 60–74; and folk medicine, 141–42; and food boycotts, riots, and strikes, 176–83; and garment industry, 24–26; as homeworkers, 121–26; household culture of, *see* Household culture; and husband's wages, 102–4; impact of modernization on, 265–68; and midwives, 131; migration patterns of Eastern European Jews, 52–55; migration patterns of Italians, 50–52; and modification of Old World diet, 172–76; and money sent to families in Old Country, 104–5; mourning by, 238–39; and neighborhood social life, 166–67; as peddlers, 168–69; pimps and, 209–10; and rent strike of 1907, 126–27; responsibilities of, 100;

settlement workers and, 76–91; single, 108–9; as union organizers, 253–55. *See also* Immigrant daughters; Immigrant mothers

Ince, Thomas, 220

Industrial accidents, 249, 251

Industrialization: changes caused by, 21–22; and Eastern European Jewish migration, 52; impact on immigrant working-class women, 15–16. *See also* Consumerism; Factory work; Mass production

Infant care: and contaminated milk, 137–38; cultural conflict over, 135–39

Installment salesmen, 170–71

Insurance, family economy and, 113–15

Intermarriage, between Jews and Italians, 13

International Ladies' Garment Workers' Union (ILGWU), 106, 193

Italy, impact of migration to U.S. on, 50–51

Jewish Daily Forward, 72, 140, 180, 217, 229, 230

Jewish holidays, factory workers and, 249–50

Jews Without Money (Gold), 141–42. *See also* Gold, Mike

Kittredge, Mabel, 157, 160, 161

Landlords, attitudes toward, 116–18. *See also* Rent strikes

Landsmanshaft societies, 113–15; and social life of immigrant daughters, 210

Laundry, in Old and New Worlds compared, 148–50

Lefkowitz, Louis, 151, 153

Lindsay, Vachel, 219

Lottery tickets, 170

Love. *See* Romantic love

Lower East Side, New York: as amalgam of old and new, 16; first impressions of, 60–74; health care in, *see* Health care; industrialization and, 243; Jewish and Italian population in 1920, 21; organization of labor unions on, 252–62; population density in, 26; rent strike of 1907, 126–27; rents in, 116; small shops in 1913, 167. *See also* New York City; Settlement houses; Settlement workers

Marketplace, in Eastern European Jewish culture, 38; role on Lower East Side, 168–71
Marriage: changes in, 227–35; desertion and, 230; father-daughter conflicts over, 227–28; immigrant men's attitudes toward, 230–32; in Italian community, 232–35; in Jewish community, 44–46, 229–32; as motivation for immigration, 53, quitting jobs after, 230–32, 233–35, 250–51; women's fear of, 229–30. *See also* Arranged marriage
Mass production: and garment industry, 25; transformation of American household culture and, 148. *See also* Industrialization
Matchmakers, 227–28; in Eastern European Jewish culture, 44–46; in Italian peasant culture, 36
Medical care. *See* Health care
Melting pot myth, 13–14
Middle-class American women: compared with immigrant working-class women, 22–24; impact of consumer society on, 77–78; lack of contact with new immigrants, 76; settlement movement publicity and, 81–82; shirtwaist strike and, 256–57, 258. *See also* Middle-class Americans; Settlement workers
Middle-class Americans: and abandonment of Lower East Side, 27;

attitudes toward early movies, 219; attitudes toward married women working, 230; attitudes toward working class immigrants, 69–70; and concept of adolescence, 99
Midwifery: abortion and, 133; attitude of medical establishment toward, 134–35; cost of, 132; culture and, 131–32; decline of, 135; on Lower East Side, 130–35; role in Italian peasant culture, 33
Mikveh baths, 46, 140
Milk, contaminated, 137–38
Model-tenement movement, program of, 160–61
Modernization, impact on women, 265–68. *See also* Industrialization
Money: immigrant mothers and control of, 98–106; as motivation for immigration, 55; sent to Old World, 121. *See also* Family economy
Moral philanthropy, settlement house movement and, 78–79
More, Louise Bolard, 83, 102, 104
Mothers' Anti-High Price League, 178–79, 181
Movie houses, changes in, 223–24
Movies: content changes after 1920, 222–24; immigrant stars in, 217–18; immigrant themes in, 220; and sexual values, 218, 219, 222–24
Moving, 154; jumping rent by, 116–17; selection of neighborhoods for, 166–67
Mutual-benefit societies, 113–15

Name changes, and Americanization, 72–73
National Aid League, 180
National Desertion Bureau, 230
National Industries Conference Board, 176
New York City: development of ethnic neighborhoods in, 63; first impressions of, 60–74; ready-made clothing industry

and, 25; separation of classes in, 26–27. See also Lower East Side

Eastern European Jewish culture, 39–41; family finances and, 98–104; in Italian peasant communities, 34–36; and male and female boarders, 120; middle-class American women and, 77–78; middle-class values and, 87–88; settlement work and, 78–79, 82–83

Sexism: and attitude toward married women working, 231; and attitudes toward sons' and daughters' wages, 105–6; education and, 89–90, 194–96; in social work movement, 82; in trade union movement, 259–60

Sexual abuse, in factories, 249

Sexual attitudes: and generational conflict, 107; Italian parents and, 210–14; and movies, 218, 219, 222–24

Shirtwaist strike of 1909, 256–58

Shopkeeping, by immigrants, 167–71

Sickness. *See* Health care

Simkhovitch, Mary Kingsbury, 16, 76, 80, 81, 84, 87, 89, 90, 97, 102, 157–58, 175–76, 268

Singing, in factories, 248, 251, 252

Single men or women: boarding with family, 120; and immigration to U.S. from Italy, 51–52

Social classes, creation of, urban consumer economy and, 24–26. *See also* Middle-class Americans; Middle-class women; *and entries beginning with "Immigrant"*

Social life of immigrants, 166–67, 203–5; and bargaining, 169–70; and celebrations, *see* Celebrations; changes in U.S., 24; and culture, 216; of daughters, 208–24; and factory work, 248–49, 250–52; family recreation, 214–15; of fathers, 103–4; funerals and, 238–39; Italian parents and, 210–14; and marketplace, 169–72; and movies, 216–24; protest

movements and, 176–83; role of food in, 174–75; and social clubs, 211; visits to parks, 214–15; weddings and, 235–37

Social workers: 175; attitudes toward housework, 159–61; attitudes toward immigrant daughters' wages, 105–6; attitudes toward midwives, 134–35; attitudes toward nursing, 135–39; attitudes toward poor, 205; attitudes toward street life of Lower East Side, 166; conflict with immigrant mothers over child-rearing practices, 138–39; and diet of immigrant families, 173–74, 175–76; and establishment of health care services, 143–44; gender differences within movement of, 81–83; on generational conflict, 107; on homework, 123, 124, 125–26; and milk stations, 137–38; perception of immigrant mothers, 96–97; Progressive ideology and, 84–85. *See also* Settlement workers

Socialism: in Eastern European Jewish culture, 43–44; impact on immigrant women, 90. *See also* Radicals; Socialist Party

Socialist Party, and food riots, 180

Standard of living: foods and, 172–73; inflation and, 176–78; of native-born and immigrant families, 113

Steamship companies, profits from immigration, 55–56

Strikes, 254, 255; cloakmakers in 1910, 256; kosher meat strike, 176–83; and liberal bosses, 261; shirtwaist strike of 1909, 256–58; and tension between male trade union officials and women workers, 259–60; at textile mills in Lawrence, Massachusetts, 258. *See also* Food boycotts; Rent strikes

Subcontracting system, in garment

industry, 247–48

Suicide, in Eastern European Jewish culture, 45

Sullivan, G. Gardner, 220

Survey magazine, 17, 71, 73, 81, 87, 96, 127, 137, 140–41, 145, 158, 176, 181, 188–89, 209, 216, 257–58

Swanson, Gloria, 222

Tenement House Commission, 82

Trade unions. *See entries beginning with "Union"*

Tresca, Carlo, 134

Triangle Waist Company, 256–57; fire at, 259–60

Union business agents, 254

Union organizing, 252–62; in garment industry, 254–62; impact on immigrant women, 90; and "runaway shops," 262

Union-sponsored social events, 210

U.S. Immigration Commission, 156

U.S. Peddling Commission of Greater New York, 169

University Settlement House, 88

Valentino, Rudolf, 217–19

Wages: children giving to family, 98, 100–101, 104–6; children witholding from family, 106–8; for factory work, 246, 247; in garment industry, 25; sexism and, 260

Wald, Lillian, 21, 76, 80, 81, 84, 86, 134, 137, 139, 156, 175, 193, 199–200, 202, 216

Washing clothes. *See* Laundry

Working-class immigrants. *See entries beginning with "Immigrant"*

Wedding gifts, 237, 250–51

Weddings, 235–37; cost of, 236–37; in Eastern European Jewish culture, 46; factory workers and, 251

Widows: immigration to U.S. from Italy, 52; and taking in boarders, 121

Women's liberation movement, link to past, 268

Women's suffrage: passage of referendum on, 260; trade union organization and, 258–59

Women's Trade Union League, 256–57, 258

Workman's Circle, 114

Yezierska, Anzia, 54–55, 60–61, 117, 138, 139, 170, 199, 200–1, 202, 203, 204–5, 217, 227

Zukor, Adolph, 217